DERRIDA READS SHAKESPEARE

EDINBURGH CRITICAL STUDIES IN SHAKESPEARE AND PHILOSOPHY
Series Editor: Kevin Curran

Edinburgh Critical Studies in Shakespeare and Philosophy takes seriously the speculative and world-making properties of Shakespeare's art. Maintaining a broad view of 'philosophy' that accommodates first-order questions of metaphysics, ethics, politics and aesthetics, the series also expands our understanding of philosophy to include the unique kinds of theoretical work carried out by performance and poetry itself. These scholarly monographs will reinvigorate Shakespeare studies by opening new interdisciplinary conversations among scholars, artists and students.

Editorial Board Members
Ewan Fernie, Shakespeare Institute, University of Birmingham
James Kearney, University of California, Santa Barbara
Julia Reinhard Lupton, University of California, Irvine
Madhavi Menon, Ashoka University
Simon Palfrey, Oxford University
Tiffany Stern, Shakespeare Institute, University of Birmingham
Henry Turner, Rutgers University
Michael Witmore, The Folger Shakespeare Library
Paul Yachnin, McGill University

Published Titles
Rethinking Shakespeare's Political Philosophy: From Lear to Leviathan
Alex Schulman
Shakespeare in Hindsight: Counterfactual Thinking and Shakespearean Tragedy
Amir Khan
Second Death: Theatricalities of the Soul in Shakespeare's Drama
Donovan Sherman
Shakespeare's Fugitive Politics
Thomas P. Anderson
Is Shylock Jewish?: Citing Scripture and the Moral Agency of Shakespeare's Jews
Sara Coodin
Chaste Value: Economic Crisis, Female Chastity and the Production of Social Difference on Shakespeare's Stage
Katherine Gillen
Shakespearean Melancholy: Philosophy, Form and the Transformation of Comedy
J. F. Bernard
Shakespeare's Moral Compass
Neema Parvini
Shakespeare and the Fall of the Roman Republic: Selfhood, Stoicism and Civil War
Patrick Gray
Revenge Tragedy and Classical Philosophy on the Early Modern Stage
Christopher Crosbie
Shakespeare and the Truth-Teller: Confronting the Cynic Ideal
David Hershinow
Derrida Reads Shakespeare
Chiara Alfano
Conceiving Desire: Metaphor, Cognition and Eros in Lyly and Shakespeare
Gillian Knoll

Forthcoming Titles
Making Publics in Shakespeare's Playhouse
Paul Yachnin
The Play and the Thing: A Phenomenology of Shakespearean Theatre
Matthew Wagner
Immateriality and Early Modern English Literature: Shakespeare, Donne and Herbert
James A. Knapp
Shakespeare's Staging of the Self: The Reformation and Protestant Hermenuetics
Roberta Kwan

For further information please visit our website at edinburghuniversitypress.com/series/ecsst

DERRIDA READS SHAKESPEARE

◆ ◆ ◆

CHIARA ALFANO

EDINBURGH
University Press

Edinburgh University Press is one of the leading university presses in the UK. We publish academic books and journals in our selected subject areas across the humanities and social sciences, combining cutting-edge scholarship with high editorial and production values to produce academic works of lasting importance. For more information visit our website: edinburghuniversitypress.com

© Chiara Alfano, 2020, 2021

Edinburgh University Press Ltd
The Tun – Holyrood Road
12(2f) Jackson's Entry
Edinburgh EH8 8PJ

First published in hardback by Edinburgh University Press 2020

Typeset in 12/15 Adobe Sabon by
IDSUK (DataConnection) Ltd

A CIP record for this book is available from the British Library

ISBN 978 1 4744 0987 2 (hardback)
ISBN 978 1 4744 9184 6 (paperback)
ISBN 978 1 4744 0988 9 (webready PDF)
ISBN 978 1 4744 0989 6 (epub)

The right of Chiara Alfano to be identified as the author of this work has been asserted in accordance with the Copyright, Designs and Patents Act 1988, and the Copyright and Related Rights Regulations 2003 (SI No. 2498).

CONTENTS

Acknowledgements vi
Series Editor's Preface viii

1. What is Shakespeare's Genius? 1
2. Deconstructing (with) Shakespeare 31
3. *Flèches* and the Wounds of Reading 65
4. Porpentine 101
5. Giving the Greatest Chance to Chance 135
6. The Politics of Re-reading 173
7. Conclusion, or *Génie qui es tu* 215

Works Cited 227
Index 242

ACKNOWLEDGEMENTS

I would like to thank the publishers and editors who granted permission to reprint material that appeared in earlier incarnations elsewhere. An earlier version of Chapter 4 was first published as 'Porpentine', *The Oxford Literary Review* 34, no. 1 (July 2012): 109–22. Parts of Chapter 5 and the Conclusion were first published as 'Freud's Cadence: Taking Chances with *Julius Caesar*', in *Freud after Derrida*, special issue (Part II) of *Mosaic* 44, no. 4 (2011): 63–78. Chapter 6 is based on 'Strange Frequencies: Reading *Hamlet* with Derrida and Nancy', in *Where Ghosts Live*, special issue of *Derrida Today* 5, no. 2 (November 2012): 214–31.

Writing this book as been an exercise in 'contretemps'. The birth of two boys drew out work on this book to such a degree that I convinced myself that the time for writing it had passed. I would like to thank my students on Kingston's Literature and Philosophy MA for convincing me otherwise. I would also like to thank Kevin Curran, the series editor of Edinburgh Critical Studies in Shakespeare and Philosophy, and Michelle Houston at Edinburgh University Press for bearing with me.

Much of this book is the result of conversations about Derrida and the relationship between literature and philosophy, which I have been having almost my entire adult life, starting from when Clare Connors smuggled 'Aphorism Countertime' into one of our tutorials. I will always be grateful to her for this act of readerly rebellion. Nick Royle patiently oversaw my graduate work on Derrida. My examiners, Peter Boxall and Sarah Wood, raised follow-on questions which I am still thinking about seven years on. I would also like to thank Liz Sage for encouraging me to embark on this project in the first place. Other conversations, too, have borne on it, whether they were held at conferences, symposia, reading groups, meetings, at the pub, over a plate of food, over email or in response to conference papers, articles and drafts. In this sense, I would like to thank: Graham Allen, Alice Andrews, Matías Bascuñán, Andrew Benjamin, Geoffrey Bennington, Matthew Birchwood, Hugo Blumenthal, Tina Chanter, David Coughlan, Pleshette DeArmitt, Sarah Doebbert Epstein, Ilit Ferber, Mauricio Gonzalez, Sam Haddad, Martin Hägglund, Werner Hamacher, Margit Hesselager, J. Hillis Miller, Daniel Hoffman-Schwartz, Peggy Kamuf, Oisín Keohane, Zora Kostadinova, Adam Lipszyc, Martin McQuillan, Sarah Kathryn Marshall, Ronald Mendoza-De Jesús, Simon Morgan Wortham, Forbes Morlock, Michael Naas, Joe Palmer, John Phillips, Juliane Prade-Weiss, Adam Rosenthal, Kas Saghafi, Nassima Sahraoui, Roy Sellars, Mauro Senatore, Shela Sheikh, Timo Uotinen, Francesco Vitale and Richard Wilson. I would also like to thank all those who have helped by simply being lovely: my friends and my family, and in particular my parents, Stef and my sons.

SERIES EDITOR'S PREFACE

Picture Macbeth alone on stage, staring intently into empty space. 'Is this a dagger which I see before me?' he asks, grasping decisively at the air. On one hand, this is a quintessentially theatrical question. At once an object and a vector, the dagger describes the possibility of knowledge ('Is this a dagger') in specifically visual and spatial terms ('which I see before me'). At the same time, Macbeth is posing a quintessentially *philosophical* question, one that assumes knowledge to be both conditional and experiential, and that probes the relationship between certainty and perception as well as intention and action. It is from this shared ground of art and inquiry, of theater and theory, that this series advances its basic premise: Shakespeare is philosophical.

It seems like a simple enough claim. But what does it mean exactly, beyond the parameters of this specific moment in *Macbeth*? Does it mean that Shakespeare had something we could think of as his own philosophy? Does it mean that he was influenced by particular philosophical schools, texts and thinkers? Does it mean, conversely, that modern philosophers have been influenced by *him*, that Shakespeare's plays and poems have been, and continue to be, resources for philosophical thought and speculation?

The answer is yes all around. These are all useful ways of conceiving a philosophical Shakespeare and all point to lines of inquiry that this series welcomes. But Shakespeare is philosophical in a much more fundamental way as well. Shakespeare is philosophical because the plays and poems actively create new worlds of knowledge and new scenes of ethical encounter. They ask big questions, make bold arguments and develop new vocabularies in order to think what might otherwise be unthinkable. Through both their scenarios and their imagery, the plays and poems engage the qualities of consciousness, the consequences of human action, the phenomenology of motive and attention, the conditions of personhood and the relationship among different orders of reality and experience. This is writing and dramaturgy, moreover, that consistently experiments with a broad range of conceptual crossings, between love and subjectivity, nature and politics, and temporality and form.

Edinburgh Critical Studies in Shakespeare and Philosophy takes seriously these speculative and world-making dimensions of Shakespeare's work. The series proceeds from a core conviction that art's capacity to think – to formulate, not just reflect, ideas – is what makes it urgent and valuable. Art matters because unlike other human activities it establishes its own frame of reference, reminding us that all acts of creation – biological, political, intellectual and amorous – are grounded in imagination. This is a far cry from business-as-usual in Shakespeare studies. Because historicism remains the methodological gold standard of the field, far more energy has been invested in exploring what Shakespeare once meant than in thinking rigorously about what Shakespeare continues to make possible. In response, Edinburgh Critical Studies in Shakespeare and Philosophy pushes back against the critical orthodoxies of historicism and cultural studies to clear a space for scholarship that confronts aspects of literature that can neither be reduced to nor adequately explained by particular historical contexts.

Shakespeare's creations are not just inheritances of a past culture, frozen artefacts whose original settings must be expertly reconstructed in order to be understood. The plays and poems are also living art, vital thought-worlds that struggle, across time, with foundational questions of metaphysics, ethics, politics and aesthetics. With this orientation in mind, Edinburgh Critical Studies in Shakespeare and Philosophy offers a series of scholarly monographs that will reinvigorate Shakespeare studies by opening new interdisciplinary conversations among scholars, artists and students.

Kevin Curran

Per Mamma e Papà

CHAPTER 1

WHAT IS SHAKESPEARE'S GENIUS?

Quarrelling Again

The ancient quarrel between literature and philosophy has, it seems, all but subsided and it has become widely accepted that the two disciplines can cohabitate fruitfully. In fact, a glut of work that dwells in the interdisciplinary space between philosophy and literature has been published in the last decade.[1] Despite this, assumptions about the rapport between these two disciplines are taken to task surprisingly seldom, as we still struggle to establish a consensus of what constitutes rigorous interdisciplinary approaches and what these should be aiming to do. Philosophers may now no longer disagree that literature can at times be philosophically valuable, but they do, however, still quarrel about what constitutes literature's usefulness for philosophy.

Nowhere is the unresolved status of the ancient quarrel felt more than in philosophy's attitudes towards Shakespeare. Historically, Shakespeare's plays have had an almost unparalleled grip on philosophers' imaginations, yet philosophers have not been able to give a clear, let alone unanimous, account of what makes the plays such particularly fertile ground for philosophical rumination. Indeed, what seems to have made Shakespeare's plays worthy of philosophical attention has, perhaps, been the fact that they have been written by an undisputed literary genius. Shakespeare's role within the wider field of literature and philosophy is therefore neither simply exemplary nor exceptional; accentuating some of the widely acknowledged benefits that a serious consideration of literature can have for philosophy, it far exceeds others. We may celebrate Shakespeare as an example of what literature can do for philosophy, but it is the exceptional status of the work that leads philosophers to him in the first place. And yet, the alacrity with which some philosophers turn to Shakespeare might just be as suspect as the stubbornness with which many have insisted that philosophy has nothing to learn from literature.

When Derrida reads Shakespeare, he is, of course, in illustrious company.[2] In this book, it is not my intention to argue that Derrida reads Shakespeare better than any other philosopher. More than most philosophical engagements with the Bard, however, Derrida's readings invite us to ponder the conditions of their own existence *as* philosophical readings. Put differently, although the readings Derrida offers of *Hamlet*, *Romeo and Julie*t, *The Merchant of Venice* or *King Lear* contain many original and often surprising insights, their most original contribution to the fields of Shakespeare studies and philosophy, as well as that of philosophy and literature, lies in their performance of a different *mode* of philosophical-literary reading. What I would like to suggest, then, is that the way Derrida reads Shakespeare outlines a new and utterly original way of conceiving of why literature and philosophy would do well to turn to each other. And because it challenges long and deeply held views about Shakespeare and great literary works in general, as well as what contact with 'literary excellence' might do for philosophy, the interest of this readerly encounter far exceeds what some may wish to describe as the parochial, and perhaps outdated, concerns of so-called 'deconstructionists'. In this book, I will show that the originality of Derrida's contribution to the intersecting fields of literature and philosophy is in great part a function of Derrida's incisive critique of our notions of literary genius, and his concomitant invitation to reimagine where the 'genius' of a work, and a language such as Shakespeare's, might lie. The central argument of this book is, therefore, that the way Derrida reads Shakespeare fundamentally unsettles how we have traditionally come to think of the relationship between literature and philosophy, by inviting us to rethink the *kind* of attention we have become used to give to a canonical work such as Shakespeare's.

Before turning to the way Derrida reads Shakespeare in earnest in the next chapter, my concern in this first chapter is to set the stage, to sketch out the environs on to which Derrida's texts on Shakespeare appear – like disruptive spectres. In what follows, I will spend some time considering why scholars might feel that it is at times productive, or perhaps even necessary, to turn to Shakespeare in order to do philosophy. It is not my aim here to give an exhaustive overview of the particular insights philosophers have over the years won from an engagement with Shakespeare. In line with the meta-philosophical, even meta-philosophical-literary, focus of Derrida's texts on Shakespeare, my emphasis falls on how recent philosophical engagements with Shakespeare are framed. In particular, I am interested in the preconceptions – both good and bad – that the stories that philosophers tell about Shakespeare expose. Indeed, what interests me most is in how far, when it comes to thinking about the relationship between Shakespeare and philosophy, we are still indebted to the idea of Shakespeare's *genius*, in this context a byword for the Bard's almost superhuman insight into the human condition, as well as a marker of literary excellence so superior as to be put perennially beyond the reach of any serious critique. It is in Derrida's reluctance to subscribe to such a notion of genius, indeed in his attempt to, to use his own word, *overwrite* what Shakespeare's genius might be and do, that the most powerful move of the way he reads Shakespeare lies. Whether or not one agrees with Derrida, the originality of his vision of what happens philosophically when we read Shakespeare provides a unique opportunity to reconsider this relationship from afresh and to rid ourselves of the baggage that we bring to Shakespeare. Exit Derrida, then, for now.

How Not to Read Shakespeare

Philosophers do not always know what to do with Shakespeare. As much is at least suggested by Martha Nussbaum in a review of three books written on Shakespeare and philosophy – A. D. Nuttall's *Shakespeare the Thinker*, Colin McGinn's *Shakespeare's Philosophy* and Tzachi Zamir's *Double Vision: Moral Philosophy and Shakespearean Drama* – published in May 2008 in the *New Statesman*. Nussbaum characteristically does not mince her words: 'Philosophers often try to write about Shakespeare. Most of the time they are ill-equipped to do so.'[3] Although 'there is something irresistibly tempting in the depth and the complexity of the plays', Nussbaum believes that most philosophers 'lure[d]' into responding 'to that complexity with abstract thought' are 'for the most part . . . utterly unprepared, emotionally or stylistically, to write about literary experience'.[4] She continues: 'armed with their standard analytic equipment, they frequently produce accounts that are laughably reductive, contributing little or nothing to philosophy or to the understanding of Shakespeare'.[5] Nussbaum has strong opinions on how philosophers fail to think with Shakespeare, but she also outlines clearly how philosophers might do better. 'Stages of Thought' names three criteria that a worthwhile philosophical engagement with Shakespeare should fulfil:

First and most centrally, it should really do philosophy, and not just allude to familiar philosophical ideas and positions. It should pursue tough questions and come up with something interesting and subtle – rather than just connecting Shakespeare to this or that idea from Philosophy 101. A philosopher reading Shakespeare should wonder, and ponder, in a genuinely philosophical way. Second, it should illuminate the world of the plays, attending closely enough to language and to texture that the interpretation changes the way we see the work, rather than just uses the work as grist for some argumentative mill. And finally, such a study should offer some account of why philosophical thinking needs to turn to Shakespeare's plays, or to works like them. Why must the philosopher care about these plays? Do they supply to thought something that a straightforward piece of philosophical prose cannot supply, and if so, what?[6]

One might, of course, not subscribe to Nussbaum's particular vision of the relationship between literature and philosophy. Equally, we might believe her criteria to be neither exhaustive nor sufficient. But Nussbaum's review as a whole, and the formulation of these three criteria especially, are useful, because they help us get a better handle on the assumptions that underlie much of our thinking about what literature, and Shakespeare in particular, can do for philosophy. These are, of course, as we shall see, those very same assumptions that Derrida's way of reading Shakespeare challenges.

In Nussbaum's view, something in our philosophical ways of reading Shakespeare has gone awry. If I had to choose one word to characterise the sorry state of affairs Nussbaum's review describes it might be: imbalance. Each one of Nussbaum's criteria, indeed, calls for the remedy of a lopsided approach to interdisciplinarity, where one discipline's insights become subservient to the other discipline's goals. Her critique thus aims not merely at Nuttall and McGinn (as we shall see, Zamir fares much better) but at the field of literature and philosophy as a whole. Take, for example, philosophical readings of Shakespeare that do not *do* philosophy but which bring previously and independently elaborated philosophical themes or insights to the plays. Here, philosophy does not need literature to do its job; rather than an equal discipline, literature becomes, in Nussbaum's words, the grist for philosophy's mill.[7] Such philosophical projections also do not tell us anything new about the literary work. In a particularly brusque moment, Nuttall is, for example, criticised for being unable to contribute significantly to an understanding of Shakespeare in general, or the respective plays he is taking on in particular. For Nussbaum, his analysis of the plays speak of a critic 'who is no longer electrified by the dramas and who finds the task of interpretation rather boring'.[8] His readings also, and this is perhaps the most constructive part of Nussbaum's critique, do ultimately not answer or even pose the question what precisely one discipline could not do without the other. For Nussbaum, then, the interdisciplinary relationship between literature and philosophy, as it is mostly understood and practised, is not merely out of kilter but also fundamentally unproductive: it does not make anything new happen.

In 'Adventures of Reading', Toril Moi asks: 'What is the point of reading literature if all we manage to see in it is a theory we already know? Why not simply stick to reading theory and philosophy if that's what we really want to do?'[9] Like for Nussbaum, for Moi the viability or value of any interdisciplinary encounter between literature and philosophy depends first and foremost on finding a balanced reading approach:

> How can we read philosophically without reducing the text to a witting or unwitting illustration of a pre-existing theory? How can we read literature with philosophy in ways that suggest that the writer may actually have something

to tell the philosopher? And more radically: Is there a way to read philosophically without having recourse to a given philosophy at all? Can criticism itself be philosophy?[10]

Nachträglichkeit is a useful concept to think about the difference between already knowing something (philosophically) before discovering it through (a literary) reading. Sigmund Freud (and the fact that I shall be returning to Freud throughout this book already tells us something about the peculiar kinships of Derrida's approach to Shakespeare) coins this word to describe a particular psychoanalytic conception of time, a complex and possibly reciprocal movement according to which a past event is reinvested with meaning. The German word *nachträglich* means 'later' or 'subsequently', and 'additional' or 'supplementary', while the German verb *nachtragen* means 'to hold a grudge' – literally, to carry something after somebody. Interestingly, Freud did not himself seem to give the term a great importance, and never dedicates an entire essay to it. The explosiveness of Freud's concept only goes off *nachträglich*. In the *Language of Psychoanalysis*, Jean Laplanche and Jean-Bertrand Pontalis follow Jacques Lacan and render the term as *après-coup*, a phrase indicating something being 'too late' or 'after the fact'. Like many translations of Shakespeare, this translation has turned out to be itself so seminal as to trigger a third generation of translations or readings: from the German *Nachträglichkeit* to the French *après-coup* to 'afterwardness', rather than James Strachey's 'deferred effect'.[11] Laplanche dedicates some of his later work to the exploration of *après-coup*. In 'Notes on Afterwardness', he suggests that its reinvesting movement can stem from both the past and the present.[12] In a deterministic scenario the past event only goes off, so to say, in the present; in this case the psychic causality between past and present is hence entirely determined by the past. In a hermeneutic scenario the psychic causality is reversed: the past regains meaning by means of a present reading.[13]

Nussbaum and Moi caution against readings that favour the hermeneutic over the deterministic approach, where, in other words, too great a focus on present philosophical interpretations crowd out a work's own insight (whatever that may be). Both Nussbaum and Moi wish to replace such partial blindness with an approach where philosophical and literary insights do not merely exist side by side but also augment and merge into each other, perhaps just like past and present mingle in Freud's *Nachträglichkeit*. The mingling of perspectives and modes of thinking is at the heart of Zamir's *Double Vision*, which Nussbaum reviews favourably. This engagement with Shakespeare meets all three of her criteria: it offers new insights into the plays, it actually does philosophy, and it gives an account for why – and in what manner – philosophy must turn to Shakespeare. Such 'integrated "philosophical criticism"', in other words an active philosophical engagement with literary works, can, Zamir writes, 'substantially compensate for some limitations of nonliterary philosophical argumentation'.[14] Zamir succeeds in 'allowing the two distinct outlooks of philosophy and literature to interplay', thus facilitating the emergence of 'a kind of thought – a form of double vision – that opens up important modes of understanding'.[15] In this perspective, it is only when literature's and philosophy's distinct modes of understanding become conducive to each other that doing philosophy *with* Shakespeare becomes possible.

Bardolatry

But why do philosophers read Shakespeare in the first place? Is it because Shakespeare is particularly, or uniquely, useful to philosophers? Zamir chooses Shakespeare primarily because of 'the gratifying insights that his writings yield when brought into close dialogue with philosophical concerns' – because, in other words, the nature of his writing, so different from philosophy, yields insights that it cannot find alone.[16] Paul Kottman's acknowledgement that 'students of the plays invariably find themselves wrapped up . . . in philosophical questions' because of the dramatic nature of Shakespeare's work similarly seems to locate Shakespeare's philosophical value in a more generalised understanding of what distinguishes literary from philosophical discourse.[17] More often than not, however, Shakespeare is deemed not only to be representative of literature's value for philosophy, but is thought to far exceed it. In fact, the second reason Zamir gives for focusing on Shakespeare is that his work 'exemplifies literary excellence' and that 'the uncontested aesthetic value of his plays enables investigations into what makes up that value without the need to prove first that it exists'.[18]

Ideas of literary excellence – from the Latin *excellens*, meaning to be elevated or exalted – are closely bound up with the notion of canonicity. The most notorious advocate of a thinking of canonicity is Harold Bloom, of course, and it will come as no surprise that he places Shakespeare at the very heart of his canon. Shakespeare is thus also at the very centre of the attack on great literature by what Bloom characterises as the 'School of Resentment'. For Bloom, the 'School of Resentment' is a catch-all term for all those scholars who 'value theory over literature itself' and who illegitimately bring their own 'political stance' to bear on it.[19] (As I will show in the last chapter, for Derrida, ways of reading are indeed fundamental to taking a political stance, albeit differently from what Bloom imagines here.) Although Bloom is not directly speaking about the relationship between literature and philosophy, there is an echo here of Nussbaum's or Moi's lament about the lopsidedness of many philosophical approaches to literature. In what Bloom calls 'French

Shakespeare' the philosophy is, for example, placed before the text:

> The procedure is to begin with a political stance all your own, far out and away from Shakespeare's plays, and then to locate some marginal bit of English Renaissance social history that seems to sustain your stance. Social fragment in hand, you move in from outside upon the poor play, and find some connection, however established, between your supposed social fact and Shakespeare's words.[20]

Like Nussbaum, Bloom does not believe that such approaches add something to the study of Shakespeare: 'You can bring absolutely anything to Shakespeare and the plays will light it up, far more than what you bring will illuminate the plays.'[21] For these 'professional resenters' Shakespeare is 'only a cultural phenomenon, produced by sociopolitical urgencies. In this view, Shakespeare did not write Shakespeare – his plays were written by the social, political, and economic energies of his age.'[22]

Despite Bloom's initial fears for the canon's fragility and thus the necessity and urgency to protect it tooth and nail, he also believes that the plays' intrinsic aesthetic value is so beyond question that 'Shakespeare's eminence is . . . the rock upon which the School of Resentment must at last founder.'[23] Shakespeare is thus Bloom's trump card, just as he is for Zamir. While for the former Shakespeare is the bedrock upon which the canon will stand, for the latter Shakespeare will silence those who question the value literature might have for philosophy in general. In both argumentative manoeuvres, Shakespeare's *excellence* is key. In Bloom's account, in particular, Shakespeare's eminence is put so beyond the reach of doubt as to raise the issue of idolatry. Bloom is absolutely unapologetic about his adoration of Shakespeare: 'Bardolatry, the worship of Shakespeare, ought to be even more a secular religion than it already is.'[24] For Bloom,

Shakespeare's achievements are both literary and intellectual. Shakespeare not merely 'wrote the best poetry and the best prose in English, or perhaps in any Western language', he also 'thought more comprehensively and originally than any other writer'.[25] Most importantly, however, Shakespeare 'essentially invented the human as we continue to know and value it'.[26] While for Moi an unbalanced approach to literature and philosophy risks perhaps nothing more than futility (although, as we shall see, for Nussbaum the dangers might, in truth, be far greater), for Bloom, overly theorised readings, blind to Shakespeare's true value, risk losing something far greater and far more precious. When 'resenters' put theory before the text, they risk not merely hollowing out Shakespeare but hollowing out something about our very idea of the human. Because who, Bloom, asks, 'besides Shakespeare can continue to inform an authentic idea of the human?'[27]

('I knew very well there was a ghost waiting there, and from the opening, from the raising of the curtain.'[28] Despite my best intentions to defer Derrida until later, he is already here haunting Bloom's reading of Shakespeare, haunting Bloom's idea of the human. Although Bloom's critique of French readings of Shakespeare is primarily aimed at Foucault, 'Derrideanism', as he calls it at one point in *The Invention of the Human*, also falls foul of valuing theory more than Shakespeare. The disagreements between Bloom and Derrida are far more nuanced than they might seem. As Agata Bielik-Robson ponders, might it be 'a case of mutual misunderstanding, first on the part of self-proclaimed deconstructionists who condemned [Bloom] to psychological fallacy, and then on the part of his advocates, who defended his allegedly old-school humanist approach?'[29] Bloom was, in fact, an early supporter of deconstruction and his attack is primarily aimed not at Derrida or de Man or other 'high-deconstructive giants',[30] but rather at a related 'ideologically mobilized, academic mass movement'.[31] The sea-change brought on by Derrida's work indeed laid the foundation for the 'School of Resentment' in many ways. As Simon Glendinning notes, deconstruction's habit to focus on the margins 'seemed to provide a theoretical reference point for anyone who wanted to pay exclusive attention to *non*-canonical texts and literatures', and, I would add, it also gave justification to those who wanted to look at canonical texts differently.[32] While we might be too quick to characterise Bloom's view of Derrida as entirely antagonistic, it would perhaps be impossible to exaggerate the differences between their conception of what constitutes Shakespeare's genius: for Bloom it is Shakespeare the man, perhaps even, to echo Emerson, the representative man; for Derrida it is the Thing Shakespeare. But I am skipping ahead too quickly.)

Surprisingly, perhaps, bardolatry also exists in philosophy. Take, for instance, the common practice of identifying philosophical stances in the plays and then ascribing them to Shakespeare the man himself. In *Shakespeare's Philosophy: Discovering the Meaning Behind the Plays*, unfavourably reviewed by Nussbaum, Colin McGinn attempts 'a systematic treatment of the underlying philosophical themes of the plays', including 'skepticism and the possibility of human knowledge; the nature of the self and personal identity; the understanding of causation; the existence and nature of evil' and 'the formative power of language', which he claims are 'woven deeply into Shakespeare's plots and poetry'.[33] This search for philosophical themes soon gives way to a sort of philosophical man hunt: 'part of my aim in this book is to work out exactly what his view was, insofar as it is represented in the plays'.[34] Thus, despite his own initial reservations, Shakespeare gets cast as a '"naturalist"', a 'clear-eyed observer and recorder, sensitive to the facts before his eyes, not swayed by dogma or tradition'.[35] There is a similar oscillation in David Bevington's *Shakespeare's Ideas: More Things in Heaven and Earth*. Despite declaring at the beginning of his book that Shakespeare never 'speaks in his own voice ... on what we would broadly call his "philosophy"',[36] he concludes with a chapter perhaps humorously but for that no less remarkably entitled 'Credo', which lists a whole litany of beliefs supposedly espoused by the Bard.[37]

Even the most level-headed philosophical examinations of Shakespeare's plays, where no overt attempt is made to identify the man's *own* beliefs, tend towards a sort of 'identity philosophy' and Shakespeare gets recruited as the unwitting pre-cursor of this or that philosophical school. While Millicent Bell acknowledges that 'what he is "trying to say" in his plays is hardly distinguishable in the chorus of ideas that his poetry and dramatic structures make us hear', she goes on to offer a sceptical Shakespeare, 'a doubter of many received views about humanity and the universe'.[38] In *Shakespearean Metaphysics*, Michael Witmore first resists labelling Shakespeare as anything other than a Shakespearean, but nonetheless notes that his metaphysics can be explicated 'with the help of other writers in the metaphysical tradition', because 'his metaphysics shares a common thread of interest' with Whitehead, Bergson and Spinoza.[39] Another example is Julia Reinhard Lupton's wonderful *Thinking with Shakespeare*, in which she argues for readings of Shakespeare that resist 'turning into what Ian Kott calls '"costume drama" ... constrained' not merely by a strict historicisation but also 'by the corsets and laces of their own apparatus, whether the interpretation is flooded by too much context or left high and dry by too much concept'.[40] For Shakespeare to truly be our contemporary we must not merely situate his work in our now, we must also allow ourselves to think with him about issues that concern us now, and to do so in a manner in which our engagement with conceptual (or philosophical) and the textual (or literary) aspects of the text pull our thinking in the same direction. *Thinking with Shakespeare* is in this sense less concerned with 'reconstructing the significance of Shakespeare for later traditions of thinking or staging his uncanny echoing of current events' than with excavating those 'constellations' or 'ensembles of meaning, character and setting' that *'persist*, that appear in, before, and after Shakespeare'.[41] What Reinhard Lupton is after is thus 'a kind of thinking with Shakespeare' which 'not analyzing Shakespeare per se, but following the rhythm and images of thought in Shakespeare in order to achieve original interpretative ends, effe[ct] a kind of renaissance in and through them'.[42] For Reinhard Lupton, then, a philosopher would do well to turn to Shakespeare not because his plays are a 'thesaurus of eternal messages', but because they are able 'to establish real connections with the successive worlds shared and sustained by actors and audiences over time'.[43] For her, thinking with Shakespeare is 'ideally, not to instrumentalize the plays in the service of an ideological program (as one drives in a nail "with" a hammer), but rather to think alongside Shakespeare about matters of shared concern (as one speaks "with" a friend)'.[44] This approach to Shakespeare is framed by Hannah Arendt's notion of the table as a place that *'affords* conversation among equal partners'.[45] Arendt, in fact, very much sets the table of Reinhard Lupton's thinking with Shakespeare, also in the sense that throughout the book Arendt is Reinhard Lupton's and Shakespeare's equal partner in thinking.

What to do with these by no means exhaustive but I believe rather representative philosophical portraits of Shakespeare the sceptic, the metaphysician or the Arendtian? Their diverse and contradictory nature shows that, although, as Agnes Heller writes, 'no one will solve the riddle of the sphinx called Shakespeare', most are not able to resist at least trying.[46] If the challenge for Reinhard Lupton has been 'to approach the texts with a light touch, using frameworks provided by Arendt and her readers in order to respond freshly to the texts rather than simply discover my preoccupations there', it remains unclear whether maintaining such a light touch is at all possible.⁴⁷ Although books such as *Shakespeare's Guide to Life* which search the sonnets and the plays for philosophical tenets or 'wisdoms' to be transformed into readily available and easily quotable, and thus marketable, snippets are, of course, much less sophisticated than McGinn's, Bevington's or Nuttall's well-informed studies, they do in a very real sense share something in common: the desire to go back to the man Shakespeare. As in Henry James's short story 'The Birthplace', there is a persistent desire to anchor the value of the work in the man who wrote it, perhaps in the belief that *man* is able to produce such a work.⁴⁸

Marjorie Garber has written incisively on the mechanisms of self-validation that underlie our collective tendency to quote Shakespeare to clinch an argument. We have a 'penchant for quoting Shakespeare out of context, as a testimony simultaneously to the quoter's own erudition and the truth of the sentiment being uttered'.⁴⁹ Chopped up into small, palatable nuggets of wisdom, Shakespeare is used to give a certain unquestionable ring of authority to one's statement: 'Shakespeare said it: therefore it must be true. True, somehow, to human nature, whatever that is. Universally, transhistorically true.'⁵⁰ It would be overly simplistic to ascribe this tendency, whether within or outside philosophy, to a mere narcissistic desire to find our own beliefs confirmed and thus validated by none other than Shakespeare. There is more going on here. Shakespeare emerges from many of these philosophical readings as infinitely wise and prescient; he not only knows better, but he repeatedly anticipates the history of ideas. Ralph Waldo Emerson famously noted that Shakespeare's achievements are so great that he transcends the horizon of human understanding: 'now, literature, philosophy, and thought are Shakespearized. His mind is the horizon beyond which at present we do not see. Our ears are educated to music by his rhythm.'⁵¹

Bloom agrees: 'He is a system of northern lights, an aurora borealis visible where most of us will never go.'[52] Millicent Bell, too, places Shakespeare far beyond the human horizon: 'I began to suspect, as some others have, that Shakespeare's was one of those rare minds that get around to the other side and see the moon's other face, where, until space travel, no crater had a name.'[53] But it is precisely in testing and widening the limits of human achievement that Shakespeare's work tells us something about what it means to be human: 'The plays remain the outward limit of human achievement: Aesthetically, cognitively, in certain ways morally, even spiritually. They abide beyond the end of the mind's reach; we cannot catch up to them.'[54] It is precisely in exceeding the human that, the astral imagery Bell and Bloom use suggests, Shakespeare becomes our perimeter. Unlike Neil Armstrong, whose small step became humanities' ability to not only name but walk the moon's craters, Shakespeare's extraordinariness *becomes* ours. It is in Shakespeare's ability to transcend humanity that he becomes, to use Emerson's word, representative, or Garber's turn of phrase, 'the abiding, ventriloquized voice of us all'.[55] Each time we celebrate Shakespeare we celebrate human genius and thus ourselves. More than this, Shakespeare becomes the means by which we shore up our idea of ourselves. These are precisely the walls of certainty that Derrida's way of reading Shakespeare assails.

"Who's there?" (*Hamlet*, I, i, 1). Re-enter Derrida, again.

Reading Derrida Reading Shakespeare

At the beginning of 'Let's Start Again', Sarah Wood suggests that we cannot start again without also listening to the other words folded up inside this monosyllabic word:

> v. i. *to shoot, dart, move suddenly forth, or out . . . to break away: to make a sudden or involuntary movement as of surprise or becoming aware: to spring open, out of place,*

or loose: . . . *to set forth on a journey, race, career.* – v. t. *to begin: to set going: . . . to startle* (obs.) . . . – n. *a sudden movement: a sudden involuntary motion of the body: a startled feeling: a spurt: an outburst or fit . . .: a beginning: a setting in motion.*[56]

As soon as we start, the start runs away with itself, taking us to places we did not anticipate. To start is always to make an incision and, at the same time, to allow yourself to be wounded by whatever will start and shoot off. Starting is not easy. I recognise my anxiety in Sean Gaston's deceptively titled *Starting with Derrida*.[57] If anything, Gaston's book, as well as the significant number of other introductory books on Derrida, makes you realise that you will never finish with starting with Derrida, never finish with wondering how Derrida starts. We cannot start, Wood reminds us, without starting *again*.[58] (As we shall see, every start shoots off a teleiopoetic arrow, blurring the possibility of any linearity between beginning and end. And, as we shall also see, this is precisely the movement that is contained in Derrida's thinking about the 're-', the essential repeatability of the act of reading, which haunts this reading of Derrida reading Shakespeare.)

So, let's start then, again, as it is customary to do in introductions, with something like the end. Derrida's writing on Shakespeare is neither prolific nor systematic. In his published work, Shakespeare is only referred to in seven pieces: 'Aphorism Countertime', 'My Chances', *Specters of Marx*, 'What is a "Relevant" Translation?', 'The Time is Out of Joint', *Geneses, Genealogies, Genre, and Genius* and '"This Strange Institution Called Literature"'. There is something of what 'Cogito and the History of Madness' calls the 'palintrope' in Derrida's writing about Shakespeare.[59] When writing about Derrida, it is perhaps particularly appropriate to start with the end, because palintrope is at work *within* these texts. It is, for instance, at work in the strange preface to *Specters*, the 'Exordium', as well as, on a purely syntactical level, the knot of reported speech that kicks it off: '*I would like to learn to live finally [je voudrais apprendre à vivre enfin].*'[60] Similarly, 'Aphorism Countertime' begins with its hypothesis and conclusion: '1. Aphorism is the name.'[61] Here, words and themes are always forwarding and rewinding to somewhere else in the text or stretching their antennae to a different part of Derrida's oeuvre. As Derrida writes in 'Living On: Border Lines': 'Each "text" is a machine with multiple reading heads for other texts.'[62] As Gaston points out, when reading Derrida we thereby not only start with the end, but this work is always starting *again* differently, thereby 'startling' itself and losing its 'logos', frustrating, in other words, any desire to hold, understand or define it once and for all.[63] Derrida's work on Shakespeare, too, is palintropic in the very sense outlined above: in resisting a linear account, in starting and restarting again differently with Shakespeare, it loses its *logos*, and we lose the very possibility of gathering these disjointed and disjointing texts together. It is, however, precisely in this impossibility of offering a simple, linear answer to what he does to Shakespeare (and the other way around) that the thrill and the promise of the Derridean act of reading lies.

How would Derrida fare by Nussbaum's criteria? As I will show, Derrida's works on Shakespeare *do* philosophy, illuminate the plays, and give reasons why the philosopher should care about Shakespeare. For him, literature is not a simple reflection of the 'philosophy' espoused by its author. He 'offer[s] some account of why philosophical thinking needs to turn to Shakespeare's play, or to works like them'.[64] More importantly, he does not see literature merely as a repository for convenient illustrations philosophers can draw on. Not interested in claiming Shakespeare as a Derridean *avant la lettre*, he is instead concerned with showing how an engagement with Shakespeare can open a sort of thinking that cannot simply be put into the service of *one* programme of thought. As I will show, this thinking is not rooted in a quasi-religious trust in Shakespeare's wisdom or his supreme 'humanness'; it is rather a thinking which, being inaugurated by a reciprocal textual haunting, a transposition or dissemination, and the uncanny, transformative afterlife of the Shakespearean idiom, explodes traditional philosophical or literary paradigms. In this view, Shakespeare, like other great works of literature, in the end resists even being fully subsumed by Derrida's own 'programme'.

Interdisciplinarity is on everyone's lips. In a recent and important contribution to the thinking of (and beyond) interdisciplinarity, Peter Osborne has suggested that, rather than the transformative and transgressive programme that it is often celebrated to be, it is a simple extension or modulation of disciplinary hegemony. For Osborne, the discipline of '"English" (or, in the USA, Comparative Literature)' is an example of such a 'hegemonic form, incorporating whole hosts of new theoretical developments from without into radically expanded versions of their former selves'.[65] Put differently, in most cases interdisciplinary approaches do not query but reaffirm the orthodoxies of dominant disciplines. The demand to be interdisciplinary is therefore the demand to transgress – only not 'too flagrantly'.[66] More importantly, most interdisciplinary approaches do not query the deeply embedded certainties that underpin the ways we think in and beyond disciplines, but also about ourselves.

I understand Osborne's call to the transdisciplinary rather than the interdisciplinary as a call to question what modes of thinking an engagement with literature can afford, rather than simply putting them in service of a new master. This transdisciplinarity is perhaps what Martin Heidegger had in mind when in *What is Called Thinking* he called for philosophy not as a research programme but as a handicraft. A research programme is predetermined: it might not know what answers it will find but it knows the realm in which these answers will appear. The frame for thinking is set at the beginning. In contrast, thinking-as-handicraft does not yet know what awaits it; it does not yet know what horizons will border it. It follows the logic of 'start'. Derrida's way of reading Shakespeare shows us that the value of literature for philosophy lies in its ability to surprise us and to fissure any certainty that we might bring to it. What we call literature is philosophically important because it remains, to use Frank Kermode's beautifully apt phrase, 'strange, sublime, uncanny, anxious'.[67]

Although this project is the first to consider Derrida's readings of Shakespeare at some length, it joins an already considerable and ever-growing number of studies on Derrida and Shakespeare. Shakespeare studies has long registered Derrida's work but I will here keep company mostly with scholars who look at this relationship from the other side of the disciplinary divide.[68] Among them are Derek Attridge, Peggy Kamuf, Nicholas Royle and Sarah Wood, as well as, of course, Hélène Cixous, on whose 'Shakespeare Ghosting Derrida' I shall draw repeatedly. I focus on this segment of work on Derrida and Shakespeare because it more easily opens avenues to thinking about the *how* rather than merely the *what* of Derrida's engagements with the plays.

This book is about *how* Derrida reads Shakespeare. It is not primarily about *what* he finds in Shakespeare. I will address the philosophical and literary insights that spring from their encounter, but my main concern will be to gain a clearer understanding of textual practices and conceptual models that underlie Derrida's way of approaching Shakespeare. Although the how and what of an act of reading, particularly an act of reading such as Derrida's, can never be easily separated, it is in the how of Derrida's reading of Shakespeare that his challenge to traditional ways of conceiving of the relationship between literature and philosophy lies. This approach is also justified by Derrida's way of engaging with literature. Derrida is always drawn to texts that 'bear within themselves' the question of what literature is and what we should be doing with it.[69] Despite the generality and ambitiousness of this underlying question, Derrida does not shirk engagement with the singular particularities of the Shakespearean play he reads. It is as if, for Derrida, each of the plays he reads poses this question anew:

> What is fascinating is perhaps the event of a singularity powerful enough to formalize the questions and theoretical laws concerning it. No doubt we shall have to come back to this word *power*. The 'power' that language is capable of, the power that *there is*, as language or as writing, is that a singular mark should also be repeatable, iterable, as mark. It then begins to differ from itself sufficiently to become exemplary and thus involve a certain generality. This economy of exemplary iterability is of itself formalizing.[70]

As I have suggested, philosophical readings of Shakespeare have a tendency to focus on whether a particular philosophical tenet is present in or illuminated, perhaps even foreshadowed, by Shakespeare. The biggest temptation to resist when writing a book on Derrida and Shakespeare might therefore have been to argue that, depending on where one's allegiances lie, Shakespeare is really a Derridean or that Shakespeare said everything Derrida says better and before him to boot. As it turns out, the hurdle to clear was quite another one. The principal challenge of writing this book has been how to do justice to Derrida's habits of reading, without aping, simplifying or formalising them, without, in short, losing their quicksilveryness. The aim is also to write about how Derrida reads Shakespeare, how he dodges philosophical bardolatry for something altogether more alive and motile, without falling into a hagiographic register of a different sort.

The more time I spend in the company of Derrida and with the texts he wrote on and with and in the company of

Shakespeare, the more I realise that trying to write about only one of these texts is all but impossible. Even when I speak of one of his texts on Shakespeare, of a single theme addressed in it, an isolated word or sound, another of his texts (whether on Shakespeare or something else) will always be resonating just out of our earshot. The mission is to impose an order on to this intricate net of harmonies, resonances without muffling them, which would amount to a kind of embalming, a deadening. It seems nearly impossible to render the performativities of Derrida's acts of reading in the constatives that straightforward academic prose demands. I am, of course, not alone in having this difficulty. Derrida faced a similar one when writing *Dissemination*, for example. As the translator Barbara Johnson remarks, 'to perfectly disseminate the exposition of dissemination would require a kind of textual mastery that would belong among the recuperative gestures that dissemination undercuts'.[71] Derrida's readings of Shakespeare, indeed the role Shakespeare comes to play in his writings, undercuts our desire to master either discourse. However, although it disseminates, Derrida's writing on Shakespeare neither shatters nor scatters. It does not, as many would have us believe, dissolve into the thin air of mystification or obscurantism. Dissemination does not mean dispersion, and with every cross-reference, resonance and echo, his writing, which is also always an act of reading, hurtles itself ever more violently towards us and therefore towards the 'to come', which thus becomes the vanishing point of his rendezvous with Shakespeare and with literature.

Perhaps all one can hope for in thinking about Derrida is to put reading heads into motion. Rather than aspire to an unattainable textual mastery, I have therefore resorted to a more palintropic, and hopefully more resonant, mode of exposition. The impossibility of, at least for me, talking about the palintropes of Derrida's acts of reading Shakespeare in a linear fashion is marked throughout by inserting comments (parenthetical and other) which point backwards and forwards to nodal points in the argument, where different strands criss-cross and intersect. Although none can serve as a master-term to unlock what is at stake in Derrida's reading of, and writing with, Shakespeare, I also use a series of what Derrida in 'Différance' calls 'nonsynonymous substitutions' and which surface in Derrida's Shakespearean reading acts to guide me.[72] In response to Derrida's acts of reading, themes and figures like contretemps, the time is out of joint, arrows (*flèches*), peepholes (*meurtrières*), porpentine, chance and frequencies emerge to illuminate different aspects of the way Derrida reads Shakespeare. According to the logic traced by these 'nonsynonymous substitutions', neither can supplant nor supersede the other. Indeed, for Johnson, the merit of Derrida's writing lies 'in its *inscription* of the ways in which all theoretical discourse – including its own – for ever remains both belated and precipitous with respect to the textual practice it attempts to comprehend'.[73] Reminding ourselves of the particular character of these acts of reading – of their openness to what is uncanny, anxious and surprising, and their willingness to find affirmation in such radical openness which, as I will suggest, amounts to a different kind of readerly mastery – is finally, I believe, also the best strategy to give Derrida what is his due, and nothing more. What follows is a brief road map to the rest of the book.

Through a reading of 'Aphorism Countertime' and 'The Time is Out of Joint', Chapter 2 – 'Deconstructing (with) Shakespeare' – gives a succinct overview of Derrida's thought. By means of a discussion of the role the 'textual' has had in previous accounts of the relationship between literature and philosophy – most importantly in Nussbaum's critiques of Butler and Derrida – this chapter will also address common misconceptions about 'deconstruction' and its relation to literature. The last section of the chapter draws on Derrida's 'Signature Event Context' to illuminate Derrida's notion of Shakespeare as an iterable signature, which is crucial to understanding his often seemingly irreverent approach to the Bard.

In Chapter 3 – 'Flèches and the Wounds of Reading' – I suggest that any attempt to delineate a primacy or hierarchy between Derrida and Shakespeare is foiled by Derrida's notion of the palintropic unfolding of time and textual transmission. I discuss the latter through an analysis of the striking resonance between his image of Shakespeare shooting arrows at us in *Specters of Marx* and Friedrich Nietzsche's 'teleiopoetic' arrow in *Politics of Friendship*. In the second half of the chapter, I juxtapose the image of Shakespeare's arrow with *Monlingualism of the Other*'s account of how Derrida is wounded by the arrow (*flèche*) of the French language in order to formulate Derrida's understanding of reading as an event, and as a wound. I then go on to demonstrate that Derrida loves Shakespearean drama not despite but because of its Englishness. Indeed, what enflames what he calls his violent and jealous love of the Bard is in fact Shakespeare's idiom, the very materiality and body of Shakespeare's English. Brought into conversation with his understanding of the wounds of reading, most beautifully described in his work on Paul Celan, Derrida's play on Shakespeare's arrows therefore also alters what we may think of as the body, and hence also the genius, of a text.

'Porpentine', Chapter 4, considers the importance and function of Shakespeare's idiom in Derrida's work on Shakespeare – and beyond – through an analysis of the 'performative translation' of the word 'porpentine' in *Specters of Marx*. I begin by arguing, through a juxtaposition of his parenthetical non-translation of Hamlet's porpentine in Act I, scene v with Karl Marx's translation of Hamlet's mole in 'The Eighteenth Brumaire', that, like Marx's translation, Derrida's interference is performative but that, unlike Marx's, it retains its English idiom even in French.

Drawing parallels between Shakespeare's porpentine and the poematic hedgehog at the heart of 'Che cos'è la poesia?' and '*Istrice 2: Ick bünn all hier*', I go on to suggest that, for Derrida, the idiom's translatability is dependent on its idiomacity, on the singular signifier–signified combination which would appear to escape translation. The chapter concludes with a discussion of 'What is a "Relevant" Translation', a text which also includes a reading of *The Merchant of Venice*, and specifically with an analysis of the philosophical significance of the homonymic and paronomastic effects brought into play by the frequent parenthetic insertion of untranslated Shakespeare into Derrida's French.

Chapter 5 – 'Giving the Greatest Chance to Chance' – turns to the role of chance in the way Derrida reads Shakespeare. It begins with a consideration of Derrida's extremely brief and enigmatic mention of *King Lear* in 'My Chances/ Mes Chances: A Rendezvous with Some Epicurean Stereophonies'. Here, I ask what chances Derrida takes, or almost takes, with Shakespeare. I show that in proposing but failing to read *King Lear* beyond Freud's reading of the play in *The Theme of the Three Caskets* (1913) and Heidegger's treatment of Moira in 'Moira (Parmenides, Fragment viii, 34–41)', Derrida is for the greatest part concerned with querying the idea of mastery that characterises Heidegger's and Freud's stances as readers. In the second part of the chapter, I explore the complex dynamics between Freud's instrumentalisation of the chances of reading and his desire for mastery by tracing his seemingly fortuitous uses of Shakespeare in the interpretation of his '*Non Vixit* Dream' in *The Interpretation of Dreams*. In the chapter's last section, I turn to Derrida's inheritance of Freud and his understanding of literature's ability 'to give the greatest chance to chance', as well as his radical commitment to the uncanny mastery of the text as a counterpoint to ideas of Shakespeare's supremely human genius.

Chapter 6 – 'The Politics of Re-reading' – thinks about the political aspirations of Derrida's work on Shakespeare. I argue that any misreading of *Specters of Marx*, and what Derrida is doing with Marx, is also based on a misunderstanding of the role the Shakespearean references play in this text. We cannot, I argue, understand Derrida's re-politicisation if we do not understand it as an act of re-reading, which in the essay 'Marx & Sons' is also comprehended in terms of 'differential tones'. Taking Derrida's aural hint, I propose the term 'frequencies', as it emerges in *Specters of Marx*, in order to show how the Thing Shakespeare also works 'philosophonically'. With a reading of how Derrida plays on the appearance and disappearance of *Hamlet*'s Ghost in *Specters*, and more precisely of how he paraphrases one reappearance as '*Re-enter the Ghost*', I argue that it is precisely in this '*re-*' that we can hear the 'political' tones of Derrida's reading resonate.

The conclusion returns to the question of what Shakespeare's genius might be.

Notes

1. Apart from numerous studies on distinct encounters between a particular philosophy and a particular author, in the past decade an impressive number of studies and collections have been dedicated to the relationship between literature and philosophy more in general; see, for example: Peter Lamarque, *The Philosophy of Literature* (Oxford: Wiley-Blackwell, 2009); Richard Eldridge, ed., *The Oxford Handbook of Philosophy and Literature* (Oxford: Oxford University Press, 2009); Terry Eagleton, *The Event of Literature* (New Haven: Yale University Press, 2012); Anthony Cascardi, *The Cambridge Introduction to Literature and Philosophy* (Cambridge: Cambridge University Press, 2014).
2. Paul A. Kottman's *Philosophers on Shakespeare* (Stanford: Stanford University Press, 2009) collects excerpts of many philosophical engagements with the Bard.

3. Martha Nussbaum, 'Stages of Thought: Review of A. D. Nuttall, *Shakespeare the Thinker*; Colin McGinn, *Shakespeare's Philosophy*; and Tzachi Zamir, *Double Vision: Moral Philosophy and Shakespearean Drama*', in *Philosophical Interventions: Reviews 1986–2011* (Oxford: Oxford University Press, 2012), 367.
4. Ibid. 367.
5. Ibid. 367.
6. Ibid. 367.
7. Ibid. 367.
8. Ibid. 368.
9. Toril Moi, 'The Adventure of Reading: Literature and Philosophy, Cavell and Beauvoir', in *Stanley Cavell and Literary Studies: Consequences of Skepticism*, ed. Richard Eldridge and Bernie Rhie (London: Continuum, 2011), 18.
10. Ibid. 19.
11. Jean Laplanche and Jean-Bertrand Pontalis, *The Language of Psychoanalysis* (London: Karnac Books, 1988).
12. Jean Laplanche, 'Notes on Afterwardness', in *Essays on Otherness* (London: Routledge, 1999), 261.
13. Ibid. 264–5.
14. Tzachi Zamir, *Double Vision, Moral Philosophy and Shakespearean Drama* (Princeton: Princeton University Press, 2007), xiii.
15. Ibid. xv.
16. Ibid. xiii.
17. Paul A. Kottman, ed., *Philosophers on Shakespeare* (Stanford: Stanford University Press, 2009), 1.
18. Zamir, *Double Vision*, xiii.
19. Harold Bloom, *Shakespeare: The Invention of the Human* (London: Fourth Estate, 1999), 9.
20. Ibid. 9.
21. Ibid. 9.
22. Ibid. 16.
23. Harold Bloom, *The Western Canon: The Books and School of the Ages* (New York: Harcourt Brace & Company, 1994), 25.

24. Bloom, *Shakespeare: The Invention of the Human*, xvii.
25. Ibid. xviii.
26. Ibid. 290.
27. See Dominic Pettman, *Human Error: Species-Being and Media Machines* (Minneapolis: University of Minnesota Press, 2011), 12–19, for an incisive account of Bloom's vision of Shakespeare as the midwife of 'the human'.
28. Jacques Derrida, *Specters of Marx: The State of the Debt, the Work of Mourning and the New International*, trans. Peggy Kamuf (London: Routledge, 2006), 2.
29. Agata Bielik-Robson, *The Saving Lie: Harold Bloom and Deconstruction* (Evanston: Northwestern University Press, 2011), 79.
30. Ibid. 77.
31. Ibid. 76.
32. Simon Glendinning, *Derrida: A Very Short Introduction* (Oxford: Oxford University Press, 2011), 8.
33. Colin McGinn, *Shakespeare's Philosophy: Discovering the Meaning Behind the Plays* (New York: Harper Collins, 2006), viii.
34. Ibid. 15.
35. Ibid. 15.
36. David Bevington, *Shakespeare's Ideas: More Things in Heaven and* Earth (Oxford: Wiley-Blackwell, 2008), 1.
37. Ibid. 213–17.
38. Millicent Bell, *Shakespeare's Tragic Skepticism* (New Haven: Yale University Press, 2002), 1.
39. Michael Witmore, *Shakespearean Metaphysics* (London: Continuum: 2008), 3.
40. Julia Reinhard Lupton, *Thinking with Shakespeare: Essays on Politics and Life* (Chicago: University of Chicago Press, 2011), 18.
41. Ibid. 18.
42. Ibid. 20.
43. Ibid. 18.
44. Ibid. 23.

45. Ibid. 13.
46. Agnes Heller, *The Time is Out of Joint: Shakespeare as Philosopher of History* (Lanham: Rowman & Littlefield Publishers, 2002), 1.
47. Reinhard Lupton, *Thinking with Shakespeare*, 23.
48. Henry James, 'The Birthplace', in *The Better Sort* (New York: Charles Scribner's Sons: 1903), 245–311.
49. Marjorie Garber, *Symptoms of Culture* (New York: Routledge, 2000), 155. See also Marjorie Garber, '*Bartlett*'s Familiar Shakespeare', in *Profiling Shakespeare* (New York and London: Routledge, 2008), 278–301.
50. Ibid. 155.
51. Ralph Waldo Emerson, *Representative Men* (London: J. M. Dent & Co, 1901), 158.
52. Bloom, *Shakespeare: The Invention of the Human*, 3.
53. Bell, *Shakespeare's Tragic Skepticism*, x.
54. Bloom, *Shakespeare: The Invention of the Human*, xvii–xviii.
55. Garber, *Profiling Shakespeare*, 122.
56. Sarah Wood, 'Let's Start Again', *Diacritics* 29, no. 1 (1999): 1.
57. Sean Gaston, *Starting with Derrida: Plato, Aristotle and Hegel* (London and New York: Continuum, 2007).
58. Wood, 'Let's Start Again', 1.
59. Jacques Derrida, 'Cogito and the History of Madness', in *Writing and Difference*, trans. Alan Bass (London and New York: Routledge, 2001), 76.
60. Derrida, *Specters of Marx*, xvi; Jacques Derrida, *Spectres de Marx: L'État de la dette, le travail du deuil et la nouvelle Internationale* (Paris: Galilée, 1993), 13.
61. Jacques Derrida, 'Aphorism Countertime', trans. Nicholas Royle, in *Acts of Literature*, ed. Derek Attridge (London: Routledge, 1992), 416.
62. Jacques Derrida, 'Living On: Border Lines', trans. James Hulbert, in *Deconstruction and Criticism* (New York: Seabury Press, 1979), 107.
63. Gaston, *Starting with Derrida*, viii.
64. Nussbaum, 'Stages of Thought', 367.

65. Peter Osborne, 'Problematizing Disciplinarity, Transdisciplinary Problematics', *Theory, Culture and Society* 32, nos. 5–6 (2015): 5.
66. Ibid. 7–8.
67. Frank Kermode, 'Strange, Sublime, Uncanny, Anxious', *London Review of Books*, 22 December 1994, https://www.lrb.co.uk/v16/n24/frank-kermode/strange-sublime-uncanny-anxious
68. Shakespeare scholars including Malcom Evans ('Deconstructing Shakespeare's Comedies'), Howard Felperin ('"Tongue-tied our queen?": The Deconstruction of Presence in *The Winter's Tale*') and the contributors to *Shakespeare and Deconstruction* (ed. G. Douglas Atkins and David M. Bergeron, 1988), as well as Richard Wilson (*Shakespeare in French Theory: King of Shadows*, 2007) have considered 'deconstruction's' reverberation in Shakespeare studies.
69. Jacques Derrida, '"This Strange Institution Called Literature": An Interview with Jacques Derrida', trans. Geoffrey Bennington and Rachel Bowlby, in *Acts of Literature*, ed. Derek Attrige (London: Routledge, 1992), 41.
70. Ibid. 42–3.
71. Jacques Derrida, *Dissemination*, trans. Barbara Johnson (London, New York: Continuum, 2004), xxxiv.
72. Jacques Derrida, 'Différance', trans. Alan Bass, in *Margins of Philosophy* (Chicago: University of Chicago Press, 1982), 12.
73. Derrida, *Dissemination*, xxxiv.

CHAPTER 2

DECONSTRUCTING (WITH) SHAKESPEARE

Shakespeare à contretemps

How does Derrida read Shakespeare? If his teacher's judgement on Derrida's *khâgne* assignment on Shakespeare's idea of kingship – recently surfaced from University of California, Irvine's collection of his papers – is anything to go by, it is 'quite unintelligible'. His reading of *Romeo and Juliet* in 'Aphorism Countertime' is exemplary of Derrida's approach to the Shakespearean corpus. As Derek Attridge notes, this piece disrupts the 'homogenous spatiotemporal continuum' of the 'traditional critical essay'.[1] This short but incisive text is thus not least remarkable because of Derrida's decision to write in aphorisms. What is an aphorism? 'As its name indicates, aphorism separates, it marks dissociation (*apo*), it terminates, delimits, arrests (*horizō*). It brings to an end by separating, it separates in order to end – and to define [*finir – et définir*].'[2] This is what 'Aphorism Countertime' does to *Romeo and Juliet*. It separates, it dissociates, but it is perhaps because of this that this short piece is so arresting. Like thirty-nine arrows, its aphorisms puncture our understanding of what a philosophical reading of Shakespeare might be, indeed what reading Shakespeare in general might entail.

Its form is not the only unusual thing about 'Aphorism Countertime'. It also marks a highly uncommon way of approaching Shakespeare. In French, *contretemps* means 'mishap', as well as 'out of time' or, more literally, 'against time' (*Collins-Robert French Dictionary*). Doing something *à contretemps* means going against the grain. Apart from the fact that 'Aphorism Countertime' is at odds with the way Shakespeare is usually read, reading Shakespeare is also a highly unusual thing for Derrida to do. It is difficult to find a pattern to the philosophical texts Derrida feels drawn to; the shared characteristics of the literary texts he turns to are more obvious. They are, in Attridge's words, 'mostly twentieth-century, and mostly modernist, or at least nontraditional (many would say "difficult") in their use of language and literary conventions: Blanchot, Ponge, Celan, Joyce, Artaud, Jabès, Kafka'.[3] Two notable exceptions are Melville and Poe. And Shakespeare, of course. So unusual seems Derrida's choice that it prompts Attridge to ask Derrida in an interview published as '"This Strange Institution Called Literature"' whether 'a literary work as historically and culturally distant as this one pose[s] any problems for your reading of it?'[4] Derrida replies:

> As you have noticed, I did not read *Romeo and Juliet* as a sixteenth-century text, I was incapable of it. The title was, after all, 'countertime.' And also the aphorism, which means that I did not even claim to read the work itself as an ensemble. Not that I am only interested in modern texts, but I did not have the necessary competence to read this play 'in its period.'[5]

In fact, Derrida goes on to admit that he would not have written about the play had he not been invited to do so:

> Spontaneously, I would never have had the audacity to write on *Romeo and Juliet* or anything at all of Shakespeare's. My respect for an oeuvre which is one of the 'greatest' in

the world for me is too intimidated, and I consider myself too incompetent. In this case, I was asked for a short, oblique texts to accompany a production. In this sketch of a reading of *Romeo and Juliet*, I privileged the motifs of the contretemps and anachrony, which I was interested in anyway, and precisely in this place where they intersect with the question of the proper name.[6]

The fact that Derrida declares himself incompetent is to be understood less in terms of a *captatio benevolentiae*, than as an honest admission of his limitations as a Shakespeare scholar. He makes no secret of the fact that he does not have the competency or, perhaps, the desire to consider the play in its 'proper' historical context. This, however, does not mean that he dismisses Shakespeare. On the contrary:

Having said this, I would very much like to read and write in the space or heritage of Shakespeare, in relation to whom I have infinite admiration and gratitude; I would like to become (alas, it's pretty late) a 'Shakespeare expert'; I know that everything is in Shakespeare: everything and the rest, so everything or nearly.[7]

Being a Shakespeare expert in this sense would mean to think about the plays not merely in their immediate historical and textual contexts, but to delve into everything and the rest that is what we call *Shakespeare*. Here, Derrida seems to come dangerously close to an almost 'Bloom-esque' idealisation of the Shakespearean corpus as a seemingly endless well of wisdom and truth. Any trace of bardolatry is, however, expunged immediately: 'But after all, everything is also in Celan, and in the same way, although differently, and in Plato or in Joyce, in the Bible, in Vico or in Kafka, not to mention those still living, everywhere, well, almost everywhere . . .'[8] When Derrida says that he would like to become a Shakespeare expert, he is neither aspiring to an early modern specialisation, nor is he falling into bardolatry; he is rather recommitting to what reading-writing-thinking can do. Derrida is, in short, not hailing the human genius of Shakespeare, but the genius of that strange institution we call literature.

There are three important things to highlight about Derrida's way of approaching Shakespeare. Firstly, by his own admission, Derrida writes about motifs – such as contretemps and anachrony – in which he was interested in anyway. These are, in other words, concerns that he brings to rather than finds in Shakespeare. Secondly, he admits that he has not 'the necessary competence to read [*Romeo and Juliet*] "in its period"'.[9] Most importantly, he does not seem in the slightest bothered about his limitations as a Shakespeare scholar or his predetermined approach to *Romeo and Juliet*: 'No one is obliged to be interested in what interests me.'[10] Thirdly, Derrida does not merely fail to read *Romeo and Juliet* in its historical context, he also does not read it as a cohesive dramatic piece. 'Aphorism Countertime' does not venture to give an exhaustive, or even a general reading of *Romeo and Juliet*. While, as Hélène Cixous notes in 'Shakespeare Ghosting Derrida', 'it is to Shakespeare and Company that he wishes to face owing [*se veut devant*]', he does not read '"all" Shakespeare', but only 'some of the plays, a few features, a few tropes, a few words. Almost nothing, apparently. And yet . . .'[11] Like in his readings of Joyce (where Derrida focuses on just two words, *yes yes*), Celan (in which he thinks about the word *Shibboleth*) or Blanchot (where the word *pas* is his focus) when reading Shakespeare Derrida isolates, cuts, separates. Here, Shakespeare is, as the very form of 'Aphorism Countertime' seems to indicate, cut up, distorted, un-hinged and desynchronised. This is Shakespeare deconstructed.

Is the way Derrida reads Shakespeare problematic? Some might argue that, in Derrida's decontextualised, hypertextual way of looking at Shakespeare, there literally is nothing but the text, the problem being that not much of Shakespeare's text is actually read. *Romeo and Juliet*, they might argue, is here only the backdrop for a deconstructive performance with the main character being not Shakespeare but Derrida himself. In this sense, the seemingly rather innocent question 'What does Derrida do with Shakespeare?' gains a frustrated, even accusatory emphasis: What (on earth!) does he *do* with Shakespeare? Or, taking some steps back to consider not merely the question of the role of literature in his philosophical project, but his philosophical project in itself: What does his philosophy do *really*?

There is so much there, a certain well-rehearsed argument goes, that is not worthy of the proper name of philosophy: the flamboyance of subject matter, the lack of rigour, the overwrought style, the obfuscation. Derrida is, many would gladly argue, not a serious philosopher, understood to mean both that he lacks seriousness in the manner in which he does philosophy and that, in the aims of the latter, he quickly loses what really matters – Truth, the Human – from sight in favour of a brilliant but ultimately empty display of intellectualism. In fact, this pretension is not merely deemed to divert Derrida from doing worthy philosophical work, but the very way he engages with philosophy in itself is characterised as ethically pernicious. The signatories of the open letter to *The Times* during the 1992 Cambridge affair characterised his work as 'semi-intelligible attacks' not merely upon 'scholarship' but also on 'the values of reason [and] truth'.[12] Meanwhile, writing in *Der Spiegel*, Sarah Richmond worried that Derrida's work would poison young minds.[13]

Despite the fact that these criticisms did not hold enough ground to stop Derrida getting his *doctor honoris causa* from Cambridge in the end, criticisms of the same ilk still stubbornly persist. Chances are that even if you have never read any Derrida you will have a vague idea of him as the author of a recalcitrant corpus. Equally, if you have read him and are open to reading with him further, you will have a sense of why such criticisms are often founded on the unstable ground only a cursory engagement with his work can provide. In these readings of Derrida, justice is not seasoned with mercy (and as we shall see in Derrida's reading of *The Merchant of Venice*, such 'seasoning' is the key ingredient to an act of reading worthy of the name). Paradoxically, if the often injudicious manner in which his works have been widely denounced has achieved anything, it is a broadening of support, a boldening of position and a further entrenchment of those many who believe themselves to be thinking in his wake. If self-professed 'Derrideans' and his most vociferous critics are ships that pass in the night, they do so with guns blazing.

The entrenchment of the debate makes it imperative to consider criticisms of Derrida seriously, no matter how unfounded we might believe them to be, because they are informed by a certain understanding of the relationship between literature and philosophy that his work queries. Derrida's philosophical project has to be understood in terms of an engagement with literature. Literature here is not understood as a canonical body of texts to be read, but as, for lack of a better term, the textual – what both within and beyond literature calls for a certain readerly attention. It is because of this that critiques of Derrida often take, whether explicitly or implicitly, the form of a denunciation of the role of both literature and the textual in philosophy. Before returning to 'Aphorism Countertime', let us then return once again to the question about the relationship between the philosophical and the textual.

Bloodlessness

In the Cambridge affair, Derrida's critics focused, in particular, on the fact that they deemed his work to be 'too literary' to do proper philosophical work.

> M. Derrida describes himself as a philosopher, and his writings do indeed bear some of the marks of writings in that discipline. Their influence, however, has been to a striking degree almost entirely in fields outside philosophy – in departments of film studies, for example, or of French and English literature.[14]

Paradoxically, interdisciplinary approaches are often founded on the conviction that the business of doing philosophy and the business of reading literature are, although at times mutually informative, ultimately distinct. Friendly disciplines they might be, but separate they must remain. In the open letter an undue literary influence is closely linked to a work's failure to 'meet accepted standards of clarity and rigour'.[15] If philosophy wishes to answer questions that are of importance to humans, these voices claim, it needs to turn not to literature or literary strategies but to science and objectivity. This position is not isolated. For Arthur Danto, for instance, a belief that philosophy can be literature and vice versa does violence to the notion of scientific rigour central to what philosophy should be: 'to acquiesce in the concept of philosophy-as-literature just now seems tacitly to acquiesce in the view that the austere imperatives of philosophy-as-science have lost their energy'.[16] Echoing Bloom's nostalgia for an uncorrupted canon, Danto writes: 'considering what has been happening to texts when treated in recent times, our canon seems suddenly fragile, and it pains the heart to think of them enduring the frivolous sadism of the deconstructionist'.[17] While in Bloom such textual sadism is also fuelled by identity politics, here it is fed further by an egomaniacal desire to inscribe oneself on to the text. In contrast to this is the analytic ideal (to which Danto does, by the way, not fully subscribe) that philosophy should be shorn from all traces of the philosopher's identity:

> if, under the constraints of blind review, we black out name and institutional affiliation, there will be no internal evidence of authorial presence, but only a unit of pure philosophy, to the presentation of which the author will have sacrificed all identity.[18]

If, for Danto, philosophy is 'universal in the sense of being about every possible world insofar as possible', literature is specific in that it is 'about each reader who experiences it'.[19] Each literary work thus functions 'as a kind or mirror', allowing the reader to 'identif[y] himself not with the implied reader for whom the implied narrator writes but with the actual subject of the text in such a way that each work becomes a metaphor for each reader'.[20] Like for Bloom, such a recognition is, however, not merely constative but performative in that it 'transform[s] the self-consciousness of the reader who in virtue of identifying with the image recognizes what he is'.[21]

Danto's view that philosophy or science speaks generally of human truths while literature does so specifically is shared by Richard Eldridge for whom 'philosophy foregrounds result, impersonality, and attention to general discursive and practical commitment, while literature foregrounds process, personal engagement, particularity, and perplexity'.[22] It is in this attention to the particular that literature's ability to teach us something about 'human commitments and passions' lies.[23] Eldridge ultimately believes that literature and philosophy are attentions to different aspects of human life that can learn from each other. It is the otherness of literature, precisely the fact that it is *not* philosophy, that makes it so useful. Anthony Cascardi, too, believes the difference between the disciplines to be productive: 'to erase all their differences would be to deprive ourselves of whatever light they can shed on each other from positions that are always partly strange to one another'.[24] Stephen Mulhall similarly sees literature and philosophy as two distinct 'elements in the human rational armoury'.[25] He thus envisions 'a dialogue, in which philosophy and literature participate as each other's other – as autonomous but internally related'.[26] Mulhall is 'not suggesting that philosophy can or should become literature'; in fact, it is the difference between their modes of thinking that makes integrating these two disciplines so fruitful.[27]

Nussbaum's own work is testament to the fact that she believes that at times only literature can solve some of philosophy's problems. In *Love's Knowledge*, Nussbaum for instance, aims

> to establish that certain literary texts (or texts similar to these in certain relevant ways) are indispensable to a philosophical inquiry in the ethical sphere: not by any means sufficient, but sources of insight without which the inquiry cannot be complete.[28]

For Nussbaum, however, literature does not merely help philosophy do its work but it, most importantly, helps redefine what that work may be. This reorientation does not happen along pre-determined or pre-existing disciplinary lines but in response to demands that are rooted in the more general experience of being human. While 'philosophy has often seen itself as a way of transcending the merely human, of giving the human being a new and more godlike set of activities and attachments', doing philosophy with literature (in the way Nussbaum suggests) allows philosophers to relearn 'a way of being human and speaking humanly'.[29] Bringing human literary insights to philosophy therefore does not only mean 'to bring them to some academic discipline which happens to ask ethical questions. It is to bring them into connection with our deepest practical searching, for ourselves and others . . .'[30]

To varying degrees, all these thinkers and scholars acknowledge the value literature can have for philosophy. But all remain securely within an interdisciplinary framework, in that they focus on the value of literature for philosophy, rather than querying, as Osborne invites us to do, the hegemonic dynamics that structure our understanding of interdisciplinarity. On the surface, only Nussbaum allows for the fact that an engagement with literature might actually change the very idea of what philosophy is. Hers is, however, not a transdisciplinary project in Osborne's sense, because, while literature is not put in philosophy's service, both are put into service of a certain humanism. In fact, literature can help philosophy become more attuned to the human because it is viewed as a more effective vehicle for its expression. It is an attention to textuality, as opposed to Great Literature, that can work a transdisciplinary shift able to question the underlying organizing principle of 'the human'.

The degree of attention paid to the question of the textual in the way we read and write is a fault line dividing both the study of literature and the doing of philosophy. In the case of the latter, it is often, not very helpfully, called the disagreement between analytic and continental traditions. In literature, it is characterised, not any more helpfully, in terms of a difference between historicist and theorist approaches. The questions that are at stake in both cases are, however, the same: what can writing do? Can it, at its most lucid, be a perfectly reliable vessel of the author's intentions, arguments and thoughts? Does it speak to a specific historical context? Do its effects also incalculably exceed authorial and historical circumstance? Does it further the expression of human genius? Does it give habitation to that anxious, uncanny genius which for Kermode constitutes true canonicity?[31] The question of reading follows hot on the heels of the question of writing, as either notions of writing bring with them drastically different ideas of what reading is: is reading an endeavour of comprehension, or can it be more? Can, as Moi asks, criticism itself do philosophical work? In one word: yes. For Derrida, each act of reading has philosophical repercussions; in fact, the act of reading *is* the philosophical repercussion. Derrida, like Paul de Man, understands reading 'as an act which responds to those aspects of a text which cannot be defined grammatically (that is, according to a general code or program) . . . forcing one to face the paradox that reading in the strict sense is called for by that which is *unreadable* in a text'.[32] In his 'Introduction' to Derrida's *Acts of Literature*, Attridge draws attention to the 'polysemy of the term *act*: as both "serious" performance and "staged" performance, as a "proper" doing and an improper or temporary one, as an action, a law of governing actions, and a record of documenting actions'.[33] In this sense, his acts of reading may be understood, to use Colin Davies's terms, as acts of '*overreading*' which entail 'a willingness to test or to exceed the constraints which restrict the possibilities of meaning released by a work' and which at times 'depend upon what might appear to be bizarre, disorientating interpretive leaps'.[34]

Whether or not we accept such acts of overreading as philosophically valuable is crucial for how much patience we will have for the way Derrida reads Shakespeare. Take, for example, the approach taken by Nussbaum in her notorious critique of Judith Butler in 'The Professor of Parody'. The question of style is at the heart of Nussbaum's critique. What Nussbaum wants but what she does not find in Butler is a kind of writing that leaves as little as possible between itself and what it is tasked to convey. Opaque writing, such as Butler's, she claims, holds grave consequences not merely for the philosopher herself but also for the reader, who will be kept from probing whether its claims are credible. For example, after trudging through her 'verbosity', Butler's reader has, Nussbaum argues, no time or energy left for 'assessing the truth of the claims'.[35] Again, the parallels to criticisms of Derrida voiced during the Cambridge affair are striking:

> M. Derrida's voluminous writings in our view stretch the normal forms of academic scholarship beyond recognition. Above all – as every reader can very easily establish for himself (and for this purpose any page will do) – his works employ a written style that defies comprehension . . . Many of them seem to consist in no small part of elaborate jokes and puns ('logical phallusies' and the like), and M. Derrida seems to us to have come close to making a career out of what we regard as translating into the academic sphere tricks and gimmicks similar to those of the Dadaists or of the concrete poets.[36]

Like Derrida's, Butler's self-involved, reference- and term-encrusted style, Nussbaum argues, is thus a two-pronged strategy seeking first to evade critique and second to foreground the originator of an idea at the expense of the idea itself. Criticism cannot gain any fraction, cannot do its work if its object is obscure enough, and its author canny enough, to plead simply to having been misunderstood. This is what John Searle has, loosely quoting Foucault, called the terrorism of obscurantism.[37] The two elements highlighted by Nussbaum are naturally interrelated: if ideas are not spelled out clearly, they can also not function independently of the thinker who originated them. It is because of this that, so Nussbaum continues, 'some precincts of the continental philosophical tradition, though surely not all of them, have an unfortunate tendency to regard the philosopher as a star who fascinates, and frequently by obscurity, rather than as an arguer among equals'.[38]

An attention to how something is said at the expense of what is being said, is not only a distraction but, so Nussbaum argues, an escape mechanism, freeing the writer from the responsibility of getting up from her desk and fighting for change in the real world. Indeed, Nussbaum's criticism of Butler's way of writing and doing philosophy in 'The Professor of Parody' is part of a wider attempt to grapple with what might be called the 'symbolic' turn in feminism; the critique is in this sense aimed more at Butler the feminist than Butler the theorist. For Nussbaum, traditional feminist theorists, such as Catherine MacKinnon for example, have long understood that feminist theory is 'not just fancy words on paper' but 'connected to proposals for social change'.[39] In contrast, for symbolic feminists, such as Butler, 'doing fancy things with words on paper' in itself constitutes the doing of feminist politics. For Nussbaum this is emphatically not so. (I will return to the question of whether 'fancy words on paper' can engender political change in Chapter 6 when I discuss Derrida's re-reading of Marx with Shakespeare.)

It is not my concern here to defend Butler. She is not in need of my assistance; the quirks in Butler's writing do ultimately not detract from the very real impact Butler's work has had on how gender is thought about today. Despite the admiration one might have for Butler's work, it would nevertheless be wrong to argue that she is Derrida's equal either in terms of importance of their work or, since we are here dealing with the question of style, regarding the question of who is the better stylist. In fact, just like Derrida's work haunts the debate about the relationship between Shakespeare and philosophy, he is also present in the background of Nussbaum's critique of Butler. The rise of 'symbolic' feminism in fact 'owe[s] much to the recent prominence of French postmodernist thought' and 'the extremely French idea that the intellectual does politics by speaking seditiously, and that this is a significant type of political action'.[40]

Nussbaum does not mention Derrida's writings on Shakespeare at all in 'Stages of Thought', but, given that she thinks that 'Derrida on truth is simply not worth studying', it does not take much imagination to guess what her verdict would have been had she turned to his work in the context of the question of what philosophy might learn from Shakespeare.[41] In a brief aside on Derrida's work on Nietzsche in *Love's Knowledge*, Nussbaum talks about how much hard work reading him is, although she is less severe with Derrida than she is with Butler:

> The sense that we are social beings puzzling out, in times of great moral difficulty, what might be, for us, the best way to live – this sense of practical importance, which animates contemporary ethical theory and has always animated much of great literature, is absent from the writings of many of our leading literary theorists. One can have no clearer single measure of this absence than to have the experience of reading Jacques Derrida's *Éperons* after reading Nietzsche. Once one has worked through and been suitably (I think) impressed by Derrida's perceptive and witty analysis of Nietzsche's style, one feels, at the end of all the urbanity, an empty longing amounting to a hunger, a longing for the sense of difficulty and risk and practical urgency that are inseparable from Zarathustra's dance.[42]

Like Butler, Derrida is, so Nussbaum argues, not ready to engage with the urgent and practical questions that most concern us as humans: 'After reading Derrida and not Derrida alone, I feel a certain hunger for blood; for, that is, writing about literature that talks of human lives and choices as if they matter to us all.'[43] This image of bloodlessness is intimately connected with the notion of 'deconstruction' as a mechanistic and soul-less approach to reading. The 'deconstructed' text is 'deadened' (to echo a word Zamir significantly uses to characterise postmodern thought), a conduit of an uncanny textual, deconstructive machinery, devoid of any attempt to grapple with the (human) questions that truly matter.[44]

In Butler and in Derrida the elevation of the textual is thus seen as intrinsically questionable because it draws our attention away from what should mainly concern us, not merely as human beings, but also as citizens. In *Love's Knowledge*, Nussbaum laments, along similar lines, the failure of literary theory to take a sustained interest in ethical questions. Theory

> has been constrained by pressure of the current thought that to discuss a text's ethical or social content is somehow to neglect 'textuality,' the complex relationships of that text with other texts; and of the related, though more extreme, thought that texts do not refer to human life at all, but only to other texts and to themselves.[45]

What, the argument goes, literary theory misses is any sense of urgency to think about the questions that really matter to us. It is noteworthy, also in relation to the almost prophetic powers often ascribed to Shakespeare, that this double gesture – the attack on 'theory' is *at the same time* a defence of the human – is also a function of a division of great literature from 'mere' mechanisms of textuality. The 'sense of practical importance' which fuels the inquiry into what 'the best way to live' may be has 'always animated much of great literature'.[46] And further: 'I imagine, instead, a future in which our talk about literature will return, increasingly, to a concern with the practical – to the ethical and social questions that give literature its high importance in our lives'.[47] A true Aristotelian, Nussbaum does not merely want us to know good but to do good.

In what follows, I would like to suggest that Derrida's deconstructive reading of *Romeo and Juliet* does not make us care less about what happens in the play. It does not make us care less about the 'practical' issues that Shakespeare's play raises. In fact, as I will show, his against-the-grain *contretemporal* reading is full of strikingly original insights into love and death which might inform how we choose to live (as he confesses at the beginning of *Specters of Marx*, Derrida, after all, would like to learn how to live finally). In Derrida, however, these insights are closely connected to questions pertaining to our love for and the survival of the play *Romeo and Juliet* itself. To put it differently: in Derrida attention to the textual is not an avoidance of those issues that matter to us and to the way we live with others, but presents an opening towards thinking about them anew.

Out of Joint, or Something Like an Introduction to Deconstruction

Let's start again. According to the *Oxford English Dictionary*, deconstruction is 'a method of critical analysis of philosophical and literary language which emphasizes the internal workings of language and conceptual systems, the relational quality of meaning, and the assumptions implicit in forms of expression'. Misconceptions of deconstruction as a programmatic, mechanistic, tool-kit approach to literature are rooted in such a mischaracterisation of deconstruction as a 'set method'. But if it is not a method, what is deconstruction? Derrida's thought is notoriously difficult to summarise. Despite what those who opposed Derrida's honorary doctorate argued and despite what many of his critics still might want you to believe, this does not mean that he is not worth studying. This difficulty does in and of itself also not warrant giving his work particular preference. Derrida 'fascinates' not because he is difficult – as Nussbaum's image of obscure fascination might suggest – but because his work both theorises and performs a near-impossible responsiveness to the singularity of the other. It is in this affirmation of the demand and impossibility of absolute responsiveness that his value for literary scholars and philosophers lies. Paradoxically, it is precisely because of this commitment to respond that Derrida's work resists summary. If there were a law or a tenet, it would be something like this:

> My law, the one to which I try to devote myself or to respond, is *the text of the other*, its very singularity, its idiom, its appeal which precedes me. But I can only respond to it in a responsible way (and this goes for the law in general, ethics in particular) if I put in play, and in guarantee [*en gage*], my singularity, by signing, with another signature; for the countersignature signs by confirming the signature of the other, but also by signing in an absolutely new and inaugural way, both at once, like each time I confirm my own signature by signing once more: each time in the same way and each time differently, one more time, at another date.[48]

In Derrida the act of reading (which as we shall see also means countersigning) *is* the act of doing philosophy and thus every attempt to distil an essence or philosophical tenet from his singular acts of reading must in the end fail. The notion of Derrida 'originating' anything like a monolithic 'school of thought' called 'deconstruction' is deeply unsympathetic to Derrida's sense of each act of reading, each philosophical engagement with a text, as a singular, and potentially momentous, event. The very word used to describe the school of thought he is believed to have originated – deconstruction – for example, emerges from a very specific engagement with Heidegger's *Konstruktion* and *Destruktion*. This, of course, does not mean that Derrida's different acts of readings do not share significant and typical characteristics; they, in fact, often do follow a similar-yet-different argumentative rhythm or movement. Nor does it mean that this rhythm, or approximations of this rhythm, cannot be found in some of the best work by what some might call 'deconstructionists'. What it does mean is that every summary of or introduction to Derrida must negotiate the fact that his work presents itself not as a set of theses but as a series of close engagements (Derrida calls them *corps à corps*, and the importance of this bodily image, with all the physicality and viscerality that this entails, will become apparent in the next chapter) with texts.

The downside of this stubborn resistance to summary is that it is difficult to defend Derrida without inviting his detractors to read over his shoulder, as it were. And as the fact that, as the Cambridge affair proved, criticisms of Derrida are seldom heavily referenced shows this might prove to be an impossible task in itself.[49] Yet, because every single one of Derrida's acts of reading not only performs impossible and absolute responsiveness but also theorises the conditions that constitute the encounter between reader and text, between subject and other, each one also functions as an introduction. Not only that, but since every act of reading and every textual encounter is an event which is both unforeseeable and unrepeatable 'we must', as Derrida writes in *Of Grammatology*, 'begin *wherever we are* . . .'[50] For a very short introduction to deconstruction, if there is such a thing, we must then not look further than his reading of *Romeo and Juliet*.

In 'Aphorism Countertime', Derrida reads *Romeo and Juliet à contretemps*, meaning out of or against time. There is something disjointed about the way Derrida approaches the play, but there is of course also something out of joint about the play itself. *Romeo and Juliet* is full of mishaps, missed connections, bad timings. Although this play has often been 'represented as the scene of fortuitous contretemps, of aleatory anachrony', nothing, 'the failed rendezvous, the unfortunate accident, the letter which does not arrive at its destination, the time of the detour prolonged for a *purloined letter*, the remedy which transforms itself into poison . . .' comes as a result of a freakish conjuration of time and chance against Romeo and Juliet; instead, for Derrida, all these things are symptoms of a more essential contretemps.[51] What indeed would Romeo and Juliet's love have been without contretemps? Derrida argues that Romeo and Juliet's love is not thwarted by contretemps; instead their love depends on 'the essential impossibility of any absolute synchronization'.[52]

Similarly, their love is not truncated by death, but death conditions it. When '*the impossible happens*', when Romeo and Juliet 'live *in turn* the death of the other, for a time, the contretemps of their death', for Derrida, this illustrates a fact about love, namely that

> right from the pledge which binds together two desires, each is already in mourning for the other, entrusts death to the other as well: if you die before me, I will keep you, if I die before you, you will carry me in yourself, one will keep the other, will already have kept the other from the first declaration.[53]

This in-built desynchronisation of love is what conditions it. Derrida: 'There would have been no love, the pledge would not have taken place, nor time, nor its theater, without discordance.'[54] From the beginning love is disjointed; we love, because we know with 'absolute certainty . . . that one must die before the other', that 'one of us, only one of us, will carry the death of the other – and the mourning'.[55] The essential impossibility of synchronisation Derrida recognises in the play is in fact bound to the ineluctable eventuality of our death, and to the similarly ineluctable fact that our death will not coincide with the death of those we love. *Romeo and Juliet* shows that love is inaugurated by the possibility, and indeed by the anticipation, that the other will die before me, or that I will die before him. Again, this is something that

Derrida also thinks about in 'Envois' where the I knows that to love is always to be in mourning: '*no my love that's my wake*'.⁵⁶ I love you because your time is not mine, he seems to say, because one of us will die before the other, because, although we are together now, one of us will – eventually – survive the other.

Romeo and Juliet demonstrates that love is conditioned by what seems to disrupt it; it also shows that the same is true of time. The story of Romeo and Juliet 'confounds a philosophical logic which would like accidents to remain what they are, accidental', by marking 'the absolute interruption of history as deployment of *a* temporality, of a single and organized temporality'.⁵⁷ Here, Derrida seems to ventriloquise Hamlet's 'the time is out of joint' analysed not merely in his *Specters of Marx* but also in his less well-known, later 'The Time is Out of Joint' (I, v, 186). But what exactly is Hamlet saying? Hamlet's famous statement is usually read as primarily indicating that the age is out of joint, that something is rotten in the state of Denmark. For Derrida, however, it points us towards the fact that in his state of mourning Hamlet's perception of time is somehow out of kilter, disjointed from the passing of time that the other characters perceive. As Derrida observes in 'The Time is Out of Joint', Hamlet 'is mad about dates', more precisely about the date of his father's death.⁵⁸ He, Derrida continues, 'seems no longer to know *when* his father died. On what date? Since when?'⁵⁹ Derrida notes that as 'time passes', for Hamlet time 'disappears . . . ceases to take place . . . it shrinks': two months become a month, and then 'the less than a month of the "within a month"' hastily becomes '"within two hours"'.⁶⁰ The time of mourning is strange. As Derrida writes in *The Work of Mourning*, the death of the other (a friend, a lover, a father, a mother) marks 'each time another end of the world', almost the end of time itself.⁶¹ And yet, as *Romeo and Juliet* illustrates, mourning is also its beginning, it prepares the path for love, makes it a possibility.

When Derrida speaks of the out-of-jointness of time, he is speaking of fissuring or an interruption of time, which just like Romeo and Juliet's contretemps is not accidental but essential. Introducing such 'interruption' as 'both textual strategy and as feature of temporalisation' allows, Joanna Hodge suggests, 'a rethinking of an asymmetry between past and future'.[62] This disjunction – Hodge calls it a 'syncopation of non-simultaneity' – disrupts any thinking about time in terms of a linear connection between before and after.[63] Time, Derrida writes in '"I Have a Taste for the Secret"', is 'outside itself, beside itself, unhinged; it is not gathered together in its place, in its present'.[64]

For Derrida, this out-of-jointness of time affects not merely love; it is rather the symptom of a fundamental out-of-jointness of being. Derrida indeed suggests 'that time itself, the present indicative of the verb to be in the third person singular, the "is" that says what time is, this tense of time is out of joint, itself and by itself out of joint'.[65] And this concept of time breaks what 'The Time is Out of Joint' calls the 'shock waves' that create the tremor at the very 'heart of the question "to be or not to be"'.[66] What is disjointed is, in short, not only Hamlet's perception of time, the time of mourning, but also 'a very little word, the miniscule coupling of *two letters*', in short 'a *minuscopule*': to be.[67] Here then is deconstruction's fissuring of ontology.

Throughout this brief reading of 'Aphorism Countertime', I have drawn on other works by Derrida where he grapples with the same issues. This foundational out-of-jointness is not merely at work in *Romeo and Juliet*, but traverses the entirety of Derrida's oeuvre. Like all of his acts of reading, 'Aphorism Countertime' is an inquiry into what, for lack of a better term, we might call that 'logic' which Derrida discusses using a chain of 'nonsynonymous substitutions', for example trace, supplement and, most notoriously, *différance*.[68] One way of thinking about the movement of *différance* might be a sort of inversion at the heart of presence, being or identity. Another way might be that something which is usually thought to be secondary or even parasitic to Presence or Being (note the capitals!) in fact turns out to be fundamental to and constitutive of it: time is constituted by interruption, love by the end of love, and being by difference. It is important to note, however, that Derrida does not speak here of difference from something else, but of a fundamental and foundational difference *from* itself. To quote Simon Glendinning: 'the "otherness" that is implied in every identity' is not the otherness of the other, 'but a certain otherness within itself, *the other in the same*'.[69] Otherness to itself also affects Derrida's writings. This is why, although there is a certain repetitiveness to Derrida's oeuvre, what is repeated is always new.

'Aphorism Countertime' is exemplary of Derrida's approach to thinking as handicraft. The rhythms and repetitions of Derrida's treatment of love, time and being in *Romeo and Juliet* and *Hamlet* give us a good sense of the iterative nature of his thought. Although the movement of *différance* is at work in all, his meditations on love, time and being are not mere repetitions. Even repetition itself is subject to *différance* and thus is never simply the same; there is always the other in sameness and a new arrival in every return. This is the reason why we must speak of a *quasi*-synonymous chain of, for lack a better word, reading hinges, such as *différance and* trace *and* supplement *and* contretemps, and so on. 'And' is perhaps the most important word to understand what 'deconstruction' does. Derrida thinks about the 'impossible synchronization' between Romeo and Juliet in terms of the 'and' which simultaneously con- and disjoins them. Like *Romeo and Juliet*, deconstruction, if there is such a thing, is perhaps nothing but a 'theater of this "and"', this hinge of impossible synchronisation.[70] In 'Et Cetera . . .' Derrida writes: 'And in the beginning, there is the *and*.'[71] 'In the beginning' of deconstruction, 'there is an and', Derrida observes. The iterative nature of Derrida's work is testament to the fact that there is also such a disjunction at play in and between deconstructive readings themselves: we read with *and* against a text, and each deconstructive reading is same *and* other. No deconstruction, then, without the *and*, the conjoining disjunction of the mark and writing and trace and *différance* and any other of the terms in Derrida's chain of non-synonymous terms. The theatre of the 'and' orchestrates the impossible synchronisations, the ontological leap, fissure or rhythm that these terms denote. The same logic also dictates that this chain is not pleonastic, that, in other words, it is not the 'trite repetition of the same' that the idea of deconstruction as a tool-kit implies. Each act of reading performs repetition and renewal: iteration. (To put it in terms that I will pick up again in the last chapter, each reading is already a *re*-reading).

Iterable Shakespeare

What does *différance* mean for the way we read Shakespeare? 'Aphorism Countertime' is an extraordinary meditation on love, on the *and* between Romeo *and* Juliet. We must, however, listen for the silent slippage between Romeo *and* Juliet *and Romeo and Juliet*; whatever Derrida writes happens between Romeo and Juliet also happens between us and the play. Derrida is not only, and perhaps not even mainly, concerned with the contretemps of Romeo and Juliet, but with the contretemps of the play itself. We could not love *Romeo and Juliet* if it were not for its contretemps. Just as 'I love because the other is the other, because its time will never be mine', we can love *Romeo and Juliet* because its contretemps does something to time.[72] Just as the 'very presence of [the other's] love remains infinitely distant from mine', the contretemps of *Romeo and Juliet* 'cuts into the fabric of durations'.[73] What he is concerned with is, therefore, 'the double survival, the contretemps, in short the aphorism of *Romeo and Juliet*. Not of Romeo and of Juliet but of *Romeo and Juliet*, Shakespeare's play of that title.'[74]

If 'this drama has . . . been imprinted, superimprinted on the memory of Europe, text upon text', it is not only because the 'anachronous accident comes to illustrate an essential possibility', but also because it is saying something about its own survival, the play's capacity to be reiterated text upon text, staging upon staging, adaption upon adaption.[75] And because 'the survival of a theatrical work implies that, theatrically, it is saying something about theatre itself, about its essential possibility', Derrida's reading of *Romeo and Juliet* in 'Aphorism Countertime' tells us not merely something about love and time in the play and more in general; it also tells us something about how a work like *Romeo and Juliet* behaves in time.[76] It might give an explanation of how something so steeped in its historical and literary context lends itself to such degrees of reimagining. Indeed, as Derrida tells Attridge, who demonstrates better than Shakespeare 'that texts fully conditioned by their history, loaded with history, and on historical themes, offer themselves so well for reading in historical contexts very distant from their time and place of origin?'[77] In this sense, each reading, each production of this play, is a nonsynonymous substitution. Each repetition is new and, in some ways, surprising, unprecedented, unthought and itself unrepeatable. *Différance* and iteration are at play – in the play.

When Attridge asks whether *Romeo and Juliet* 'merits special attention in terms of [his] interests and goals', Derrida concedes that its thematisation of proper names is no doubt 'exemplary' for 'the effect of the same a-logical "logic" of the singular and iterable mark'.[78] And this 'a-logical "logic"' also affects the way we might think about the play as a whole. Just as Juliet loves Romeo not despite but because of his name, the play's survival, Derrida suggests, would not 'have been possible "without that title," as Juliet put it'.⁷⁹ Let's ask with Juliet: What is a title's play? It is not premise nor end, nor any part belonging to a play. What, then, is it? It is, perhaps, that thing which marks out a literary work from other texts and a work by Shakespeare from other literary texts. The title is, in this sense, not merely subject to canonisation but an agent of it.

Something which comes to us bearing the Shakespearean signature also comes bearing the baggage that that entails. For Derrida, however, the literary work abides by the same paradoxical rules as the signature:

> So by *oeuvre* I mean something that remains, that is absolutely not translatable, that bears a signature (the signature is not necessarily the narcissism of the proper name or the reappropriation of something that belongs to me); in any case, something that has a place, that has a certain consistency, that is recorded, to which one can return, that can be repeated in a different context, that can be read in the future in a context where reading conditions have changed.⁸⁰

In order to be recognisable, a signature has to have a 'repeatable, iterable, imitable form; it must be able to be detached from the present and singular intention of its production'.⁸¹ The 'absolute singularity of a signature-event' is precisely constituted by the 'pure reproducibility of a pure event'.⁸² It is a spacing which not only separates the mark 'from other elements of the internal contextual chain (the always open possibility of its disengagement and graft), but also from all forms of present reference (whether past or future in the modified form of the present that is past or to come), objective or subjective'.⁸³ Just like a signature, a singular literary work is therefore marked by 'iterability', that 'logic that ties repetition to alterity'.⁸⁴ Just like a signature, a literary work would not be one if it could not survive beyond its intended or implied sender and receiver.⁸⁵ *Romeo and Juliet* therefore 'subsists' because it 'does not exhaust itself in the moment of its inscription', and because it 'can give rise to an iteration in the absence and beyond the presence of the empirically determined subject who, in a given context, has emitted or produced it'.[86] Derrida's reading of *Romeo and Juliet* is hence founded on and justified by the iterable structure of the text, 'its iterability, which both puts down roots in the unity of a context and immediately opens this non-saturable context onto a recontextualisation'.[87] None of the play's printing and superimprinting could be possible, Derrida suggests, without the singular Shakespearean signature of *Romeo and* Juliet: that which 'giv[es] rise every time to the chance of an absolutely singular event as it does to the untranslatable idiom of a proper name, to its fatality (the "enemy" that I "hate"), to the fatality of a date and of a rendezvous'.[88]

Nussbaum's worry about bloodlessness, just like Bloom's worry about the treatment of Shakespeare by the 'Resenters', is linked to a fear of losing the value a literary work, at its best, can have for us humans. Which is also a fear of losing our idea of the human itself. As I have argued in the previous chapter, often the tendency of much work on Shakespeare that appeals to his human representativeness is exhibited in an attachment to the fantasy of Shakespeare the person as a monolithic, if unknown, repository of wisdom (although this is not Nussbaum's case). Derrida's way of reading Shakespeare and other literary or philosophical texts is based on the assumption that these texts owe their power to the fact that their link to their point of origin remains open to iteration. Derrida's 'Signature Event Context' contains perhaps his most powerful and best-known critique of the assumed close bond between writing and authorial intention, between text and blood so to say. It is, of course, also one of the crucial texts in the continental–analytical controversies, in as much as its reading of Austin led to a heated exchange with John Searle who felt that Derrida had completely misread or misinterpreted speech act theory. Incidentally, the strength of Searle's reaction itself is testament to the hold that the idea of an author's intentions and consequential idea of propriety – my real Austin versus your fake Austin – has on philosophy as understood by some. Derrida was in truth much more taken with Austin's speech act theory that he is given credit for.[89] What Derrida *did* criticise Austin for is that he did not take into account the '*graphematic in general*' in his account of performatives.[90] Another way of putting this criticism would be that Austin stakes too much credence in the transparency of writing, that our intentions are transparent in our words.[91] In an almost perfect symmetry, Derrida is thus criticising Austin precisely for what Nussbaum and others find him lacking of.

'Signature Event Context' argues that, very much contrary to what was believed throughout the history of philosophy, writing is not a simple means of communication. For an example of philosophy's notion of writing, Derrida turns to Condillac's *Essay on the Origin of Human Knowledge*, in which writing as communication is seen as different and distinct from the process of thinking. For writing to be purely a means of communication, what is to be communicated must already and in advance be transparent to the self-present writer.[92] For Condillac, writing is a means of communication, a means for a self-present and self-transparent sender of reaching an addressee who, for whatever reason, is not present and hence unable to receive the communication immediately and in person. In this picture, writing bridges absence. For Derrida, too, writing is haunted by absence, but very differently than imagined by Condillac; who is absent from the writing is not merely the addressee but also the writer. The sender is as absent 'from the mark that he abandons' as the reader.[93] The mark thus 'cuts itself off from him and continues to produce effects independently of his presence and of the present actuality of his intentions [*vouloir-dire*], indeed even after his death, his absence'.[94]

Similarly to his reading of time, love and being in 'The Time is Out of Joint' and 'Aphorism Countertime', this disjunction at the origin of writing is not pernicious or accidental but is understood to be essential to the survival of a text through time:

> For a writing to be a writing it must continue to 'act' and to be readable even when what is called the author of the writing no longer answers for what he has written, for what he seems to have signed, be it because of a temporary absence, because he is dead or, more generally, because he has not employed his absolutely actual and present intention or attention, the plenitude of his desire to say what he means, in order to sustain what seems to be written 'in his name'.[95]

For Derrida, Condillac's condition of the absence of the receiver becomes both structuralised and generalised. Writing does not work despite this absence, but because of it. Writing is only recognisable as such in as much as it relies on the absence of both the sender and the receiver:

> It is at this point that the *différance* [difference and deferral, *trans*.] as writing could no longer (be) an (ontological) modification of presence. In order for my 'written communication' to retain its function as writing, i.e., its readability, it must remain readable despite the absolute disappearance of any receiver, determined in general. My communication must be repeatable – iterable – in the absolute absence of the receiver or of any empirically determinable collectivity of receivers. Such iterability – (*iter*, again, probably comes from *itara*, *other* in Sanskrit, and everything that follows can be read as the working out of the logic that ties repetition to alterity) structures the mark of writing itself, no matter what particular type of writing is involved

(whether pictographical, hieroglyphic, ideographic, phonetic, alphabetic, to cite the old categories). A writing that is not structurally readable – iterable – beyond the death of the addressee would not be writing.[96]

For Derrida, the texts we call Shakespeare's are just such iterable signatures. Each word, in fact, is a Shakespearean signature, a singular event calling for singular reiterations and countersignatures. Literature is perhaps the singular event *par excellence*, inviting us to follow it to places neither we nor the work itself have yet discovered. For Derrida, whatever is yet to come is made possible by this encounter between two irreducible and yet iterable singularities: text and reader.

Shakespeare is iterable. Derrida's acts of reading themselves are iterable, tracing the movement of what is most commonly called *différance* through separate acts of reading; they are each time the same *and* different. It is precisely because of this iterability that Derrida's readings of Shakespeare are not acts of illegitimate appropriation or narcissistic self-reflection. Rather, Derrida's engagements with Shakespeare perform the very thing that they so often, and in their many different idioms, state, namely that each encounter with a text opens up to a singular, othering, unprecedented, unforeseeable and unrepeatable event. It is to this act of reading, understood as the event of a meeting of two iterable singularities, that I shall turn to next.

Notes

1. Jacques Derrida, 'Aphorism Countertime', trans. Nicholas Royle, in *Acts of Literature*, ed. Derek Attridge (London: Routledge, 1992), 415.
2. Ibid. 416.
3. Jacques Derrida, '"This Strange Institution Called Literature": An Interview with Jacques Derrida', trans. Geoffrey Bennington and Rachel Bowlby, in *Acts of Literature*, ed. Derek Attridge (London: Routledge, 1992), 41.

4. Ibid. 62.
5. Ibid. 62.
6. Ibid. 63.
7. Ibid. 67.
8. Ibid. 67.
9. Ibid. 62.
10. Ibid. 65.
11. Hélène Cixous, 'Shakespeare Ghosting Derrida', trans. Laurent Milesi, *The Oxford Literary Review* 34, no. 1 (2012): 2.
12. Barry Smith, 'Letter to *The Times*', *The Times*, 9 May 1992.
13. Benoît Peeters, *Derrida: A Biography*, trans. Andrew Brown (Cambridge: Polity Press, 2013), 447.
14. Smith, 'Letter to *The Times*'.
15. Ibid.
16. Arthur C. Danto, 'Philosophy and/as/of Literature', in *A Companion to the Philosophy of Literature*, ed. Garry L. Hagberg and Walter Jost (Oxford: Wiley-Blackwell, 2010), 53.
17. Ibid. 53.
18. Ibid. 54.
19. Ibid. 63.
20. Ibid. 64.
21. Ibid. 64.
22. Richard Eldridge, 'Introduction', in *The Oxford Handbook of Philosophy and Litertaure*, ed. Richard Eldridge (Oxford: Oxford University Press, 2009), 7.
23. Ibid. 4.
24. Anthony J. Cascardi, *The Cambridge Introduction to Litertaure and Philosophy* (New York and Cambridge: Cambridge University Press, 2014), 187.
25. Stephen Mulhall, *The Wounded Animal: J. M. Coetzee and the Difficulty of Reality in Literature and Philosophy* (Princeton: Princeton University Press, 2009), 9.
26. Ibid. 3.
27. Ibid. 3.
28. Martha Nussbaum, *Love's Knowledge: Essays on Philosophy and Literature* (Oxford: Oxford University Press, 1990), 23–4.

29. Ibid. 53.
30. Ibid. 24.
31. Frank Kermode, 'Strange, Sublime, Uncanny, Anxious', *London Review of Books*, 22 December 1994, https://www.lrb.co.uk/v16/n24/frank-kermode/strange-sublime-uncanny-anxious
32. Derek Attidge, 'Introduction: Derrida and the Questioning of Literature', in *Acts of Literature*, ed. Derek Attridge (London: Routledge, 1992), 2.
33. Ibid. 2.
34. Colin Davis, *Critical Excess: Overreading in Derrida, Deleuze, Levinas, Žižek and Cavell* (Stanford: Stanford University Press, 2010), ix, xii.
35. Martha Nussbaum, 'The Professor of Parody: Review of Four Books by Judith Butler, *Excitable Speech*; *The Psychic Life of Power*; *Bodies that Matter*; *Gender Trouble*', in *Philosophical Interventions: Reviews 1986–2011* (Oxford: Oxford University Press, 2012), 203.
36. Smith, 'Letter to *The Times*'.
37. Gustavo Faigenbaum, *Conversations with John Searle* (Buenos Aires: LibrosEnRed, 2003), 169.
38. Nussbaum, 'The Professor of Parody', 202.
39. Ibid. 198.
40. Ibid. 199–200.
41. Martha Nussbaum, *Cultivating Humanity: A Classical Defense of Reform in Liberal Education* (Cambridge, MA: Harvard University Press, 1998), 41.
42. Nussbaum, *Love's Knowledge*, 170–1.
43. Ibid. 171.
44. 'Reflection through literature thus presents an alternative to the false rigour of analytical philosophy without adopting the deadening skepticism that underlies so much postmodern thought.' Tzachi Zamir, *Double Vision, Moral Philosophy and Shakespearean Drama* (Princeton: Princeton University Press, 2007), 44.
45. Nussbaum, *Love's Knowledge*, 170.
46. Ibid. 170–1.
47. Ibid. 168.

48. Derrida, '"This Strange Institution Called Literature"', 66–7.
49. As Peeters notes, the phrase 'logical phallusies' never appears in Derrida's oeuvre. Peeters, *Derrida: A Biography*, 447. Also see Johann Gregory, 'Wordplay in Shakespeare's *Hamlet* and the Accusation of Derrida's "Logical Phallusies"', *English Studies* 94, no. 3 (2013): 313–30.
50. Jacques Derrida, *Of Grammatology*, trans. Gayatri Chakravorty Spivak (Baltimore: Johns Hopkins University Press, 2016), 177.
51. Derrida, 'Aphorism Countertime', 419.
52. Ibid. 418.
53. Ibid. 422.
54. Ibid. 420.
55. Ibid. 422.
56. Jacques Derrida, 'Envois', in *The Postcard: From Socrates to Freud and Beyond*, trans. Alan Bass (Chicago and London: University of Chicago Press, 1987), 141.
57. Derrida, 'Aphorism Countertime', 420.
58. Jacques Derrida, 'The Time is Out of Joint', trans. Peggy Kamuf, in *Deconstruction is/in America: A New Sense of the Political*, ed. Anselm Haverkamp (New York: New York University Press, 1995), 17.
59. Ibid. 22.
60. Ibid. 23.
61. Jacques Derrida, *The Work of Mourning*, ed. Pascale-Anne Brault and Michael Naas (Chicago: University of Chicago Press, 2003), 95.
62. Joanna Hodge, *Derrida on Time* (London: Routledge, 2007), 22.
63. Ibid. x.
64. Jacques Derrida, '"I Have a Taste for the Secret"', trans. Giacomo Donis, in *A Taste for the Secret*, ed. Giacomo Donis and David Webb (Cambridge: Polity Press, 2001), 6.
65. Derrida, 'The Time is Out of Joint', 29.
66. Ibid. 29.
67. Ibid. 16.
68. Jacques Derrida, 'Différance', trans. Alan Bass, in *Margins of Philosophy* (Chicago: University of Chicago Press, 1982), 12.

69. Simon Glendinning, *Derrida: A Very Short Introduction* (Oxford: Oxford University Press, 2011), 62.
70. Derrida, 'Aphorism Countertime', 419.
71. Jacques Derrida, 'Et Cetera ... (and so on, und so weiter, and so forth, et ainsi de suite, und so überall, etc.)', trans. Geoffrey Bennington, in *Deconstructions: A User's Guide*, ed. Nicholas Royle (Basingstoke: Palgrave, 2000), 282.
72. Derrida, 'Aphorism Countertime', 420.
73. Ibid. 420, 421.
74. Ibid. 433.
75. Ibid. 420.
76. Ibid. 419.
77. Derrida, '"This Strange Institution Called Literature"', 63.
78. Ibid. 62, 66.
79. Derrida, 'Aphorism Coutertime', 433.
80. Derrida, '"I Have a Taste for the Secret"', 14.
81. Jacques Derrida, 'Signature Event Context', trans. Samuel Weber and Jeffrey Mehlman, in *Limited Inc*, ed. Gerald Graff (Evanston: Northwestern University Press, 1988), 20.
82. Ibid. 20.
83. Ibid. 9–10.
84. Ibid. 7.
85. Ibid. 8.
86. Ibid. 9.
87. Derrida, '"This Strange Institution Called Literature"', 63.
88. Derrida, 'Aphorism Countertime', 419.
89. Derrida, 'Signature Event Context', 14.
90. Ibid. 14.
91. Ibid. 14.
92. Ibid. 4.
93. Ibid. 5.
94. Ibid. 5.
95. Ibid. 8.
96. Ibid. 7.

CHAPTER 3

FLÈCHES AND THE WOUNDS OF READING

Téléiopoièse

Criticisms of Derrida often hinge on the belief that he advocates that a text can mean whatever we want it to. Implied in this critique is that Derrida reads literature as a kind of vanity project, and that under his gaze every literary or philosophical work, no matter how great, becomes a mirror reflecting nothing but himself. It is, so the critique goes, because of this fatal self-absorption that this Narcissus – deconstruction – must ultimately fail to achieve anything but its own demise. As I have argued in the last chapter, the 'logic' of contretemps Derrida dissects in his reading of *Romeo and Juliet* speaks of an essential contretemps of time and being. Moving in this chapter to Derrida's understanding of the act of reading Shakespeare itself, I will show that this generalised out-of-jointness, to couch it in the terms of his reading of *Hamlet*, also bears on the act of reading, and since, for Derrida reading *is* philosophising, on the very act of doing philosophy itself.

As discussed in the previous chapter, *Romeo and Juliet*, Shakespeare's drama of double survival, inaugurates a new 'logic', namely that accidents are anything but 'accidental'.[1] It is worth taking another, closer look at what exactly Derrida writes about contretemps in 'Aphorism Countertime': 'This logic, at the same time, throws out into the unthinkable an anachrony of structure, the absolute interruption of history as deployment of *a* temporality, of a single and organized temporality.'² In Derrida's French this sentence reads: 'Cette logique, du même coup, rejette dans l'impensable une anachronie de structure, l'interruption absolue de l'histoire en tant que déploiement d'*une* temporalité, d'une temporalité une et organisée.'³ Derrida's word choice *rejeter* is striking. *Rejeter* means both (1) 'to reject' or 'throw out', as well as (2) 'to throw back' or (3) 'discharge' (*Collins-Robert French Dictionary*). While holding on to the idea of throwing, Nicholas Royle's translation of *rejeter* as 'to throw out' loses the word's negative inflection, as well as the pluri-directionality the French word comprises: the anachrony of structure is both *thrown out* into the unthinkable, and *thrown back* – but thrown back or towards what? Who shoots off and who is hit? Who sends and who receives? Who reads or writes whom? Together with time, agency, address and the vectors of reading are warped.

Contretemps throws and hurtles; it shoots (itself) off. The *jet* in *rejeter* refers us to an idea of speed and force, even of violence. *Rejeter* also chimes with the *coup* of 'du même coup' at the start of the sentence.⁴ In French *coup* is a (1) 'knock' or 'blow' and (2) a 'stroke' or 'shot' (*Collins-Robert French Dictionary*). Throwing or shooting is what the aphorisms of *Romeo and Juliet* do. Aphorism 4:

> An aphorism is exposure to contretemps. It exposes discourse – hands it over to contretemps. Literally – because it is abandoning a word [*une parole*] to its letter.
>
> (Already this could be read as a series of aphorisms, the alea of an initial anachrony. In the beginning there was contretemps. In the beginning there is speed. Word and deed are *overtaken*. Aphorism outstrips.)⁵

In French, these last two, punctuated sentences read: "La parole et l'acte sont *pris de vitesse*. L'aphorisme gagne de vitesse."[6] Aphorism is an exposure to *alea*, it *throws* the dice of chance (*alea iacta est*). (Chance, to which I shall be turning in Chapter 5, is an irreducible, perhaps unexaminable, part of Derridean acts of reading.) Aphorism is also a question of speed. Contretemps *and* speed at the beginning. It is because of this initial contretemporal speed that word and deed are overtaken *in the very moment of their inscription*.

Sont pris de vitesse: this simple present passive construction is more ambiguous than it might at first seem. Literally, it indicates that word and deed are overtaken, maybe surprised, by speed. *Prendre de vitesse*, however, also means to gain speed. Word and deed are surprised and overtaken by speed; at the same time, they also do the overtaking. At the beginning of the aphorism, before it can outstrip and beat somebody to the finish line (like *Hamlet*'s mole, but I shall come to that), word and deed are not only overtaken, but also gather or increase speed. Word and deed in the aphorism are already exposed to the outstripping movement of contretemps. Contretemps *and différance and* trace *and* so on (goes the chain of 'ands' of the quasi-synonymous substitutions) places the essential possibility of unfamiliar, othering readings at the very heart and origin of the literary work.

Here, Derrida not only links *Romeo and Juliet*'s openness to iteration (and hence to readings that depart from its 'immediate' historical context) to an *essential* contretemps, but also suggests, as I have argued in the previous chapter, that it is the play's iterability which welcomes readings such as Derrida's. With contretemps our image of an unfolding of a text through time that is, if not smooth, then at least linear and progressive no longer holds. Whatever allows Derrida to read *Romeo and Juliet* is not extrinsic to this play but intrinsic. Indeed, its 'anachrony' of structure is something that radiates from it, that the play *throws out*, into the unthinkable, towards those readers who are yet unthought of, as well as those readers who might do the unthinkable to

Shakespeare. The anachrony of structure which contretemps describes both radiates *from* and is projected *back to Romeo and Juliet*; it is both the result and the cause of Derrida's aphoristic reading.

For Derrida, texts are not, Clare Connors writes, the 'static structures' or 'guaranteed movements' that they are for structuralists but 'dynamic and puissant adventures'.[7] In all of his acts of reading, Derrida seeks to reckon with the outstripping speed of the contretemporal text and with what it throws at us. We may, for example, recognise shadows of this outstripping movement in his discussion of missiles in 'No Apocalypse, Not Now', or in his discussion of missives in *The Post Card*. In relation to Shakespeare (but not only to him, as I will show), this movement is mostly thought about in terms of an arrow.

In *Specters* everything turns on the desire to respond to a 'magisterial locution', or 'watchword', which shoots forth 'from the lips of the master' and 'vibrates like an arrow in the course of an irreversible and asymmetrical address, the one that goes most often from father to son, master to disciple, or master to slave'.[8] When speaking of the vibrating arrow of the master's locution, he is not only speaking of the Ghost's locution in *Hamlet*, or indeed in Marx's texts themselves, but also, and I would argue, most importantly of the vibrating arrow that the Shakespearean oeuvre shoots at us:

> 'The time is out of joint': time is *disarticulated*, dislocated, dislodged, time is run down, on the run and run down [*traqué et détraqué*], *deranged*, both out of order and mad. Time is off its hinges, time is off course, beside itself, disadjusted. Says Hamlet. Who thereby opened one of those breaches [*brèches*], often they are poetic and thinking peepholes [*meurtrières*], through which Shakespeare will have kept watch over the English language; at the same time

> he signed its body, with the same unprecedented stroke of some arrow [*et à la fois signé son corps, du même coup sans précédent, de quelque flèche*].⁹

Every time Shakespeare shoots an arrow at us, its trajectory is unthinkable and every time it hits us, our wounds are unprecedented: *sans précédent*. Like we were with the aphorisms of 'Aphorism Countertime', we are here in the strange temporality of the stroke or *coup*, where every hit is new and different and yet anticipated from the arrow's very start. And, as Wood reminds us, of course, the start is never inaugural, but always a restart.¹⁰

The act of reading, the trajectory of this arrow, is singular, othering, unprecedented, unforeseeable and unrepeatable because it is teleiopoietic. 'It is the arrow of this teleiopoesis that we have been following, waiting for, preceding for such a long time – the long time of a time that does not belong to time. A time out of joint.'¹¹ All this time we have been following the tra*je(t)*ctory of what *Politics of Friendship* calls the 'arrow of teleiopoesis' (as Derrida argues elsewhere, there is no work of genius without the '*jet*', the throwness of reading).¹² Just like in *Specters* and 'Aphorism Countertime', the metaphor of the arrow in *Politics of Friendship* traces a text's trajectory from its original contretemps to the moment in which it traverses the reader. 'Here is an arrow whose flight would consist in a return to the bow: fast enough, in sum, never to have left it.' ¹³ Despite the fact that it is thus 'withdrawn', its return 'will nevertheless have reached us, struck home'.¹⁴

What is thrown or shot into the unthinkable in *Politics of Friendship* is not some aphoristic fragment of a Shakespeare play, nor the asymmetrical demand of a ghost, but rather a 'shudder of a sentence' from Friedrich Nietzsche's *Beyond Good and Evil*: '"Alas! if only you knew how soon, how very soon, things will be – different! –' (– *Ach! Wenn ihr wußtet, wie es bald, so bald schon – anders kommt!*).'¹⁵ This sentence flies like an arrow 'of which it is still not known where and how far it will go', its trajectory is perhaps unprecedented like Hamlet's 'the time is out of joint'.¹⁶ At stake here is what Martin McQuillan dubs 'a structure of writing-for-the-future'.¹⁷ It is a writing for or towards the *avenir*. At the same time, its trajectory loops backward placing the *avenir*, that which will always remain to come, at its start.

Téléiopoièse is the word that Derrida chooses 'to formalize this absolute economy of the feint, this generation by joint and simultaneous grafting of the performative and the reportive, without a body of its own'.¹⁸ The term *téléiopoièse* traces the arrow's economy of feint through the flicker of an ambiguously inserted letter, *lettre* or vowel. As Derrida writes in *Politics of Friendship*, '*teleiopoiós* qualifies, in a great number of contexts and semantic orders, that which *renders* absolute, perfect, completed, accomplished, finished, that which *brings* to an end'.¹⁹ Corinne Scheiner notes that '*téléiopoièse* references the adjectival stem *teleio* deriving from the adjective *teleios* (complete), and therefore translates as the making of things complete'.²⁰ In *téléiopoièse*, poetry (*poesis*) and a creative act (*poeiesis*) are therefore brought to fruition, if you will. As such, *téléiopoièse* is part of those acts called performative, or rather perlocutionary; it is what '*renders* absolute, perfect, completed, accomplished, finished, that which *brings* to an end'.²¹ For Derrida, however, the tele*i*opoetic always reverberates with the teleopoetic: it 'permi[ts] us to play too with the other *tele*, the one that speaks to distance and the far-removed'.²² What brings *poiesis* to an end (*teleio*) is indeed not itself, but something other, something distant (*tele*), something even at its own end. As Derrida writes in *Politics of Friendship*, what is at stake is 'a poetics of distance' which is at the same time one of 'acceleration', whereby something 'begins at the end, it is initiated with the signature of the other'.²³

It is this telescoping of end and beginning which is written into the teleio- and teleopoetic that Derrida's talk of speed in 'Aphorism Countertime' and elsewhere grapples with. The distance covered by the arrow of *téléiopoièse* is unthinkable, at the same time immeasurably big and small. Again, like in 'Aphorism Countertime' and the beginning of *Specters of Marx*, speed expands and outstrips itself:

> Infinite or nil speed, absolute economy, for the arrow [*flèche*] carries its address along and implies in advance, in its very readability, the signature [*la signature*] of the addressee. This is tantamount to saying that it withdraws from space by penetrating it. You only have to listen. It advances backwards; it outruns itself by reversing itself. It outstrips itself [*elle se gagne de vitesse*].[24]

What reading is for Derrida can perhaps be summed up in this idea of *gagner de vitesse*, which appears not merely in relation to the arrow of Nietzsche's sentence here, but also, as we have seen, in relation to Shakespeare, the Ghost's and Marx's magistral locution in *Specters*. Like the aphorism, the arrow of teleiopoiesis outstrips itself, overtakes itself and thus strips itself bare, annuls itself. It is the speed of the *rejeter* that kicks this reading scene off, that allows Derrida to read Shakespeare *à contretemps*.[25]

What does such a conception of the behaviour of a text in (relation to) time do? The teleiopoetic trajectory of the act of reading annuls time and space, but at the same time it *gives* time and space. 'Teleiopoesis makes the *arrivants* come – or rather, allows them to come – by withdrawing; it produces an event, sinking into the darkness of a friendship which is not yet.'[26] Its arrow 'withdraws from space by penetrating it'.[27] When Shakespeare's arrows are pointed at us, and eventually shot at us, they do not so much wound us as create space for us. When Derrida speaks of the penetrating *and* withdrawing arrow, he is also depicting the paradox of signature as a space for the other's signature. Speaking of Nietzsche's sentence, Derrida continues: 'for what is indeed in question here is a poetics of distance at one remove, and of an absolute acceleration in the spanning of space by the very structure of the sentence (it begins at the end, it is initiated with the signature of the other)'.[28] The phrase 'elle se gagne de vitesse', which I discussed above, in this sense not only refers to *la flèche*, but also to *la signature* of the addressee, which is teleio- and teleopoetically implied from the start. In 'Signature Event Context', Derrida speaks of the signature in similar terms to the *flèche*. It, too, has a 'breaking force [*force de rupture*]', which 'breaks with its context'.[29] It too is 'tied to the spacing [*espacement*] that constitutes the written sign'.[30] This spacing is the means by which a literary work may constitute its own poetics. The signature is the arrow, is the wound of reading.

The work's 'both unique and repeatable moment of a signature' thus 'opens the verbal body onto something other than itself', opens and carries it 'beyond itself, towards the other or towards the world'.[31] 'Address takes place', and address makes space (for the other), Derrida writes in 'Shibboleth: For Paul Celan'.[32] The same is true for time. Disrupting our idea of the linear unfolding of the time of reading, the Derridean act of reading 'will have taken some time'.[33] Covering within itself the incalculable distance between the text and reader, the text implies its reader from its very start. This is, perhaps, less a Barthes-esque annunciation of the death of the author than a proclamation of the text's survival, its incalculable and uncanny mastery, even its genius. In this view, then, the incalculable speed of reading 'will, perhaps, have changed the order of the world even before we are able to awake to the realization that, in sum, nothing will have been said, nothing that will not already have been blindly endorsed in advance'.[34]

If what we read is teleiopoietic, it traces a trajectory without fixed beginning and end: all flight and all start. It is, as McQuillan writes of the private letters of 'Envois', a missive that 'pass[es] through the various destinations of [its] readership, [is] countersigned by the reader en route, without ever coming to rest at a final address'.35 Following the trajectory of this arrow which shoots (itself) off 'one begins', 'Envoi' suggests, 'no longer to understand what to come [*venir*], to come before, to come after, to foresee [*prévenir*], to come back [*revenir*] all mean'.36 The pluridirectional *jet* of the teleiopoetic arrow makes the linearity of the act of reading quiver from the very start:

> As soon as, in a second, the first stroke of a letter divides itself, and must indeed support partition in order to identify itself, there are nothing but post cards, anonymous morsels without fixed domicile, without legitimate addressee, letters open, but like crypts.37

Perhaps, for Derrida, texts, like arrows, do not have a body of their own ('without a body of its own'), or maybe their bodies are different from what we might image, what we might call the corpus of a work.38 Let's earmark this.

A little while ago I asked what *différance and* iteration *and* contretemps and so on mean for reading Shakespeare. As Derrida's use of the arrow, in his discussion of Nietzsche or Shakespeare, for example, shows, it has a profound impact on what we think reading might do. Indeed, if we accept it, it makes any paradigmatic mode or act of reading both impossible and redundant. When, as J. Hillis Miller notes in *Speech Acts in Literature*, the consequences of 'iterabilty', the division *ab initio* of the first *stroke (coup)* of a letter, mean both 'that any utterance or writing can function in the radical absence of the sender' and that 'any utterance or writing must be able to function in the radical absence of any particular receiver', then traditional reading paradigms no longer apply.[39] How can we apply traditional interpretative methods when, as Kamuf notes, the text 'begins with this response that gives or gives *back* reason to the other'?[40] The teleiopoetic presence of the other at the *start* of a text, pivotal to Derrida's view of the act of reading, must supplant any general interpretative paradigm – including what some believe a deconstructive reading to be – with an absolute responsiveness to the singularity of the other. No one understood better than Derrida that such an absolute responsiveness is both necessary and ultimately impossible.

The arrow is in mid-air. Although we do not yet know what frequencies are 'quivering here', from what quiver the 'vibration of a shaft of writing' come from, we know that, in its flight, this arrow 'promises and calls for a reading, a preponderance to come of the interpretative decision'.[41] In the temporal limbo opened by Nietzsche, Shakespeare and other literary *génies*, in 'the long time of a time that does not belong to time', in other words a time which is 'out of joint', the arrow, like the spectre, comes back from the future;[42] although it 'begins at the end', it 'carries its address along and implies in advance, in its very readability, the signature of the addressee'.[43] As I will go on to argue in the next section, the singular response that this address demands must also be singular, perhaps like love's wound. 'O Romeo, Romeo . . .' (II, ii, 33). Just like the teleiopoetic arrow, the 'address of love' is, Kamuf argues, 'never issued by a pre-existent subject in the direction of an object, its object, or destination', but is 'determined by the other'.[44] In the words of 'Envois':

> And when I call you my love, my love, is it you I am calling or my love? You, my love, is it you I thereby name, is it to you that I address myself? I don't know if the question is well put, it frightens me. But I am sure that the answer, if it gets to me one day, will have come to me from you. You alone, my love, you alone will have known it.[45]

In the words of Shakespeare: 'Call me but love, and I'll be new baptized' (II, ii, 50).

How to Love Shakespeare

With every word or phrase Shakespeare watches over us. This is, at least, what Derrida claims. Let's go back, once more:

> 'The time is out of joint': time is *disarticulated*, dislocated, dislodged, time is run down, on the run and run down [*traqué et détraqué*], *deranged*, both out of order and mad. Time is off its hinges, time is off course, beside itself, disadjusted. Says Hamlet. Who thereby opened one of those breaches [*brèches*], often they are poetic and thinking peepholes [*meurtrières*], through which Shakespeare will have kept watch over the English language; at the same time he signed its body, with the same unprecedented stroke of some arrow [*et à la fois signé son corps, du même coup sans précédent, de quelque flèche*].[46]

Shakespeare is watching over us, but not as a good shepherd might. This does not mean to say that, for Derrida, Shakespeare, or indeed literature, cannot bring solace or counsel. One way of putting this would be that the work we call Shakespeare's is not constative (providing answers) but performative (making things happen). Indeed, more than anything else, Derrida affirms the performativity of great literary works (think back to Nussbaum's critique of fancy but inoperative words on a page), their ability to make thinking happen. When Derrida then writes that Shakespeare watches over us, he is not suggesting that we might turn to him for ready morsels of wisdom, but rather that Shakespeare's words – for example 'the time is out of joint' – allow us to take our thinking to unforeseen, unexpected, truly new places. It's a labour of love.

'Aphorism Countertime' declares that such love as exists between Romeo *and* Juliet also exists between us *and Romeo and Juliet*. In 'The Time is Out of Joint', Derrida admits that Hamlet's phrase is 'cited, recited, analyzed there [in *Specters*] like an obsession'.[47] Something about Shakespeare, something that Derrida also calls 'the force of the poem', makes him 'quote it, again and again, by an irresistible compulsion', and makes him learn it by heart.[48] In 'Deconstruction and Love', Kamuf asks whether we do violence to the concept of love, 'which has to be (does it not?) either interpersonal or at least a relation formed between animate, living beings' when we proclaim our love for a text, or even, as Derrida does in 'The Time is Out of Joint', for a phrase.[49] As I have argued in the last chapter, we can love *Romeo and Juliet* and Shakespeare with the passion only a 'singular name', or a 'signature', can ignite.

Can one love a literary work or perhaps a philosophical text? And what might the difference between these two loves be? Derrida 'love[s] very much everything that [he] deconstructs in [his] own manner'.[50] If there is deconstruction, it is a kind of obsessive love, what in *The Ear of the Other* is called a 'loving jealousy'.[51] Love is involved in the way Derrida reads Shakespeare, but also danger. Shakespeare watches over us and the English language through *meurtrières*, he writes. A *meurtrière* is an arrow slit or a loophole. It is also a *criminelle*, a murderess. *Meurtrier* is an adjective meaning deadly, lethal. As Royle points out, *meurtrières* are also death traps, making Shakespeare's a 'death-trap English'.[52] Addressing his beloved in 'Envois', the 'I' indeed writes about love in terms of *meurtrières*: 'Our delinquency, my love, we are the worst criminals and the first victims, I would like not to kill anyone, and everything that I send you goes through *meurtrières* [vertical slots in the wall of a fortification for projecting weapons; murderesses].'[53] The arrows Shakespeare sends through those *meurtrières* are also love letters wounding the body of English, which is also Shakespeare's body. This then is perhaps one way in which Shakespeare has become our horizon as Emerson imagined.

The 'stroke of some arrow' is such a fitting image not only because it delineates that space which is opened by the *brèches* of the Shakespearean signature, but also because it renders the violence that makes such openness possible. Derrida speaks of a similar violent transversal in *Monolingualism of the Other*, not, however, in the context of his relationship to Shakespeare but to the French language. Derrida speaks of how he

> seemed to be harpooned by French philosophy and literature, the one and the other, the one or the other: wooden or metallic darts [*flèches*], a penetrating body of enviable, formidable, and inaccessible words even when they were entering me, sentences which it was necessary to appropriate, domesticate, coax [*amadouer*], that is to say, love by setting on fire, burn ('tinder' [*amadou*] is never far away), perhaps destroy, in all events mark, transform, prune, cut, forge, graft at the fire, let come in another way, in other words, to itself in itself.[54]

Although the translator, Patrick Mensah, opts to speak of 'metallic darts', Derrida is speaking here of those same *flèches* that Shakespeare is shooting at the English language, at Derrida, and at us, speakers of Shakespeare's English.

This passage in *Monolingualism of the Other* is perhaps the closest Derrida comes to formulating a manifesto of what he wants to do with the French language, indeed what the French language does to him; he wants to woo, wound and change the French language as it woos, wounds and changes him. *Monolingualism* plays on the partial homophony between *amadouer*, to 'coax', and *amadou*, 'tinder': here love is never far away from destruction. In an image that uncannily echoes Derrida's *flèches*, Jean-Luc Nancy writes of love as a blade that is plunged into us, and each time in an absolutely singular manner: 'for as long as it lasts, love does not cease to come from without and to remain, not outside but this outside itself, each time singular, a blade plunged into me and that I cannot rejoin because it disjoins me'.[55] When Derrida is 'harpooned' by French philosophy and literature, the 'penetrating body' of 'enviable, formidable, and inaccessible words', words enter his body, but they also withdraw. He is not only wounded by them, but he wounds and transforms them in turn: he 'appropriates', 'transforms', 'forges' and cuts them. The resonances to Derrida's conceptualisation of the teleiopoetic arrow in *Politics of Friendship*, but also in *Specters* or 'Aphorism Countertime' are unmistakable.

We must not imagine that reading Shakespeare should leave either of us, or these texts themselves, without a scratch. For Derrida, being hit by the *flèches* of Shakespeare, or any great literary work, any work of a literary 'genius', is a process as loving as it is passionately violent: he needs to forge the harpooning *flèches* that penetrate him, he needs to 'appropriate' and 'domesticate' them, he needs to 'love' them 'by setting [them] on fire'.[56] It is this violent transversal that Derrida speaks about in *The Ear of the Other*; but this love, though violent, is not a 'negative operation'.[57] If there is a deconstructive position it would fall somewhere between the two, where we cannot '*choose* between an operation that we'll call negative or nihilist, an operation that would set about furiously dismantling systems, and the other operation'.[58] Loving a text means to allow oneself to be traversed, to create space in oneself, but it also means doing something with this *flèche*, burning it with the fire of one's wound, opening it up in turn and forging something else from it. Derrida also calls this countersigning. (I will return to this later, in the next chapter. Let's stay for now with what Derrida wants to make happen in language, not merely French or English or German, but the *plus d'un* of and in language.)

Derrida's is not a fantasy of 'harming the language', or 'of endangering or injuring it', but of making 'something happen to this language'.[59] This wish speaks of a great sensitivity to the struggle that is already happening in language and between the languages within any one language. Whenever we speak or write, whenever we idiomatise language, which cannot at bottom be appropriated we 'carry on a hand-to-hand, bodily struggle with it': a *corps à corps*.[60] Every idiom '(and the idiom, precisely means *the proper*, what is proper to) every signature is both an attempt to appropriate and at the same time an 'experience [of] the fact that language can never be appropriated'.[61] Derrida's most beautiful meditations on this *corps à corps* can be found in his work on the poet Paul Celan. Celan, perhaps, does to German what Derrida wants to do to French. Each of Celan's poems and each word marks an *Auseinandersetzung*, a combat between Celan and German but also within the differences of German itself.[62] Echoing the double meaning of *amadouer* in his discussion of French in *Monolingualism*, Derrida here imagines Celan working with the German language in a way that is both absolutely and impossibly respectful, even loving, at the same time as tampering with (*touche à*) language.[63] With each stroke. Celan then leaves upon language 'a sort of scar, a mark, a wound'.[64]

As I noted some chapters ago, when reading Derrida, Nussbaum was thirsting for blood, for what in a text really touches us and speaks to our humanity.[65] In 'Deconstruction and Love' Peggy Kamuf sums up Nussbaum's argument like this: 'too much attention to textuality leads to bloodlessness'. She then adds: 'but is this a good thing or a bad thing? Says who?'[66] As noted in the previous chapter, Derrida's work helps us challenge the widely held assumption that a sensitivity to texts *as* texts, rather than, for instance, as a mouthpiece of human genius, hinders access to the ways in which that text might help us grapple with questions that really concern or move us. As his deconstructive readings of *Romeo and Juliet* and *Hamlet* in particular show, Derrida's acts of reading do, in fact, lend insights into matters, such as the nature of love or the act of mourning, that are of wide, even general, human interest. As I have also argued in the previous chapter, this is not despite but because of Derrida's textual sensitivity, his attention to the contretemporal nature of *Romeo and Juliet* and the out of jointness of *Hamlet* the plays *themselves*. To invert Kamuf's paraphrase: attention to textuality leads not to bloodlessness but to, well, blood. What kind of blood?

For all of Nussbaum's thirst, she misses a different kind of blood that is spilled in each of Derrida's acts of reading. In 'Shakespeare Ghosting Derrida', Cixous echoes the arrow image to talk about what Derrida does with Shakespeare:

> How does Derrida read a text? Whether it is fiction or drama, he will never have read the whole or part of a volume. He stitches on the other veil (as he puts it in *Voiles* [*Veils*]) but also pinches from it (*il pique*). A genius in him guides the blind man he is, unerringly guides his hand, his beak, his quill, his stylus, his syringe towards the worm [*vers le ver*] or the *vein*.[67]

When Derrida reads *à contretemps* his pen sharpens ever more lethally – from beak, to quill, to stylus, to syringe. When Derrida reads, his pen, in a 'stroke of luck [*coup de veine*]', begins retrieving 'meaningful blood samples [*sang/sens*]'.[68] These blood samples are not distillations of human concern, even human nature, but something completely other: they are fragments of the text itself, expressive not of a truth but of its own idiomaticity (an idiomaticity furthermore that demands a singular response).

One of the ideas that perhaps takes most getting used to in Derrida is the idea that texts have bodies and that these bodies work in their own uncanny terms. A text's body is, as Derrida writes, its 'uniqueness', as it is 'incorporated, incarnated, in what one used to call the "signifiers," in the graphemes which in themselves cannot be translated'.[69] When he reads Shakespeare, he is this attuned to the violent, material effects of Shakespearean words or phrases that sign their body and the body of English, words or phrases such as 'porpentine' (which I shall discuss at some length in the next chapter) or 'the time is out of joint'. What we are dealing with is, then, the idiom. The idiom is what 'at bottom' remains 'untranslatable . . . even if we translate it'.[70] Shakespeare's idiom – 'the time is out of joint', for instance – is irreducibly his; it marks the Thing Shakespeare's particular way of inhabiting the English language as someone might inhabit one's body. This is, of course, not only true of Shakespeare. Take Celan's works, for instance, where Derrida identifies 'a certain way of "inhabiting the idiom" ("signed: Celan from a certain place in the German language, which was his property alone")'.[71]

What does it mean to say that a literary work has a body, a body, furthermore different from and completely other to the body of its author?[72] Derrida writes that Hamlet's 'the time is out of joint' has 'opened, poetic and thinking peepholes [*meurtrières*]'.[73] Peepholes suggest an enclosure, even the act of standing guard. 'The time is out of joint' is of course an opening, an invitation to thinking, but it also marks a border, a wall, if you like, that guards a secret. It is what, as he writes in 'Che cos'é la poesia' is 'an imparted secret, at once public and private'.[74] As Derrida repeatedly highlights in his work on Celan, the idiom, understood as the 'invincible singularity of the verbal body already introduces us into the enigma of testimony' and to the question of an absolute secrecy into the heart of poetry and of language.[75] There is just such secrecy, irreducibility or untranslatability at work in Celan's poem 'Aschenglorie'. Here Derrida tentatively and briefly identifies a silent reference to Hecate, more precisely to Shakespeare's Hecate. Although 'the name of the goddess Hecate is not pronounced' Derrida detects it in the poem's association to 'the moon, the Pontic and the three of the *Dreiweg*'.[76] It is under precisely this guise that 'Hecate appears in *Macbeth*'.[77] This reference remains and, Derrida is careful to point out, will remain 'ineffaceable, beneath the surface of this poem'.[78] Indeed, one might need to know that Celan translated Shakespeare in order to recognise this sepulchral reference. Derrida's aim here is less to score some points in astute hermeneutics than to say something about the signature effect, a text's absolute situatedness and secrecy at the very moment of inscription and at each moment it is read:

> It is my body, this is my body. Every poem says, 'This is my body,' and the rest: drink it, eat it, keep it in memory of me. There is a Last Supper in every poem, which says: This is my body, here and now. And you know what comes next: passions, crucifixions, executions. Others would also say resurrections . . .[79]

It is this singularity which demands that loving jealousy that Derrida writes of. Or, as he puts it in 'Che cos'è la poesia?': 'Thus the dream of *learning by heart* arises in you. Of letting your heart be traversed by the dictated dictation.'[80] This traversal is, as we have seen by following what Derrida says about the arrow, both active and passive, both wounding and wounded. 'The signature is a wound, and there is no other origin for the work of art', Derrida writes in *Glas*.[81] In fact, Shakespeare's *coup de quelque flèche* is here met by Derrida's, the reader's own *coup*. What Derrida, therefore, says about the poet must also be true for the reader:

> The poet is someone who perceives that language, his language, the language he inherits in the sense I was just emphasizing, is in danger of becoming a dead language

again, and he therefore has the responsibility, a very grave responsibility, of waking it up, of resuscitating it (not in the sense of Christian glory but in the sense of a resurrection of language), not like an immortal body or a glorious body, but like a mortal body, frail, sometimes indecipherable, as is each poem by Celan. Each poem is a resurrection, but one that engages us to a vulnerable body, one that may be forgotten again.[82]

Every time Shakespeare's arrow is pointed at us, we must, according to Derrida, respond to its singularity. In *The Singularity of Literature*, Attridge argues that the singularity of a piece of literature, like the singularity of a loved one, is not to be confused with its uniqueness or its idiosyncrasy. Singularity is not 'what Benjamin called the "aura" of the specific, unique art-object'; it is not even limited to one single piece of art, but can 'also inhere in a group of works or an entire *oeuvre*'.[83] The analogy of the singularity of a literary work and a signature works because 'in the act of reading and verifying the signature we need not be aware of the place and time (though often this is specified as well), but we must be aware of the situatedness and datedness – in one sense of the term – of the act of writing'.[84] At stake here is a more general situatedness, what in 'I Have a Taste for the Secret' is called 'this singularity of the untimely, of non-self-contemporaneity'.[85] As Hent de Vries argues, 'the date is not an indivisible *hic et nunc*, an atomic point in time and space. From its very inception, the date will always already have broken the silence of a pure singularity.'[86] For Attridge, the work's singularity, its 'signature', paradoxically, does not limit it to 'reside in the historical past', but 'bridges, in a way that is not easy to explain, past and present'.[87] He continues: 'Strictly speaking, therefore, singularity, like alterity and inventiveness, is not a property but an event, the event of singularizing which takes place in reception: it does not occur outside the responses of those who encounter and thereby constitute it'.[88]

The time of reading, like the poem itself, is dated and singular and each time happens only once. Love's arrow wounds every time as if it were the first time and each arrow is always 'sans précédent'.[89] It kicks off a *corps à corps*, a 'hand-to-hand, bodily struggle . . . an attack'[90]:

> There is as it were a duel of singularities, a duel of writing and reading, in the course of which a countersignature comes both to confirm, repeat and respect the signature of the other, of the 'original' work, and to *lead it off* elsewhere, so running the risk of *betraying* it, having to betray it in a certain way so as to respect it, through the invention of another signature just as singular.[91]

In *The Ear of the Other*, Derrida claims that all the texts that he loves are 'texts whose future . . . will not be exhausted for a long time'.[92] Their 'signature is not yet finished – that's the destiny of signatures'.[93] While, as Derrida argues in 'Signature Event Context', 'the signature also marks and retains his [the signers] having-been present in a past *now* or present [*maintenant*]', at the same time it posits that this now is also a 'future *now* or present [*maintenant*]'.[94] Here, just like at the beginning of *Specters*, Derrida is playing on the flexible duration of the present that the French word *maintenant* traces. It means (1) 'now', but it can also mean (2) 'by now' or (3) 'from now on' (*Collins-Robert French Dictionary*). Although Derrida calls it 'the transcendental form of presentness [*maintenance*]', what is at issue here is not an idea of transcendence, but rather the 'singular present punctuality' pinpointed by the signature and the singular literary oeuvre.[95] The *différance* of every now, every being unfurls towards a to come, the time where an unfurling singularity will be met with an absolutely singular response. As mentioned above, the loving arrow of reading does something to time. Each reading's and each writing's new idiom *makes things happen* [*fait arriver*], this signature brought forth [*fait arrivée*], produces events in the given language, the given language to which things must still be given, sometimes *unverifiable* events: illegible events. Events that are always promised rather than given. Messianic events. But the promise is not nothing; it is not a non-event.[96]

The wound of reading says: 'It only happens to me.' We find this sentence at least twice in Derrida's work: in 'Envois' and 'Circumfession'.[97] These texts, just like Derrida's other Shakespearean encounters, do not attempt a general reading; they respond to Shakespeare's idiom with their own.

> I wrote a text, which in the face of the event of another's text, as it comes to me at a particular, quite singular, moment, tries to 'respond' or to 'countersign,' in an idiom which turns out to be mine. But an idiom is never pure, its iterability opens it up to others.[98]

Chance plays a central role in the way Derrida reads Shakespeare. It's a stroke of luck, which becomes a *coup de veine*. In relation to 'Aphorism Countertime', Derrida admits: 'In this case, I was asked for a short, oblique text to accompany a production.'[99] As such, we owe 'Aphorism Countertime' to nothing but chance (and I will turn to role of chance in Derrida's readings of Shakespeare soon):

> If the actor-producer Daniel Mesguich had not put the play on at that point (but why did he?), if he hadn't been interested in what I write (but why? – this opens up another chain of causality), he wouldn't have asked anything of me and I would never have written this text.[100]

And yet despite, or rather because of, this chance encounter with Shakespeare, Derrida 'felt like signing and even dating' the singularity of his response 'at a past moment in December, that year, at Verona (as it says at the end of the text)'.[101] Here then is his countersignature:

> 39. The absolute aphorism: a proper name. Without genealogy, without the least copula. End of drama. Curtain. Tableau (*The Two Lovers United in Death* by Angelo dall'Oca Bianca). Tourism, December sun in Verona ('Verona by that name is known' [V, iii, 299]). A true sun, the other ('The sun for sorrow will not show his head' [V, iii, 305]).[102]

In 'Following Derrida', Attridge suggests that we turn to the French: *tableau* in French conveys a transition from the theatre to painting in a way that 'tableau' in English doesn't, being much more rooted in the world of the stage. For Attridge, 'the end of *Romeo and Juliet* . . . presents a tableau mirrored in a painting (to be seen, presumably by visitors to Verona)'.[103] But we can never hope to get to the bottom of Derrida's countersignature: for instance, why he refers to the painting by the Veronese painter Angelo Dall'Oca Bianca, whose original title, *Ultimi istanti di Giulietta e Romeo*, refers, as if by a stroke of chance, to the contretemps of the theatre of double survival. While some parts can be deciphered, others, like Celan's Shakespearean countersignature in 'Aschenglorie' remain beyond our reach.[104] Together with what Attridge calls Derrida's 'irreducibly personal memory', the aphoristic and parenthetical insertions from the end of *Romeo and Juliet* remain as incisive as they are irretrievable. All we can hope to do is countersign in turn.

Is Derrida an Anglicist?

Is it possible, or even advisable, to read Derrida in English translation only and to claim to be, in however small a way, an expert? His work on Shakespeare is living proof (yes, *living*, because texts are alive, albeit in their own uncanny ways) that Derrida was no stranger to working in, through and with translation. Addressing an English audience, he says: 'I am speaking to you in English, having written this in French, and apparently no catastrophe has resulted.'[105] What catastrophe might result when reading Shakespeare in French? What catastrophe might happen when I, a native German speaker, read Derrida in English, who in turn read Shakespeare in French? What, on the other hand, could be won by such translinguistic encounters?

Saying that Shakespeare 'watches over us', as Derrida does in *Specters*, is another way of saying that when we speak, write, and think in English we speak, write and think in Shakespeare's English. What does it mean for a French philosopher, who, by his own admission thinks and 'write[s] in French' only quoting 'the German or the English' when necessary to make such a claim?[106] Derrida is, in fact, rather apologetic about his knowledge of English, just as he is, for example, of his knowledge of German. And yet, his relationship to his 'own' language, French, is by no means uncomplicated. While *Monolingualism of the Other* is perhaps Derrida's most overt admission of his complex relationship to French, there is always a certain angularity or alienation at play when Derrida writes French. French belongs to Derrida, like English belongs to Shakespeare, which is to say that they do not belong at all, at least not in the traditional sense of propriety or even mastery. As Julian Wolfreys, John Brannigan and Ruth Robbins write in *The French Connections of Jacques Derrida*, it would be wrong to think of Derrida as a thinker who 'emerges as part of a clearly definable cultural and literary tradition'.[107] There is, they continue, 'difference and alterity within the writing that is signed "Jacques Derrida"' just as there is difference and alterity in 'the language that he calls "his", French'.[108] There are not merely differences between languages; there is *différance* within (one) language(s).

Let's then follow Thomas Dutoit and think of Derrida not as a French writer and thinker but as an Anglicist. Derrida, he claims, does not write in French but in Anglish and, furthermore, in angles. Playing on the homophones of *l'anglais* (English) and *l'anglé* (angle), Dutoit goes on to suggest that there is no language more apt to be the language of deconstruction than this anglish English.[109] English's idiomaticity, its signature, is constituted by the 'angularity and divisibility' of its 'semantics' and 'phonetics'.[110] And yet this is naturally not merely true of English, but also of German, French or indeed any language.

Derrida, the Anglicist, is sensitive and responsive to these angles of language, of any language. He is an Anglicist because language is never owned. Shakespeare, too, is an Anglicist and so is Celan, because both, like Shakespeare, know that there is always a kink in language, and that each word, each syllable or *lettre*, is a possible deviation. In this perspective, it is fully possible to be both 'monolingual . . . and speak a language that is not one's own'.[111] This is the 'multiplicity and migration of language', the 'Babel within *a single* language' discussed in depth in Derrida's reading of Celan.[112]

Diversion, distance and alienation are always at work in language from the beginning. *Monolingualism*, indeed, does not melancholically hark back to a supposed moment of jointness with a mother tongue. Alienation here denotes less an alienation from a lost presentness to or ipseity in language than the movement of distancing and othering inherent in language itself. To put it in the terms of Dutoit's apt description of Derrida's angle-icism, the angles in and of language (what perhaps in previous chapters was discussed in terms of *différance*) are not angles that keep something hidden (perhaps a secret); rather it is this angularity that creates meaning in the first place. Language's alienation or othering 'lacks nothing that precedes or follows it, it alienates no *ipseity*, no property, and no self that has ever been able to represent its watchful eye'.[113] The alienation of language is not a call or a summons to something that has been, something or someone perhaps to 'watch over its past or future'; it is a call that in summoning us, interpellates us as watchmen and watchwomen guardians, inventors and dreamers of this language.[114]

There is no Shakespeare to watch over English, unless he is understood to be an Anglicist, just like Derrida. Because language is never single or monolingual, indeed because these differences and diversions in language are the conditions of meaning, the question of Derrida's relationship to one particular language, whether it be French, English or German, is less important than might initially seem. For the vast majority of readers of Derrida who read him in English this must surely be welcome news. In fact, who better than Celan and Derrida demonstrate that it is an advantage to think in a language never fully one's own.

What is true for the French or English language is incidentally also true for French or anglophone philosophy. Thinking of Derrida as a 'French' philosopher would be just as inaccurate as thinking about him as a native French speaker. In fact, deconstruction first flourished not in France but in the United States, more precisely in Yale during the 1970s and 1980s, and not in philosophy but in literature departments. The description of a linguistic and cultural divide between anglo-analytic sobriety and French-continental flamboyance therefore ignores the very rich history that deconstruction has had in the United States. Describing someone as a French philosopher is less a comment on his or her nationality than a philosophical categorisation itself. When we say: Derrida is a French or continental philosopher we assign him to a certain branch of the philosophical tradition and to a certain way of doing philosophy. We signal to others and to ourselves that this philosophy has to be read in a certain way, and linked up to and contextualised with different ideas and methods that are part of that tradition. Here 'French' or 'continental' then is a philosophical language or idiom, a way of going about things philosophically, as well a reference horizon, a vanishing point for thinking. Because 'continental', even more obviously than 'French', is not so much a statement of the language in which philosophy is written, than a description of the language, what Wittgenstein would have called the grammar, of the philosophy itself.

There survives in certain parts of philosophy the fantasy that philosophical thought ought to be fully translatable. In this view, a philosophical thought, if it is worth its salt, should have a smoothness of meaning; put differently, its meaning would remain unaltered were it to leave the terms in which it was originally couched. Implied here is the belief that a worthy philosophical thought should survive transferal from one habitat to another. Call this the fantasy of the complete divisibility of signifier and signified, or perhaps of the transparency of language.

Conversely, in the study of literature it is widely accepted, even celebrated, that a literary text is never fully translatable: translation loses something of its original meaning but is also able to add something. Thus the original materiality of its language, its idiom – including also its specific intertextual references – is exchanged for another one, often no less rich in resonance or indeed significance. It could even be said that the study of literature is often the study of what in literary texts resists translation or transferal, what, in other words, remains untranslatable even by the most skilled translator. It is also the study of what, on the other hand, translation, no matter how flawed in the end, can and does add.

Can philosophy be translated? And if yes, what would such translation entail and what would it leave out? In a tantalisingly brief recent talk, Marian Hobson suggests that much could be won from reading philosophy *as if it* were a poem, and furthermore a translated poem: 'Now if we are not all that used to reading philosophy, reading it *as if it were* in translation, with a kind of slight suspicion, can teach us better, closer reading.'[115] I am struck by Hobson's suggestions that *slight* suspicion can make us better readers of philosophy, particularly if we are not habitual readers of philosophical works. In order to explain what she means by this, she points us towards what Derrida says in *Eyes of the University: Right to Philosophy* 2 about René Descartes's *Discourse on Method* (1637), more precisely its penultimate paragraph in which Descartes addresses his decision to write the work not, as might have been expected at the time, in Latin but in French:

> And if I write in French, which is the language of my country, rather than in Latin, which is that of my teachers, it is because I hope that those who use only their pure natural reason will better judge my opinions than those who believe only in old books, and because I am sure that those who combine good sense with scholarship, whom alone I wish to have as my judges, will not be so partial to Latin as to refuse to hear my reasons because I express them in a vulgar tongue.[116]

Here, Descartes's text speaks not only *in* French but also *about* French.[117] Extrapolating a general 'truth' from a particular instance, Derrida notes that the problem of philosophy in/as translation that Descartes points us to here is at play whenever we speak philosophically. It is at play not merely when we cross or criss-cross linguistic boundaries, as Descartes does in the *Discourse* – between French and Latin – or as Derrida does when talking about the *Discourse*. Indeed, Derrida delivered the four lectures on which the first part of *Eyes of the University: Right to Philosophy* 2 – 'Transfer *Ex Cathedra*: Language and Institutions of Philosophy' – are based at the University of Toronto and in English. When he therefore 'was preparing this seminar in [his] language, French, knowing that [he] would have to give it, once translated, in English', he already 'ran into' these problems of translation.[118] 'We are reading the *Discourse on Method* here in one language or another. I have read it in French; we are reading it in English; I have written about it in French; I am talking to you about it in English.'[119] The point about drawing our attention to the penultimate paragraph of Descartes's *Discourse* is, however, less to note a linguistic particularity common to Derrida – as I have already noted, he is more often read in translation and the fortunes of his work have been better in a non-French academic context – than to think about the tensions between the idiomacity of philosophical discourse and the universalist aspirations I touched upon a moment ago: 'How can one, starting from this example, deal with the general relations between a language and a philosophical discourse, the multiplicity of language and the universalist claim of the discourse called philosophical?'[120] Now, idiomacity here in this example is first and foremost language, but it includes also what with Derrida we might call the *event* of the writing and reading of a text, in other words the irreducible singularity of the moment of inscription, as well as of reading.

What happens to a philosophical text that speaks self-reflectively in and about its idiom when it is translated? Descartes's meta-linguistic paragraph disappears in Étienne de Courcelles's 1744 Latin translation of the *Discourse*, while Adam and Tannery's edition remarks the omission with a 'sublime' sentence: '"There was in fact no cause to translate [it]" (*il n'y avait pas lieu de [le] traduire en effet* [*Oeuvres* 6.583]).'[121] Derrida suggests that because Descartes's paragraph 'is irreducibly bound to a language that forms not only the signifying fabric of its *presentation*, but also the signified theme', any rendition in another language, even one that translates faithfully word by word, would 'obliterate' it.[122] It is precisely at this point, namely when the discourse becomes more self-consciously idiomatic, that these statements 'founder, in their form and their content, body and soul, one might say, at the instant of translation'.[123]

Why is this important when thinking about what Shakespeare can do for philosophy? What Hobson's suggestion that we, and particular those of us who are not philosophers first, should read philosophy as if it were a translated poem gets at is precisely the Derridean understanding of the importance of the idiom – the act of reading, which is an act of wrestling the idiom – for doing philosophy. Equally, this erasure by translation also highlights what in language resists translation, what cannot cross over between linguistic realms without losing something of its signifying power. Descartes's vanishing paragraph is therefore also a *remaining* paragraph, a monument to what the idiom does for philosophy. In a very true sense, each piece of philosophical writing, even the apparently most transparent one, contains what, like a poem or like Descartes's paragraph, resists transfer and translation. At the same time, it invites performative translation. Derrida's way of doing philosophy and of doing philosophy with Shakespeare in particular reminds us that, no matter how seemingly peripheral to the philosophical thought it conveys, the idiom, which by definition remains untranslatable to some degree, does important and irreducible philosophical work. Enter: the Shakespearean porpentine.

Notes

1. Jacques Derrida, 'Aphorism Countertime', trans. Nicholas Royle, in *Acts of Literature*, ed. Derek Attridge (London: Routledge, 1992), 420.
2. Ibid. 420.
3. Jacques Derrida, 'L'aphorisme à contretemps', in *Psyché: Inventions de l'autre II* (Paris: Galilée, 2003), 134.
4. Ibid. 134.
5. Derrida, 'Aphorism Countertime', 416.

6. Derrida, 'L'aphorisme à contretemps', 131.
7. Clare Connors, *Force from Nietzsche to Derrida* (London: Legenda, 2010), 103.
8. Jacques Derrida, *Specters of Marx: The State of the Debt, the Work of Mourning and the New International*, trans. Peggy Kamuf (London: Routledge, 2006), xvi.
9. Ibid. 20; Jacques Derrida, *Spectres de Marx: L'État de la dette, le travail du deuil et la nouvelle Internationale* (Paris: Galilée, 1993), 42.
10. Sarah Wood, 'Let's Start Again', *Diacritics* 29, no. 1 (1999): 1.
11. Jacques Derrida, *Politics of Friendship*, trans. George Collins (London and New York: Verso Books, 2005), 77.
12. Ibid. 77.
13. Ibid. 32.
14. Ibid. 32.
15. Ibid. 31.
16. Ibid. 31.
17. Martin McQuillan, *Deconstruction after 9/11* (London: Routledge, 2009), 58.
18. Derrida, *Politics of Friendship*, 32.
19. Ibid. 32.
20. Corinne Scheiner, 'Teleiopoiesis, Telepoesis, and the Practice of Comparative Literature', *Comparative Literature* 57, no. 3 (2005): 243.
21. Derrida, *Politics of Friendship*, 32.
22. Ibid. 32.
23. Ibid. 32.
24. Derrida, *Politics of Friendship*, 32; Jacques Derrida, *Politiques de l'amitié: suivi de l'oreille de Heidegger* (Paris: Éditions Galilée, 1994), 50.
25. Derrida, 'L'aphorisme à contretemps', 134.
26. Derrida, *Politics of Friendship*, 42–3.
27. Ibid. 32.
28. Ibid. 32.
29. Jacques Derrida, 'Signature Event Context', trans. Samuel Weber and Jeffrey Mehlman, in *Limited Inc*, ed. Gerald Graff (Evanston: Northwestern University Press, 1988), 9.

30. Ibid. 9.
31. Jacques Derrida, '"A Self-Unsealing Poetic Text": Poetics and Politics of Witnessing', trans. Rachel Bowlby, in *Revenge of the Aesthetic: The Place of Literature in Theory Today*, ed. Michael P. Clark (Berkeley: University of California Press, 2000), 180.
32. Jacques Derrida, 'Shibboleth: For Paul Celan', trans. Thomas Dutoit and Joshua Wilner, in *Sovereignties in Question: The Poetics of Paul Celan*, ed. Thomas Dutoit and Outi Pasanen (New York: Fordham University Press, 2005), 33.
33. Derrida, *Politics of Friendship*, 32.
34. Ibid. 32.
35. McQuillan, *Deconstruction after 9/11*, 58.
36. Jacques Derrida, 'Envois', in *The Post Card: From Socrates to Freud and Beyond*, trans. Alan Bass (Chicago and London: University of Chicago Press, 1987), 21.
37. Ibid. 53.
38. Derrida, *Politics of Friendship*, 32.
39. J. Hillis Miller, *Speech Acts in Literature* (Stanford: Stanford University Press, 2001), 91.
40. Peggy Kamuf, *Book of Addresses* (Stanford: Stanford University Press, 2005), 6.
41. Derrida, *Politics of Friendship*, 31.
42. Ibid. 77.
43. Ibid. 32.
44. Peggy Kamuf, 'Deconstruction and Love', in *Deconstructions: A User's Guide*, ed. Nicholas Royle (Basingstoke: Palgrave, 2000), 155.
45. Derrida, 'Envois', 8.
46. Derrida, *Specters of Marx*, 20; *Spectres de Marx*, 42.
47. Derrida, 'The Time is Out of Joint', 18.
48. Derrida, '"A Self-Unsealing Poetic Text"', 198.
49. Kamuf, 'Deconstruction and Love', 152–3.
50. Derrida, *The Ear of the Other: Otobiography, Transference, Translation: Texts and Discussions with Derrida*, trans. Peggy Kamuf, ed. Christie McDonald (Lincoln: University of Nebraska Press, 1988), 87.

51. Ibid. 87.
52. Nicholas Royle, *The Uncanny* (Manchester: Manchester University Press, 2003), 124.
53. Derrida, 'Envois', 67–8.
54. Jacques Derrida, *Monolingualism of the Other; or, the Prosthesis of Origin*, trans. Patrick Mensah (Stanford: Stanford University Press, 1998), 50–1.
55. Jean-Luc Nancy, 'L'amour en éclats', in *Une pensée finie* (Paris: Galilée, 1990), 247–8.
56. Derrida, *Monolingualism of the Other*, 50–1.
57. Derrida, *The Ear of the Other*, 87.
58. Ibid. 87.
59. Derrida, *Monolingualism of the Other*, 51.
60. Derrida, 'Language is Never Owned: An Interview', trans. Thomas Dutoit and Phillippe Romanski, in *Sovereignties in Question: The Poetics of Paul Celan*, ed. Thomas Dutoit and Outi Pasanen (New York: Fordham University Press, 2005), 99.
61. Ibid. 99.
62. Ibid. 100.
63. Ibid. 100.
64. Ibid. 100.
65. Martha Nussbaum, *Love's Knowledge: Essays on Philosophy and Literature* (Oxford: Oxford University Press, 1990), 171.
66. Kamuf, 'Deconstruction and Love', 168.
67. Hélène Cixous, 'Shakespeare Ghosting Derrida', trans. Laurent Milesi, *The Oxford Literary Review* 34, no. 1 (2012): 2–3.
68. Ibid. 4.
69. Derrida, 'The Truth That Wounds: From an Interview', trans. Thomas Dutoit, in *Sovereignties in Question: The Poetics of Paul Celan*, ed. Thomas Dutoit and Outi Pasanen (New York: Fordham University Press, 2005), 168.
70. Derrida, 'Poetics and Politics of Witnessin', trans. Rachel Bowlby in *Sovereignties in Question: The Poetics of Paul Celan*, ed. Thomas Dutoit and Outi Pasanen (New York: Fordham University Press, 2005), 67.
71. Derrida, 'Language is Never Owned', 99.

72. I talk about what the body of Derrida's texts means for the way we inherited him in 'The King is Dead. Long Live the King', in *Desire in Ashes: Deconstruction, Psychoanalysis and Philosophy*, ed. Simon Morgan Wortham and Chiara Alfano (London: Bloomsbury, 2015).
73. Derrida, *Specters of Marx*, 20; *Spectres de Marx*, 42.
74. Jacques Derrida, 'Che cos'è la poesia?' in *A Derrida Reader: Between the Blinds*, trans. and ed. Peggy Kamuf (New York: Columbia University Press, 1991), 223.
75. Derrida, '"A Self-Unsealing Poetic Text"', 67.
76. Ibid. 93.
77. Ibid. 94.
78. Ibid. 93.
79. Derrida, 'The Truth That Wounds', 169.
80. Derrida, 'Che cos'è la poesia?', 231.
81. Jacques Derrida, *Glas*, trans. John P. Leavey, Jr. and Richard Rand (Lincoln: University of Nebraska Press, 1990), 184.
82. Derrida, 'Language is Never Owned', 106–7.
83. Derek Attridge, *The Singularity of Literature* (London: Routledge, 2004), 64.
84. Ibid. 110.
85. Jacques Derrida, '"I Have a Taste for the Secret"', trans. Giacomo Donis, in *A Taste for the Secret*, ed. Giacomo Donis and David Webb (Cambridge: Polity Press, 2001), 13.
86. Hent de Vries, 'The Shibboleth Effect: On Reading Paul Celan', in *Judeities: Questions for Jacques Derrida*, trans. Bettina Bergo and Michael B. Smith, ed. Bettina Bergo, Joseph Cohen and Raphael Zagury-Orly (New York: Fordham University Press, 2007), 186.
87. Attridge, *The Singularity of Literature*, 64.
88. Ibid. 64.
89. Derrida, *Spectres de Marx*, 42.
90. Derrida, 'The Truth That Wounds', 168.
91. Jacques Derrida, '"This Strange Institution Called Literature": An Interview with Jacques Derrida', trans. Geoffrey Bennington and Rachel Bowlby, in *Acts of Literature*, ed. Derek Attridge (London: Routledge, 1992), 69.

92. Derrida, *The Ear of the Other*, 87.
93. Ibid. 87.
94. Derrida, 'Signature Event Context', 20.
95. Ibid. 20.
96. Derrida, *Monolingualism of the Other*, 66.
97. Derrida, 'Envois', 135; Jacques Derrida, 'Circumfession', trans. Geoffrey Bennington, in *Jacques Derrida* (Chicago: University of Chicago Press, 1993), 305.
98. Derrida, '"This Strange Institution Called Literature"', 62.
99. Ibid. 63.
100. Ibid. 66.
101. Ibid. 65.
102. Derrida, 'Aphorism Countertime', 433.
103. Derek Attridge, 'Following Derrida', *Tympanum: A Journal of Comparative Literary Studies. Special Edition Choraographies for Jacques Derrida on July 15, 2000*, http://www.usc.edu/dept/comp-lit/tympanum/4/khora.html (last accessible 11 April 2012).
104. Derrida, '"This Strange Institution Called Literature"', 65.
105. Derrida, 'If There is Cause to Translate II: Descartes' Romances, or The Economy of Words', trans. Rebecca Comay, in *Eyes of the University: Right to Philosophy* 2 (Stanford: Stanford University Press, 2004), 21.
106. Derrida, '"This Strange Institution Called Literature"', 60–1.
107. Julian Wolfreys, John Brannigan and Ruth Robbins, eds, *The French Connections of Jacques Derrida* (Albany: State University of New York Press, 1999), xi.
108. Ibid. xi.
109. Thomas Dutoit, 'Jacques Derrida, Anglicist', *Oxford Literary Review* 25 (2003): 323.
110. Ibid. 332.
111. Derrida, *Monolingualism of the Other*, 5.
112 Derrida, 'Shibboleth: For Paul Celan', 28.
113. Derrida, *Monolingualism of the Other*, 25.
114. Ibid. 25.

115. Marian Hobson, 'Marian Hobson on Reading Philosophy as Translation', British Academy podcast, https://soundcloud.com/britishacademy/marian-hobson-on-reading-philosophy-as-translation (last accessed 25 October 2018).
116. Derrida, 'If There is Cause to Translate I: Philosophy in its National Language (Toward a "licterature en François"), trans. Sylvia Söderlind, in *Eyes of the University: Right to Philosophy 2* (Stanford: Stanford University Press, 2004), 1.
117. Ibid. 19.
118. Ibid. 1.
119. Ibid. 2.
120. Ibid. 3.
121. Ibid. 19.
122. Derrida, 'If There is Cause to Translate II', 21.
123. Derrida, 'If There is Cause to Translate I', 19.

CHAPTER 4

PORPENTINE

These Little Moles of Language

Over the years, considerable philosophical importance has been attached to the figure of the mole in *Hamlet*. It has been argued that the mole represents a kind of consciousness, or at the very least a kind of unconscious, working somewhere beneath the surface of Shakespearean language. 'Shakespeare in the Ear of Hegel' in Ned Lukacher's *Primal Scenes*, for instance, as Royle notes in 'Nuclear Piece', 'tracks the "mole" to a number of purportedly compatible sites: something deep in Hamlet's "character" [205] . . . something that is "still burrowing" [209] . . . and – last but not least – "Shakespeare" "himself" [235]'.[1] Nothing could be further from Derrida's understanding of how Shakespeare watches over the English language. If the mole can indeed be thought of as an example of what Shakespeare's texts do, then this mole traces the 'slow mole-like advance' Derrida speaks of in 'Freud and the Scene of Writing'.[2] Margreta de Grazia has suggested that this 'mole of the unconscious moves out of sync with consciousness, erupting sporadically to break new paths, like deconstructive writing itself'.[3] In *The Uncanny*, Royle suggests that the mole-like character of Hamlet's language allows us to think beyond 'conventional boundaries of characterology, scenes and acts, and imagery', to think towards a kind of 'dramaturgic or theatrical telepathy'.[4] Such a 'telepathy' would then also account for what Royle in *Telepathy and Literature: Essays on the Reading Mind* calls 'a sort of telepathic repetition of utterance, apparent displays of telepathy or thought transmission' rife in *Hamlet* and elsewhere in Shakespeare, which 'no amount of textual scholarship or editorial argumentation will efface'.[5]

What I am concerned with on this occasion, however, is not only the mole-like, even telepathic, character of Shakespeare's language, but how it depends on the idiom's 'body', its thick net of resonating and travelling sounds, letters and syllables. This resonant modality is what, in relation to the 'imp' in Poe's writing, Stanley Cavell calls 'these little moles of language', it is 'the implanted origins or constituents of words, leading lives of their own, staring back at us, calling upon one another, giving us away, alarming – because to note them is to see that they live in front of our eyes, within earshot, at every moment'.[6] Although this impish animal is reminiscent of what Garrett Stewart calls 'lexical dismemberment' and of the inter- and intratextual travel of sounds and syllables in which Derrida is so interested, it is for Cavell ultimately a negative figure, because the lexical dismemberment that it wreaks prevents us speaking earnestly.[7] In Stewart's words, 'these disruptive "imp words" prevent us not only from saying what we mean but even from meaning it coherently'.[8] For Derrida, there is no such coherent and self-present meaning to disrupt, which does not mean that his attention to Shakespeare's little moles of language stands in the way of grappling with those questions that matter to us most. In fact, as I have argued, quite the opposite is true.

Hegel and Derrida are not the only philosophers interested in Hamlet's mole. Jacques Lacan and Sigmund Freud have used it respectively to illustrate the 'trajectory of [male] desire',[9] or the chthonic realm of the unconscious.[10] Ruth Stevenson has suggested that for all these philosophers the mole becomes a 'cultural emblem, part of a progressive symbolism contributing to a historical allegory whose meaning and function reside outside the verbal patterning of the play'.[11] Both de Grazia and Stevenson, however, distinguish between the sheer linguistic force of the mole and its philosophical use. To understand and to hear (to say it in one word of Derrida's French: *entendre*) how Shakespeare keeps watch over some parts of Derrida's philosophical writings, we must pay heed to a little catachrestic animal – not the mole or what Derrida calls the *hérisson*, but the porpentine. The porpentine epitomises, I would like to argue, the Shakespearean wounded and wounding 'signature'. It is what, like his cousin the *hérisson* – that little poematic animal at the heart of Derrida's most incisive work on poetry, 'Che cos'è la poesia?' – has 'its arrows held at the ready [*toutes flèches dehors*]'; it is what wounds its own body with the teleiopoetic arrows it shoots at us.[12] I would like to propose the porpentine, then, as an alternative to such a mole, and argue that this Shakespearean *hérisson* allows us to see how it is precisely the 'linguistic' force of Shakespeare's writing that opens up philosophical thinking space. By on the one hand considering the parenthetical supplementation of the porpentine to the French translation of *Hamlet* Derrida uses, and on the other hand by understanding the porpentine as a Shakespearean version of Derrida's *hérisson*, I will propose that it is precisely the catachresis of the Shakespearean *lettre*, the idiomatic body of his words, that allows Derrida to think and translate through Shakespeare as he does. But before we can turn to the porpentine, we must take into account the progress of Hamlet's mole in Marx's *The Eighteenth Brumaire*, since it is his performative translation of Shakespeare that frames the way, to put it in Cixous's words, 'Derrida *loves* in French Shakespeare's English.'[13]

Marx and Mole

Marx, like Derrida, loves Shakespeare: 'Oh, Marx's love for Shakespeare!'[14] In 'Recollections of Mohr', Eleanor Marx writes: 'As to Shakespeare he was the Bible of our house, seldom out of our hands or mouths.'[15] Marx also often drew on Shakespeare in his philosophical writings. His most famous citation of Shakespeare is undoubtedly his use of *Timon of Athens* in 'The Power of Money' from the *Economic and Philosophic Manuscripts* of 1844, as well as in *The German Ideology*. For Derrida, Timon's imprecation 'against prostitution – prostitution in the face of gold and the prostitution of gold itself' shows how 'the genius of Shakespeare will have understood this phantomalization of property centuries ago and said it better than anyone'.[16] Derrida again: 'What, Marx seems to say, the genius of a great poet – and the spirit of a great father – will have uttered in a poetic flash, with one blow going faster and farther than our little bourgeois colleagues in economic theory, is the becoming-god of gold.'[17] This is not bardolatry, although it may seem it. At stake in this poetic *flash* once more is the *coup de quelque flèche* through which Shakespeare will, it seems, not only have watched over the English language, but also German, and through which he will have seemed to anticipate Marx's critique of property.

Marx knew about Shakespeare's 'poetic flash' and he also harnessed it in *The Eighteenth Brumaire of Louis Napoleon*. *The Eighteenth Brumaire* is widely considered to be Marx's 'most brilliant political pamphlet' and is concerned with two things primarily: to offer a re-reading of recent French history through a satirical and critical lens, and to separate the wheat from the chaff, the good aspects of the revolution from the ones to be avoided.[18] What Marx learns from Napoleon III's rehashing of the French Revolution is firstly that repetition is always farcical: 'Hegel remarks somewhere that all facts and personages of great importance in world history occur, as it were, twice. He forgot to add: the first time as tragedy, the second as farce.'[19] His second concern is to show that, as Derrida aptly puts it, it is 'the condition of *inheritance*' that 'men make their own history'.[20] I quote from *The Eighteenth Brumaire*:

> The social revolution of the nineteenth century cannot draw its poetry from the past, but only from the future. It cannot begin with itself before it has stripped off all superstition in regard to the past. Earlier revolutions required recollections of past world history in order to drug themselves concerning their own content. In order to arrive at its own content, the revolution of the nineteenth century must let the dead bury their dead. There the phrase went beyond the content; here the content goes beyond the phrase.[21]

While Marx brushes 'the poetry of the past' to one side, the feet of his argument are firmly placed on its ground. Here the phrase haunts the content. 'Let the dead bury the dead' is of course a citation from the Gospel of Luke: 'let the dead bury their own dead' (9.2). The poetry of the past cannot quite be exorcised. In *Specters*, Derrida writes: 'And the borrowing *speaks*: borrowed language, borrowed names, *says* Marx.'[22] It is just now, as Marx is slowly enveloping himself in the poetry of the past, that *Hamlet*'s spectre makes an appearance and speaks:

> But the revolution is thoroughgoing. It is still journeying through purgatory. It does its work methodically. By 2 December 1851, it had completed one half of its preparatory work; it is now completing the other half. First it perfected the parliamentary power, in order to be able to overthrow it. Now that it has attained this, it perfects the executive power, reduces it to its purest expression, isolates it, sets it up against itself as the sole target, in order

to concentrate all its forces of destruction against it. And when it has done this second half of its preliminary work, Europe will leap from its seat and exultantly exclaim: Well grubbed, old mole!'[23]

As through a peephole or *meurtrière*, we are suddenly transported to Elsinore and to *Hamlet*'s cellarage scene. As Hamlet feverishly shifts his ground, the Ghost shape-shifts: it is a 'boy' (I, v, 150), a 'fellow in the cellarage' (I, v, 151), a 'worthy pioner' (I, v, 162) and also an 'old mole' (I, v, 161). While the reference to the cellarage places Hamlet and his Ghost firmly in the wooden reality of the early modern stage, with the reference to the mole and the pioner (a soldier who digs to lay mines), the scene becomes earthier. We are closer to the gravediggers that await us later in the play, closer to St Luke's image of dead burying their own dead.

Marjorie Garber has written eloquently on the use of quotation, especially of Shakespeare, in popular culture: 'quotations, especially disembodied quotations, can serve an educative function, providing (or counterfeiting) wisdom. Detached from their contexts they seem not only "true" but iconic, monumental.'[24] Do philosophical quotations of Shakespeare fall prey to the same monumentalising desires? Both of Marx's references to *Hamlet*'s mole and *Timon of Athens* illustrate a philosophical point: while Timon's speech illustrates the corrosive power of money, the mole epitomises revolution. The repercussions of his quotation of *Hamlet*'s mole in *The Eighteenth Brumaire*, however, explode the merely illustrative function Marx's reference to Timon seems to have. It, therefore, appears to fulfil at least one of Nussbaum's criteria in that it actually does philosophy.[25] Marx's translation of the mole, however, does not merely register a previously conceptualised philosophical point.

Hamlet's mole resurfaces, perhaps surprisingly, in another German philosophical text. In Hegel's *History of Philosophy* this mole represents spirit. In Hegel's own words:

> Spirit . . . is inwardly working ever forward (as when Hamlet says of the ghost of his father, 'Well said, old mole! canst work i' the ground so fast?'), until grown strong in itself it bursts asunder the crust of earth which divided it from the sun . . . so that the earth crumbles away.[26]

Before Marx used Shakespeare's mole to illustrate the steadily growing power of the proletarian revolution, Hegel had used the mole to make a quite different point. As Martin Harries has shown, Marx's German rendition of Shakespeare's English differs both from Hegel's and from Schlegel's then-current translation. There the mole is strangely silenced – 'Brav, alter Maulwurf! Wühlst so hurtig fort' – thus leaving room for the varieties of action imagined by Hegel and Marx: working and burrowing. Hegel translates 'Well said, old mole' as 'Brav gearbeitet, wackerer Maulwurf', while Marx quotes Hamlet as saying 'Brav gewühlt, alter Maulwurf!'[27] Marx does not use Schlegel's current translation – 'Brav, alter Maulwurf! Wühlst so hurtig fort?'[28] Instead, he changes it: 'his slight alteration makes a past principle ("gewühlt") of Schlegel's present tense verb ("Wühlst"), and moves it from the beginning of the second phrase of Schlegel's line to the second position in the first phrase'.[29] Marx's 'well grubbed, old mole' is thus only a quotation of Shakespeare, but also a (mis)quotation of Hegel, and one that contains a tightly packed parcel of subversive gestures. With the shift from present tense to past principle the mole's emergence is no longer potential: it has already happened.[30] The translation thus performs Marx's subversion of a Hegelian brand of idealism in favour of Marxist materialism. Here, Shakespeare's text is not merely an illustration of a distinct or separate philosophical point; rather, one part of the philosophical argument is made through a performative translation of Shakespeare.

Like Marx's, Derrida's thinking through Shakespeare is dictated by translation. There is, however, a significant difference between the way Derrida and Marx translate and think through Shakespeare. In Marx's performative translation, to use the powerful image suggested in 'What is a "Relevant" Translation?' the passion of translation comes to lick with a flame his and Hegel's German, and leaves the idiomatic body of Shakespeare's English intact.[31] In contrast, Derrida can only love and read a text in the manner outlined in the previous chapter. Put in terms of the twinned image of *Monolingualism*, in Derrida's act of reading and translating, Shakespeare's 'penetrating body of enviable, formidable, and inaccessible words' are 'appropriat[ed], domesticat[ed], coax[ed] [*amadouer*], that is to say, lov[ed] by [being set] on fire'.[32] Turning to *Specters*, a text in which Derrida countersigns Marx by countersigning *Hamlet*, a parenthetical insertion of a very Shakespearean *hérisson* – the porpentine – will helps us think about precisely how Derrida does this.

A *Shakespearean* Hérisson

Hamlet's strange reference to the mole is also noted by Derrida. After reaffirming his own inheritance of Marx's radical critique, Derrida inserts the first seven lines of Yves Bonnefoy's French translation of the Ghost's speech ('I am thy Father's Spirit') to Hamlet, and concludes:

> Every *revenant* seems here to come from and return to the *earth*, to come from it as from a buried clandestinity (humus and mold, tomb and subterranean prison), to return to it as to the lowest, toward the humble, humid, humiliated. We must pass by here, we too, we must pass over in silence, as low as possible to the earth, the return of an animal: not

the figure of the old mole ('Well said, old Mole'), nor of a certain hedgehog, but more precisely of a 'fretfull Porpentine' that the spirit of the Father is then getting ready to conjure away by removing an 'eternal blazon' from 'ears of flesh and blood'.[33]

De Grazia argues that Derrida substitutes 'porcupine for mole', because the old mole 'had reached the end of the teleological line'.[34] For here 'the porcupine exists in a post-molean, post-teleological era', and stands for Derrida's messianic promise.[35] De Grazia here incorrectly refers to a porcupine. What is unfortunately lost in the English translation is that Derrida opens one of these peepholes, not only when he quotes *Hamlet*, but also later when he shifts the attention away from the mole, via the *hérisson*, not to the porcupine but rather to the porpentine:

> Il nous faut ici passer, nous aussi, passer sous silence, au plus près de la terre, le retour d'un animal: non pas la figure de la vieille taupe (*'Well said, old Mole'*), ni d'un certain hérisson, mais plus précisément d'un 'inquiet porc-épic' (*fretfull Porpentine*) que l'esprit du Père alors s'apprête à conjurer, en soustrayant un 'éternel blason' aux 'oreilles de chair et de sang' (*ibid.*).[36]

As Royle notes in *The Uncanny*, the 'allusion to the mole is subsumed or encrypted, as it were, within an observation about that "fretful porpentine" (1.5.20) to which the Ghost of Hamlet's father refers'.[37] Why does Derrida supplement Yves Bonnefoy's *porc-épic* but not the 'éternel blason' or the 'oreilles de chair et de sang'? Is he pointing out the untranslatability of this Shakespearean word 'porpentine', or is he remarking on the specificity of the phrase in Shakespeare's idiom? Perhaps a bit of both. But there is more happening in this 'taupological ellipsis' than Royle suggests: the allusion to the mole is subsumed or encrypted within an observation about that 'fretful porpentine', but not without first mentioning and eliminating, or mentioning while eliminating, a certain poematic hedgehog or *hérisson*.[38] We must stay with Derrida's strange shift from the mole – via the *hérisson* – to the porpentine in order to grasp the different model for imbrication between Shakespeare and literature that Derrida is proposing in *Specters* and elsewhere.

We might almost not have heard this porpentine (but, as we shall see, what this Shakespearean signature haunts is precisely our ears). The Ghost is indeed conjuring away this porpentine by removing his narration from 'ears of flesh and blood'.[39] Shakespeare's porpentine is almost silent, almost heard, almost listening and almost deaf. Wedged between two lunulae, the porpentine also remains silent, yet strangely eloquent, in Derrida's text. Here it is only a parenthetical afterthought to the *porc-épic*, which itself is an extension, say a variation, of the *hérisson*, which, like the mole, is named and immediately silenced. The *hérisson*, Derrida implies, only has a supporting role: it has already taken centre stage in 'Che cos'è la poesia?' where it helps him think about poetry. Derrida also dwelt on this little poematic animal in an interview with Maurizio Ferraris, 'Istrice 2. Ick bünn all hier'. Although the *hérisson* is not juxtaposed with the mole, porpentine or *porc-épic* here, as it is in *Specters*, but with its German cousin the *Igel*, the differentiations and distinctions are also applied by Derrida to our porpentine.

The *hérisson*, Derrida stresses, is not related to Schlegel's prickly image of the artwork. In his *Athenaeums Fragmente*, Schlegel writes that 'a fragment, like a miniature work of art, has to be entirely isolated from the surrounding world and be complete in itself like a porcupine [*Igel*]'.[40] Derrida is suspicious of this idea of the artwork as complete in itself as a porcupine, because in its fragmentary wholeness this Igel always assumes a greater whole, an origin and a truth. Schlegel's *Igel* is thus closely related to notions of Shakespeare's genius; but what counts for Derrida is the different, uncanny genius of language itself. Unlike Schlegel's *Igel*, the *hérisson* is not part of a different whole or truth but is only idiomatic of itself. Derrida also makes it clear that his *hérisson* is not related to the *Igel* that briefly surfaces in Heidegger's reading of the Grimms' tale 'The Hedgehog and the Hare' in 'Die onto-theologische Verfassung der Metaphysik' in *Identity and Difference*.[41] Grimm's tale is a version of the story of the tortoise and the hare. This time, however, the hedgehog, to be sure of victory, sends his wife to the finishing line. From there she is already in a position to turn around to the sprinting and surprised hare and declare triumphantly: 'I have already been here.' In Heidegger's reading, the ubiquity trick of Mr and Mrs Hedgehog speaks of *Dasein*'s ability to recollect its *da* [here] and *fort* [there] to a unity and presence, or, as Derrida puts it: 'The *Da* or the *Fort-Da* of the *Dasein* would belong to this logic of destination that permits one to say, everywhere and always, "I have always already arrived at the destination".'[42] Yet, the mole's *ubiquitas* is not as easily collectable into a *hic*. The Grimms' *Igel*, indeed, has something of *Hamlet*'s mole about it: as the 'old mole', it can be 'hic et ubique'. Heidegger's mistake, Derrida continues, lies precisely in this desire to collect Mr and Mrs Igel's *fort da*, a desire that is utterly foreign to the humble little *hérisson*.

To answer the question 'What is poetry?' posed to him by the Italian journal *Poesia* in November 1988, Derrida chose the figure of the *hérisson* precisely in order to distance poetry from Heidegger's conception of *Dichtung* as a 'setting-to-work of truth'.[43] One of Derrida's reasons for speaking of poetry through the figure of the *hérisson* is precisely 'to remove what I am calling the *poem* (or the *poiemata*) from the merry-go-round or circus that brings them back in a circular fashion to *poiein*, to their poetic source, to the act or to the experience of their setting-to-work in poetry or poetics'.[44] As 'poemactics' and not as 'poetics', the *hérisson* remains profoundly alien to the setting-to-work of truth: while it is messianic, even eschatological, it is also profoundly a-teleological.[45] It is, perhaps, teleiopoetic.

Derrida's *hérisson* is neither Schlegel's artwork, nor Heidegger's *Dichtung*, and it is certainly not an animal. This word surfaces only four times in Shakespeare's works and in none of these instances does it actually denote the animal. It appears as a brothel's name in *The Comedy of Errors*. In York's speech in King Henry VI Part 2, it emerges as a simile: one man, York claims, fought so long in battle 'till that his thighs with darts / Were almost like a sharp-quilled porpentine' (III, i, 361–2). The porpentine, as a 'common spelling varian[t] of porcupine' also resurfaces in *Troilus and Cressida*. When addressing Thersites, Ajax exclaims: 'Do not, porcupine, do not. My fingers itch' (II, i, 24). Referring to Marx's three voices, as heard by Blanchot, Derrida asks in *Specters*: 'How is one to receive, how is one to understand a speech, how is one to inherit it when it does not let itself be *translated* from itself into itself?'[46] We might ask the same about this Shakespearean shape-shifter, the porpentine, which is 'indissolubly linked to the chance of a language and of signifiers that play the role of temporary proper name (first *istrice* and then its fragile translation into *hérisson*)' and 'come into being via a letter'. Yet, for Derrida, 'this "catachrestic" *hérisson* is barely a name, it does not bear its name, it plays with syllables, but in any case it is neither a concept nor a thing'.[47]

This 'animal' is, Derrida admits, 'barely a hedgehog, strictly speaking'.[48] The word *hérisson* is indeed soon substituted with the word 'letter' or *lettre* in French:[49] 'I would rather not re-semanticize this letter. It must remain of little meaning. Without secret but sealed. It is also better not to stuff polysemic vitamins down the throat of a humble little mammal.'[50] Everything rests, I believe, on Derrida's word choice here. In contrast to *mot*, *lettre* does not merely indicate 'word', but also the sounds, measure, flow and rhythm of *parole*, meaning speech, that cannot be linked to only one signification. In view of Derrida's persistent interest in human and non-human animals, this reluctance to speak of the *hérisson* in terms of animality must seem peculiar, especially since what is at stake is, in Derrida's own words, 'the return of an animal' or, as Royle paraphrases, 'the "massively unavoidable" question of animals'.[51] Perhaps a discussion too centred on the figure of an animal, even if it is only a figure for something else, would be too vulnerable to the siren call of Being or Present that the porpentine seeks to uproot. Giving the figure of the *hérisson* too much weight, conceding it an importance in itself, would perhaps defy the very reason Derrida chooses to talk about poetry in terms of this humble mammal in the first place. As Derrida puts it in 'Istrice', it 'can barely say "*Ich*" and certainly not "*bünn*," still less "*hier*" and "*da*"'.[52] Derrida's *hérisson* consequently does not gather itself up into the presence implied by the fragment or the 'always already there' of *Dasein*. Like *Hamlet*'s mole, it continuously shifts its ground, it is always *hic et ubique*, and we, like Hamlet, can barely keep up with it.

The ground on which the *hérisson* constantly shifts is not only ontological, but also linguistic. Due to the strange translinguistic publication history of this hedgehog of a text, the French word *hérisson* is simultaneously the original to be translated and the translation of an 'original'. *Poesia* originally published Derrida's French response to the question 'Che cos'è la poesia?', along with Ferraris's Italian translation, in November 1988. Before being collected in Elisabeth Weber's *Points de suspension* in 1992, Derrida's response was published in the French journal *Po&sie* in the autumn of 1989. Although in both these latter cases only the 'original' French is given, the Italian title remains, and with it the following note:

> Destinée à paraître en italien, cette 'réponse'-ci s'expose au passage, parfois littéralement, dans les lettres ou les syllabes, le mot et la chose ISTRICE (prononcer ISTRRITCHÉ), ce qui aura donné, dans une correspondance française, le hérisson.[53]

Hérisson is the 'correspondance française' of *istrice*, and although 'Che' was first published in Italian, *istrice* is the Italian translation of *hérisson*. Let us stay a while with the different catachrestic word-guises that Derrida's humble little animal assumes in 'Che', '*Istrice*' and *Specters*, be it in Derrida's original French, in Ferrari's Italian or in Kamuf's English translation. The first English translation of 'Che' appears in Peggy Kamuf's Derrida reader, *Between the Blinds*, in 1991. *Hérisson* is here translated as 'hedgehog'. The hedgehog's name is the composite of its likely dwelling place, a hedge, and its hog-like snout. According to the *Oxford Dictionary of English Etymology*, another English word for the hedgehog is 'porcupine', which is related via Middle English *porc despyne* and the Old French *porc d'espine*, denoting a pig (*porc*) with spikes (*espines*), to the French *porc-épic*. But *istrice* is, to complicate matters further, neither strictly speaking a correct translation of *hérisson*, nor vice versa. According to the *Dizionario Etimologico Italiano*, *istrice*, coming from the ancient Greek *ystricha* (*ys* for 'pig' and *thricha* for 'hair') via the Latin *hytricem*, is similar to the porcupine or *porc-épic*, although it seems to be less spiky. The Italian equivalent of porcupine would be *porcospino*. In contrast, the French word *hérisson* derives from the Latin *ericius*, which, though once used to denote the hedgehog, now denotes an altogether different animal that in Italian is not called *istrice* but *riccio*, or 'urchin' in English. It is important to point out that, in contrast to *porc-épic*, porcupine and *porcospino*, none of those words denoting this animal – *hérisson*, *istrice* or hedgehog – share an etymological root.

On the trail of the *hérisson*, we have found ourselves catachrestically criss-crossing linguistic boundaries. Derrida's insistence on the catachrestic character of the *hérisson*, his insistence on acknowledging again and again that he wrote in French but was always exposed to the Italian language, suggests that this criss-crossing of language is not an accidental but a fundamental effect of the *hérisson*. Derrida's parenthetical supplementation of Yves Bonnefoy's translation *porc-épic* with Shakespeare's porpentine also bears witness to the fact that, as the poematic hedgehog, the porpentine's catachrestic untranslatability posits an impossible injunction:

> Promets le: qu'elle se défigure, <u>transfigure</u> ou indétermine en son *port*, et tu <u>entendras</u> sous ce mot la rive du départ aussi bien que le référent vers lequel une translation se porte.⁵⁴
>
> Promise it: let it be disfigured, <u>transfigured</u> or rendered indeterminate in its *port* – and in this word you will <u>hear</u> the shore of the departure as well as the referent toward which a translation is portered.⁵⁵

Like in 'Aphorism Countertime', Derrida is here playing on the verb *porter*, playing on the resonances between 'bearing a name [*porter le nom*], as well as being in mourning [*porter le deuil*]'.⁵⁶ There is no translating, no reading of Shakespeare without hearing this *port*. We will, for instance, re-encounter this *port* when, in 'Injunctions of Marx', Derrida claims that, like *différance*, 'the time is out of joint' does not only mean 'deferral' or 'lateness'.

> Without lateness, without delay, but without presence, it is the precipitation of an absolute singularity, singular because differing, precisely [*justement*], and always other, binding itself necessarily to the form of the instant, in *imminence and in urgency*: even if it moves toward what remains to come, there is the *pledge* [gage] (promise, engagement, injunction and response to the injunction, and so forth) [même s'il se porte vers ce qui reste à venir, il y a le *gage* (promesse, engagement, injonction et réponse à l'injonction, etc.)]. The pledge is given here and now, even before, perhaps, a decision confirms it. It thus responds without delay to the demand of justice.⁵⁷

There will be no justice, no 'to come', without hearing this port. In 'Che', Derrida's translator Kamuf renders *porte* with 'portered' but leaves *port* untranslated and italicised. 'Port' is a homophone. Le *port* (in French the *t* is silent), or 'the port', denotes a haven or a harbour, also indicated in 'the shore of departure' of translation. Deriving via the Middle and Old French from the post-classical Latin *portus*, this word also reverberates with the idea of *portare*, meaning in both Latin and Italian to bring, carry or bear. The impossible injunction of the por(t)pentine has to do with this *port*, this *lettre* that I cannot help but hear in its name. This impossible injunction to the translation of the poematic porpentine is therefore also inscribed in the ear. On the high sea of translation, Derrida seems to say, your compass and navigation will be your ears, with which you will listen for your shore of departure (the 'original' text or word) and the shore towards which you are navigating.

When threatened with translation, the porpentine, like the *hérisson*, becomes prickly. Ann Thompson and Neil Taylor note that porpentine means porcupine, parenthetically adding that 'porpentine is Shakespeare's usual form'.[58] To our ears, however, there seems to be nothing usual about porpentine. The origins of the word porpentine are, according to the *Oxford Dictionary of English Etymology*, obscure. Although today this word is used solely as a Shakespearean quotation, Shakespeare did not invent this word. Skeat's *Etymological Dictionary of the English Language*, for instance, notes this version of 'porcupine' in Roger Ascham's *Toxophilus* (1545). Like porcupine, the Early Modern English word 'porpentine' derives from the Middle French *porc despyne*, borrowed from the Old French *porc espin* or *porc d'espine* (literally, 'pig of spines'), a compound of Latin *porcus* and *spina* (OED). I find myself wondering about the bifurcated evolution of the Old French *porc-espin*, leading to two English words denoting the same thing: porcupine and porpentine. According to

Skeat, there are two possible roots of this word. The earliest trace can be found in *Promptorium Parvulorum sive Clericorum Dictionarius Anglo-Latinus Princeps* (1440), which lists 'Poork-poynt, porpoynte, perpoynt, beste, Histrix'. The second trace can be found in Palsgrave's *Lesclaircissement de la Langue Francoyse* (1530), which links '*Porkepyn*, a beest' to '*porc espin*'. The last trace is to be found in Huloet's *Abecedarium Anglo-Latinum* (1552) which defines something called '*Porpyn*' as a 'beaste, havinge prickes on his backe'. Having listed these etymological traces, Skeat concludes that

> the animal had two very similar names, (1) *porkepyn*, shortly *porpin*, easily lengthened to *porpint* by the usual excrescent *t* after *n*, and finally altered to *porpentine* as a by-form of *porkepyn*'; and (2) *pork-point, porpoint*; the latter of which forms would also readily yield *porpentine*.

How either *porkepyn* or *pork-point* or *porpoint* could have 'readily' yielded porpentine, how this quintessentially English version of a French *porc-épic* shuffled vowels and syllables, shed a *c*, acquired a *t* and the suffix *-ine* remains quite enigmatic. Perhaps it was a mere slip of the tongue or swallowing of the ear that turned the spiky animal into a port-*épic*, something that bears spikes only to immediately add the suffix *-ine*, denoting again the bearing of a particular characteristic. Thus the porcupine has become the porpentine; the animal has become a name that does nothing but name, a pure signifier that defies translation. It is the idiom.

If in *Specters* Derrida prefers to speak of the porpentine rather than of a certain *hérisson*, it is because this peculiar and quintessentially English word 'porpentine' transposes what Derrida has said about the *hérisson* into the materiality of Shakespeare's idiom. It is almost as if through the parenthetical supplementation '*porc-épic* ("fretfull Porpentine")', Derrida's encounter with the *hérisson*'s catachrestic nature was transposed to his reading of Shakespeare, his irreducible, untranslatable and haunting signature. From now on we can call the Shakespearean poem porpentine:

> You will call poem from now on a certain passion of the singular mark, the signature that repeats its dispersion, each time beyond the *logos*, ahuman, barely domestic, not reappropriable into the family of the subject: a converted animal, rolled up in a ball, turned toward the other and toward itself, in sum, a thing – modest, discreet, close to the earth, the humility that you surname [*l'humilité que tu* surnommes], thus transporting yourself in the name beyond a name, a catachrestic *hérisson*, its arrows held at the ready [*toutes flèches dehors*], when this ageless blind thing hears but does not see death coming.[59]

In 'Che cos'è la poesia?', we suddenly find ourselves in the vicinity of *Hamlet* and *Specters* – back to the humus, to the mole and to the revenant. Only here it is not Shakespeare that shoots arrows, but the *hérisson*. Or perhaps it is Shakespeare after all, only in the guise of the *hérisson* or porpentine. Like the *hérisson*'s, the porpentine's poetry is a-human; it is also not an animal, nor enveloped in the *logos*. It explodes into *hic et ubique* and transports us in the name beyond a name, the pure catachresis of port-pentine. This '"demon of the heart"', Derrida writes, 'never gathers itself together . . . it would rather let itself be torn to pieces by what bears down upon it'.[60] Waiting for us in the Ghost's speech, it is a 'converted animal, rolled up in a ball, turned toward the other and toward itself'.[61] The Folio and the First Quarto read 'fretful' rather than 'fearful' (I, v, 20; V, 15). We no longer know whether the porpentine is afraid, or whether it is itself fearsome; are the quills raised in attack or in defence? Is this animal, which the Elizabethans believed to be aggressive and dangerous and which was said to 'shoot its quills out like darts', about to attack or to flee?[62] In wounding the other, this autoimmune *lettre*, wounds itself.

As I have shown in the previous chapter, the singularity of the Shakespearean oeuvre depends precisely on this violent dispersal. As Derrida suggests in 'A "Madness" Must Watch Over Thinking', 'there is singularity but it does not collect itself, it "consists" in not collecting itself'.⁶³ The *hérisson/ istrice*/porpentine has invited us to think of this disseminating effect in terms of an idiom which is never present to itself. 'The idiom is', as suggested in *'Fidelité à plus d'un'*, 'never proper or the proper identity of oneself [*à soi du propre*], it is already different from itself, it is only of difference'.⁶⁴ The idiom to be responded to, to be countersigned, is always *plus d'un*, it is more than and no more one language. In leaving the Shakespearean idiom – porpentine – intact in parenthesis, Derrida draws our attention to what 'Shibboleth: For Paul Celan' calls 'Babel within *a single* language'.⁶⁵ When reading Shakespeare, we must, therefore, following Derrida, be faithful to a language which is (no) more than one. For Cixous, 'the very operation of deconstruction ... consists in speaking in more than one language within one single language, like Shakespeare'.⁶⁶ Speaking, and allowing to be spoken to, in more than one language would entail the openness of the teleiopoetic trajectory in all its responsiveness to the other. At the same time, speaking in more than one language would also have to mean keeping watch over how this idiom finds itself in other languages. Let's then look through one of these *meurtrières*, these loving and murderous peepholes, to see how Derrida translates Shakespeare's idiom by loving his *lettre* and by allowing it to haunt him even in texts that are not written in close proximity to Shakespeare.

Taking Shakespeare at His English Word (Peepholes)

Shakespeare keeps watch over Derrida's French through *meurtrières*, or peepholes. In Kamuf's translation, there is no trace of the death trap, the murderess, of death, love and violence. 'Peepholes' drowns out the passionate, bloodier facets of this word, reinforcing instead the image's visual valence. Thus, the long slit through which watchmen might shoot arrows at approaching enemies turns into the hole we might look through before opening our door to a stranger. But for everything that is lost in a good translation, something is won; in 'peepholes', for instance, we may find traces of a vigilance 'the sense of being *on watch* for the passing of the singular other'.[67]

In Derrida's text, we may find visual traces of these round peepholes in the parentheses that frame Derrida's insertions of Shakespeare's English. In *Specters* Shakespeare's porpentine watches over Derrida's philosophy through peepholes: '"inquiet porc-épic" ("fretfull Porpentine")'.[68] At the beginning of 'What is a "Relevant" Translation?', however, the peeping is reversed. Here Derrida's French is keeping watch over Shakespeare's English. Perhaps matters are even more complicated. If, like me, you read Derrida in English first, we are peeping in on Derrida's French through Lawrence Venuti's English. Venuti, in yet another loop it seems, has written about the impossibilities of translating Derrida on translating Shakespeare: '*Then must the Jew be merciful* (Je ne traduis pas cette phrase de Portia dans *Le Merchand de Venise*)'[69] or '*Then must the Jew be merciful.* (I leave untranslated this sentence from Portia in *The Merchant of Venice.*)'[70] Peepholes are loopholes by which the translator can twist tongues; they are the phrase or word that again and again throw the translator for a loop. *Je ne traduis pas*: leaving untranslated does not mean not to translate something. It hints at the fact that, as Derrida puts it elsewhere, 'the idiom is untranslatable, ultimately, even if we translate it'.[71] Here, *je ne traduis pas* therefore has to be understood in terms of leaving the idiom, that which cannot be translated, to work. Looping peepholes show that translation never only happens between two languages. Translation – whether it be Venuti's of Derrida, or Derrida's of Shakespeare, or indeed Marx's or Hegel's – always criss-crosses between languages which are always more than one (*plus d'un*). I believe that the untranslatable Shakespearean idiom must be understood precisely in terms of such an un-collectability, precisely in terms of the porpentine's wound(ing)/(ed) *flèches*.

In all of his writing Derrida is aware of the impossible task of the translator. However, he gives his clearest description of it when, in 1998, he addresses the annual seminar of the *Assises de la traduction littéraire* at Arles, an organisation dedicated to promoting literary translation. Derrida's address, later to be published as 'Qu'est-ce qu'une traduction "relevante"?', is a crucial moment in Derrida's work on Shakespeare. This has less to do with the fact that he gives us a glimpse into how he translates him (to some extent all his texts on Shakespeare do), than with his contention that *The Merchant of Venice* tells us something about translation. In other words, 'What is a "Relevant" Translation?' is not only concerned with how Derrida translates Shakespeare, but also with how *The Merchant of Venice*, more particularly Shylock's fate, illustrates the impossible task of the translator.

Derrida swiftly sets the scene. We are at the court of the Duke of Venice. Shylock refuses Bassanio's offer of double the amount of the original loan and insists on his pound of flesh (IV, i, 84–6). Portia, disguised as Balthazar, tries a different tactic: 'Then must the Jew be merciful' (IV, i, 178). What follows is Portia's Christian interpretation of the concept of mercy, which equates mercy with supreme power. What does our translator do with Portia's 'when mercy seasons justice?' After citing it in English, Derrida 'translate[s] or rather paraphrase[s] it step by step', suggesting we substitute Victor Hugo's translation of 'to season' as 'tempère' with another translation that 'will not respond to the name *translation*' and that will work outside the economics of translation:[72] 'Je traduirai donc *seasons* par "relève": "*when mercy seasons justice*", "quand le pardon relève la justice (ou le droit)".'[73] Or, as Venuti has it: 'I shall therefore translate "seasons" as "relève": "when mercy seasons justice," "quand le pardon relève la justice (ou le droit)" [*when mercy elevates and interiorizes, thereby preserving and negating, justice (or the law)*]'.[74] No translation then because what is to be translated forever shifts and moves out of our grasp. Paradoxically, Derrida's philosophical-literary practice rests on this inaccessibility of language, the fact that language will always remain irreducibly *plus d'un*.

Between translations, italics shift and peepholes (loopholes, *meurtrières*) are added. The words – to season and *relève* – consume each other in their idiomatic singularity, cutting and burning each other, like amorous murderesses. The translator has sworn his fidelity to Shakespeare, and keeps his word. *Relever*, of course, means to season. Furthermore it 'effectively preserves the gustatory code and the culinary reference of *to season*, "assaisonner": *to season with spice*, to spice'.[75]

> It is a question of giving taste, a different taste that is blended with the first taste, now dulled, remaining the same while altering it, while changing it, while undoubtedly removing something of its native, original, idiomatic taste, but also while adding to it, and in the very process, *more* taste, while cultivating its natural taste, while giving it *still more of its own taste*, its own, natural flavour – this is what we call 'relever' in French cooking.[76]

This gustatory or culinary resonance captures the emulsion of justice and mercy Portia is after well. The second justification for this translation is that '"*relever*" effectively expresses elevation'.[77] Justice is not only qualified or 'exalted' by mercy; mercy also 'pulls and inspires justice toward highness'.[78] In short, 'mercy sublimates justice'.[79] Derrida's will therefore have been a relevant translation if it allows the idiomatic *plus d'un* to resonate, in the sense that it will have offered the 'most economic' solution, allowing the use of 'a single word to translate so many other words, even languages, with their denotations and connotations'.[80] A translation for Derrida, however, needs to do more. It needs to change itself and the other, it needs to season and to elevate: it needs to be 'relevant'.

In this cross-fertilisation of texts, Shylock's oath comes to stand for the impossible task of the translator and of the reader of Shakespeare; what it demands is an impossible fidelity, impossible because it cannot be fulfilled without some wounding, the cutting of a pound of flesh closest to the heart. Like Shylock's oath, translation demands to cut close to the heart of the idiom, but knows that this is impossible without breaking the oath. The bond of fidelity demands that the body of the word is cut open, and that it remain intact. Translation, like reading, has to engulf, love with a passion, 'consume' it, has to 'arous[e] . . . desire for the idiom', while still leaving the 'unique body of the other' 'intact'.[81] The idiom signs and wounds: 'it is only in the body of its idiomatic singularity . . . where a passion for translation comes to lick it as a flame or an amorous tongue might'.[82] What the translation between 'the pound of flesh and money' highlights, therefore, is precisely the 'required but impractical translation between the unique literalness of a proper body and the arbitrariness of a general, monetary, or fiduciary sign'.[83] Put simply, Shylock's oath reaffirms the 'law that presides over translation while commanding absolute respect, without any transaction, for the word given in its original letter [*lettre*]'.[84]

In 'Shakespeare Ghosting Derrida', Cixous writes that 'Derrida loves in French Shakespeare's English. His dream is to take Shakespeare at his English word.'[85] What would this mean to take Shakespeare at his English word? It may mean to listen beyond its meaning to the way it is posed or uttered in English. This would entail 'simultaneously subjecting the word, the subject, love to its condition *as a French word*'.[86]

Loving Shakespeare's English in French would perhaps mean transporting the Shakespearean idiom into French according to a movement in 'tr' that exceeds translation. For Cixous, Derrida indeed 'declares *his passion* first to the word, *au mot* – to the "homoword" [*au mot homo*], to the word with homonymic resources, which plays in and with itself, by itself, pivots, blinks so well that it always eludes the claws of the desire to translate, and does not let itself be clawed (back)'.[87] What Cixous calls 'au mot homo' here captures beautifully what I have been trying to think about it in terms of the catachrestic porpentine. Like the porpentine, the 'homoword' resists simple translation because some of its sound always remains to haunt its translation. A 'homophonic or homonymic effect' cannot be rendered by linear translation; it rather demands to be rendered '"one word *by* one word"', in other words in and by its singular idiomatic body.[88] In 'Translating Derrida on Translation', Venuti argues that a homophonic and plurivocal reverberation can be heard in this 'untranslatable' word 'relevant', which sounds the same as the French 'relevante'; thus, this word 'may be French and therefore translatable into English, or English yet undergoing assimilation into French and therefore resistant to translation'.[89] This Shakespearean word resists translation, because its 'unity' is 'questionable, because the signifier potentially contains more than one word insofar as it produces a homophonic or homonymic effect'.[90] This word, Venuti continues, 'derails the translation process' because it resists a conception of language that is not plurivocal.[91] As the intertextual echoes of this word 'relevant' indeed suggest, what escapes Derrida's translation and what simultaneously haunts his translations beyond Shakespeare is precisely 'the acoustic form that incorporates or signifies the indivisible unity of a meaning or concept'.[92]

Derrida claims that the English word 'relevant', which kicked off his criss-crossing translations, is a Shakespearean word.⁹³ This is strictly speaking not true; the word 'relevant' never appears in the Shakespearean corpus, including *The Merchant of Venice*. What then makes this word Shakespearean for Derrida? For this answer and for the third justification for Derrida's 'translation' we must return to Derrida's reading of Hegel:

> In 1967, to translate a crucial German word with a double meaning (*Aufheben, Aufhebung*), a word that signifies at once to suppress and to elevate, a word that Hegel says represents the speculative risk of the German language, and that the entire world had until then agreed was untranslatable – or, if you prefer, a word for which no one had agreed with anyone on a stable, satisfying translation into any language – for this word, I had proposed the noun *relève* and the verb *relever*. This allowed me to retain, joining them in a single word, the double motif of the elevation and the replacement that preserves what it denies or destroys, preserving what it causes to disappear, quite like – in a perfect example – what is called in the armed forces, in the navy, say, the relief [*relève*] of the guard. This usage is also possible in English, to relieve.⁹⁴

Again, Hegel is part of this theatre of spectres. The reason why Derrida translates 'to season' with *relever* is that he had translated Hegel's untranslatable *Aufhebung* with *relève*. 'Relevant' and 'to relieve' (as well as the noun 'relief') derive from the Latin *relevare*, meaning 'to raise again, or to alleviate'. The word 'relief' does appear in *The Merchant of Venice* (III, iv, 6). I would like to argue, however, that it is another frequency of this word which is haunting Derrida's translation of Hegel, and in turn his Hegelian translation of Shakespeare. Derrida's translation of *Aufhebung* as *relève* resonates with 'what is called in the armed forces, in the navy, say, the relief [*relève*] of the guard'.⁹⁵

Although Derrida is thinking about a frequency of this word in Joseph Conrad's 'The Secret Sharer', like Marx he also seems to 'evoke or convoke, right from the start, the first coming of the silent ghost, the apparition of the spirit that does not answer, on those ramparts of Elsinore'.[96] This is the passage from 'The Secret Sharer' he was thinking of: 'My double followed my movements; our bare feet made no sound; I let him in, closed the door with care and after giving call to the second mate returned on deck to wait for my relief.'[97] *Hamlet* and its thematisation of mourning, inheritance and debt is also at work in the subtext of Derrida's further elaboration of his word choice: 'by elevating the signifier to its meaning or value, all the while preserving the mournful and debt-laden memory of the singular body, the first body, the unique body that the translation thus elevates, preserves, and negates [*relève*]'.[98] Through this one-word peephole we are thus transported back to the beginning of *Hamlet* when one watchman asks the other: 'For this relief much thanks' (I, i, 6) or 'Who hath relieved you?' (I, i, 15). The ghosting is always reciprocal: before the French translation of the Hegelian *Aufhebung* prompted a translation for Shakespeare's English, Shakespeare's English had already haunted Derrida's translation of Hegel. What Derrida's translation of Shakespeare's 'to season' and *Aufhebung* with *relève* shows is that Shakespeare not only watches over the English language, but also Hegel's (and, as we have seen, even Marx's) German, as well as Derrida's 'native' French. The peepholes of Shakespeare's catachrestic language do not only allow him to shoot *flèches* at the (English) language, but also allow language, in the form of other translators and other readers, to penetrate the body of his work. In Derrida's hands, the effects of the catachrestic porpentine thus exceed the strict context of one discourse or one language. Moreover, they show that this haunting can also be a function of a phonic resonance: *relève*, relief, relevant, *revenant*.

Meurtrières are therefore not only for looking, but also for listening. We might say that Derrida reads Shakespeare through peepholes: not only through a phrase or a word, but also through a *lettre* or *syllabe*, and with the help of his ears. When Derrida therefore says that 'this word "relevant" carries in its body an ongoing process of translation' criss-crossing between European languages, between French, German and English in a way that does not really equal '*strictu senso* a translation', he is pointing towards the actual body or sound of the word.[99] In 'What is a "Relevant" Translation?' he writes: 'Ce mot [*relevant*] n'est pas seulement *en* traduction, comme on dirait en travail ou en voyage, *traveling, travailing*, dans un labeur, un *labour* d'accouchement.'[100] Here Derrida's string of thoughts seems to be propelled by alliteration and homophonic similarities. Traduction is not only a *travail*, but since the French 'ai' in travailing sounds like the English 'e' in travelling, translation is also travel, a voyage. This attention to sounds also makes Derrida difficult to translate. For instance, *trouvaille* is not translated with 'windfall' or 'lucky break', but with 'treasure trove'. Venuti chose this word, so he says, to render the 'alliterative series' of the 'consonant cluster "*tr*"'.[101] Another ear-led translation is Venuti's rendering of the French *travail* and *travailler* with the archaic 'travail', rather than 'work'. A 'relevant(e)' translation would therefore be a travail of ears. What we are dealing with here is therefore not translation, but another action or actions beginning in *tr*, an action that we can also hear in *meurtrières*:

> I am not sure that this transaction, even if it is the most economic possible, merits the name of *translation*, in the strict and pure sense of this word. It rather seems one of those other things in *tr.*, a transaction, transformation, travail, *travel* – and a treasure trove [*trouvaille*] (since this invention, if it also seemed to take up [*relever*] a challenge,

as another saying goes, consisted only in discovering what was waiting, or in waking what was sleeping, in the language). The treasure trove amounts to a travail; it puts to work the languages, first of all, without adequation or transparency, here assuming the shape of a new writing or rewriting that is performative or poetic, not only in French, where a new use for the word emerges, but also in German and English.[102]

Derrida's radical rethinking of translation hinges on this idea of translation as a movement in '*tr.*', a movement that inaugurates a new performative and poetic writing that transcends linguistic borders, an understanding of the poematic as an *istrice*/*hérisson*/porpentine.

As in Hegel's or Marx's translation of Shakespeare, in Derrida's translation of Hegel something more than citation or translation in the usual sense occurs: something is done, something is performed. The importance of the ear and sound in Derrida's acts of reading also shows how he exceeds Nussbaum's criteria. In forging its very own idiomatic and phonetic body of words from Shakespeare's Derridean translation is responsive to the materiality of the Shakespearean *lettre*. I have proposed the porpentine, this catachrestic *lettre*, to show how the untranslatable Shakespearean idiom watches over some of Derrida's texts. Although the porpentine is a strong visual image, it is introduced in response to an act of listening that is both actual and hypothetical. We encounter this porpentine in the Ghost's speech. The Ghost, so it tells Hamlet, is 'doomed for a certain term to walk the night', until its 'foul crimes' are 'burnt and purged away' (I, v, 10–13). The Ghost continues with a narration that resembles an apophasis, a narration that, in short, is more like an auricular infolding than an unfolding. Indeed, in the First Quarto this speech is introduced by 'Nay, pity me not, but to my unfolding / Lend thy listening ear' (V, 7–8).

GHOST		But that I am forbid
		To tell the secrets of my prison-house
		I could a tale unfold whose lightest word
		Would harrow up thy soul, freeze thy young blood,
		Make thy two eyes like stars start from their spheres,
		Thy knotted and combined locks to part
		And each particular hair to stand on end
		Like quills upon the fearful porpentine –
		But this eternal blazon must not be
		To ears of flesh and blood. List, list, O list,
		If thou didst ever thy dear father love –
HAMLET		O God!

(I, v, 13–24)

It is just as the Ghost envelopes the horrors of his prison house that the porpentine makes its appearance. Listen, the Ghost says, my story is not for your ears. But if ears of flesh and blood could hear my tale, you would be so terrified that your blood would freeze, your eyes would bulge and your hair would stick out like the quills of a porpentine. Its quills are raised in dreaded expectation of what it might hear. It is through this 'listening', through a meddling with sound that transcends linguistic borders, that this creature porters translation. When commenting on the fundamentally catachrestic nature of the *hérisson* in the first French 'monolingual' publication, Derrida insists that it is always exposing itself to the letters and syllables of the word and the thing *istrice*. As Derrida's parenthetic direction on how a Frenchman would pronounce *istrice* suggests, *hérisson* is always listening and exposing itself to the sounds of ISTRRITCHÉ. In this context, in the str-sound that Kamuf stresses in the margin of her translation 'one may hear . . . the distress of the beast caught in the strictures of this translation': it also echoes is-*tr*-ice, the hedgehog's unavoidable catachrestic shadow.[103] This little hedgehog is, as its Shakespearean relative, 'un seul trajet à plusieurs voies' or 'a single trek with several tracks' or voices.[104] Both seemingly 'come into being via a letter', both seemingly 'pla[y] with syllables'.[105] When the 'arrows' of this little porpentine are 'held at the ready', we must *listen* and expose ourselves to the pricks, spines or quills that it shoots at Derrida, and at us.[106]

Notes

1. Nicholas Royle, 'Nuclear Piece: Mémoires of Hamlet and the Time to Come', *Diacritics* 20, no. 1 (1990): 42.
2. Jacques Derrida, 'Freud and the Scene of Writing', trans. Jeffrey Mehlman, *Yale French Studies* 48 (1972): 96.
3. Margreta De Grazia. 'Teleology, Delay, and the "Old Mole"', *Shakespeare Quarterly* 50, no. 3 (1999): 260.
4. Nicholas Royle, *The Uncanny* (Manchester: Manchester University Press, 2003), 250.
5. Nicholas Royle, *Telepathy and Literature: Essays on the Reading Mind* (Oxford: Basil Blackwell, 1991), 146.
6. Stanley Cavell, *In Quest of the Ordinary: Lines of Skepticism and Romanticism* (Chicago: University of Chicago Press, 1994), 125.
7. Garrett Stewart, 'The Word Viewed: Skepticism Degree Zero', in *Stanley Cavell and Literary Studies: Consequences of Skepticism*, ed. Richard Eldridge and Bernie Rhie (London: Continuum, 2011), 80.
8. Ibid. 80.
9. De Grazia, 'Teleology, Delay, and the "Old Mole"', 261.
10. Ibid. 260.
11. Ruth Stevenson, 'Hamlet's Mice, Motes, Moles, and Minching Malecho', *New Literary History* 33 (2002): 438.
12. Jacques Derrida, 'Che cos'è la poesia?' in *A Derrida Reader: Between the Blinds*, trans. and ed. Peggy Kamuf (New York: Columbia University Press, 1991), 235/234.
13. Hélène Cixous, 'Shakespeare Ghosting Derrida', trans. Laurent Milesi, *The Oxford Literary Review* 34, no. 1 (2012): 3–4, my emphasis.

14. Jacques Derrida, *Specters of Marx: The State of the Debt, the Work of Mourning and the New International*, trans. Peggy Kamuf (London: Routledge, 2006), 10.
15. Lee Baxandall and Stefan Morawski, eds, *Marx & Engels on Literature & Art: a Selection of Writings* (St. Louis: Telos Press, 1973), 147.
16. Derrida, *Specters of Marx*, 52, 51.
17. Ibid. 51–2.
18. Karl Marx. 'The Eighteenth Brumaire of Louis Bonaparte', in *Selected Writings*, ed. David McLellan (Oxford: Oxford University Press, 2000), 329.
19. Ibid. 329.
20. Derrida, *Specters of Marx*, 134.
21. Marx, 'The Eighteenth Brumaire of Louis Bonaparte', 331.
22. Derrida, *Specters of Marx*, 136.
23. Marx, 'The Eighteenth Brumaire of Louis Bonaparte', 345.
24. Marjorie Garber, *Quotation Marks* (London: Routledge, 2003), 19.
25. Martha Nussbaum, 'Stages of Thought: Review of A. D. Nuttall, *Shakespeare the Thinker*; Colin McGinn, *Shakespeare's Philosophy*; and Tzachi Zamir, *Double Vision: Moral Philosophy and Shakespearean Drama*', in *Philosophical Interventions: Reviews 1986–2011* (Oxford: Oxford University Press, 2012), 367.
26. Georg W. F. Hegel, *Lectures on the History of Philosophy*, trans. E. S. Haldane and Frances H. Simson, 3 vols (Lincoln and London: University of Nebraska Press, 1995), 3: 546–7.
27. Martin Harries, *Scare Quotes from Shakespeare: Marx, Keynes, and the Language of Reenchantment* (Stanford: Stanford University Press, 2000), 86.
28. Ibid. 80.
29. Ibid. 86.
30. Ibid. 86.
31. Jacques, Derrida, 'What is a "Relevant" Translation?', trans. Lawrence Ventuti. *Critical Inquiry* 27, no. 2 (2001): 175.
32. Jacques Derrida, *Monolingualism of the Other; or, the Prosthesis of Origin*, trans. Patrick Mensah (Stanford: Stanford University Press, 1998), 50.

33. Derrida, *Specters of Marx*, 116–17.
34. De Grazia, 'Teleology, Delay, and the "Old Mole"', 266.
35. Ibid. 266.
36. Jacques Derrida, *Spectres de Marx: L'État de la dette, le travail du deuil et la nouvelle Internationale* (Paris: Galilée, 1993), 154.
37. Royle, *The Uncanny*, 245.
38. Ibid. 245.
39. Derrida, *Specters of Marx*, 117.
40. Friedrich Schlegel, *Lucinde and the Fragments*, trans. Peter Firchow (Minneapolis: University of Minnesota Press, 1971), 189.
41. Jacques Derrida, 'Istrice 2: Ick bünn all hier', trans. Peggy Kamuf in *Points . . . Interviews, 1974–1994*, ed. Elisabeth Weber (Stanford: Stanford University Press, 1995), 303.
42. Ibid. 304.
43. Ibid. 304.
44. Ibid. 304.
45. Ibid. 303.
46. Derrida, *Specters of Marx*, 42.
47. Derrida, 'Istrice 2: Ick bünn all hier', 303.
48. Ibid. 304.
49. Jacques Derrida, 'Istrice 2: Ick bünn all hier', in *Points de suspension: entretiens*, ed. Elisabeth Weber (Paris: Galilée, 1992), 321. Since the English and French title of this piece are the same, are in other words both in Italian and German, I will refer to the 'French' original as 'Istrice 2: Ick bünn all hier (F)'.
50. Derrida, 'Istrice 2: Ick bünn all hier', 311.
51. Derrida, *Specters of Marx*, 117; Royle, *Uncanny*, 245.
52. Derrida, 'Istrice 2: Ick bünn all hier', 304.
53. Derrida, 'Istrice 2: Ick bünn all hier (F)', 303.
54. Derrida, 'Che cos'è la poesia?', 226–8 (underline my emphasis).
55. Ibid. 227–9 (underline my emphasis).
56. Derrida, 'Aphorism Countertime', 418.
57. Derrida, *Specters of Marx*, 37; *Spectres de Marx*, 60.
58. William Shakespeare, *Hamlet*, ed. Ann Thompson and Neil Taylor (London: Arden Shakespeare, 2006), 212.

59. Derrida, 'Che cos'è la poesia?', 235/234.
60. Ibid. 235.
61. Ibid. 235.
62. Shakespeare, *Hamlet*, 212.
63. Derrida, 'A "Madness" Must Watch over Thinking', trans. Peggy Kamuf, in *Points . . . Interviews, 1974–1994*, ed. Elisabeth Weber (Stanford: Stanford University Press, 1995), 354.
64. Jacques Derrida, 'Fidèlité à plus d'un', in *Idiomes, nationalités, déconstruction – Recontre de Rabat avec Jacques Derrida*, special issue of *Cahiers INTERSIGNES* 13 (1998): 224. I am using Oisín Keohane's translation, printed in 'Tongue-tied Democracy: The Bind of National Language in Tocqueville and Derrida', *Derrida Today* 4, no. 2 (2011): 252.
65. Derrida, '*Shibboleth*: For Paul Celan', 28.
66. Cixous, 'Shakespeare Ghosting Derrida', 4.
67. Kamuf, *Book of Addresses*, 281.
68. Derrida, *Specters of Marx*, 154.
69. Jacques Derrida, 'Qu'est-ce qu'une traduction "relevante"?', in *Quinzièmes assises de la traduction littéraire* (Arles 1998) (Arles: Actes Sud, 1999), 21.
70. Derrida, 'What is a "Relevant" Translation?', 174.
71. Jacques Derrida, '"A Self-Unsealing Poetic Text": Poetics and Politics of Witnessing', trans. Rachel Bowlby, in *Revenge of the Aesthetic: The Place of Literature in Theory Today*, ed. Michael P. Clark (Berkeley: University of California Press, 2000), 181.
72. Derrida, 'What is a "Relevant" Translation?', 191, 194.
73. Derrida, 'Qu'est-ce qu'une traduction "relevante"?', 42.
74. Derrida, 'What is a "Relevant" Translation?', 195.
75. Ibid. 195.
76. Ibid. 195.
77. Ibid. 195.
78. Ibid. 195.
79. Ibid. 196.
80. Ibid. 198.
81. Ibid. 175.
82. Ibid. 175.

83. Ibid. 184.
84. Ibid. 185; Derrida, 'Qu'est-ce qu'une traduction "relevante"?', 33.
85. Cixous, 'Shakespeare Ghosting Derrida', 3–4.
86. Ibid. 3.
87. Ibid. 3.
88. Derrida, 'What is a "Relevant" Translation?', 181.
89. Lawrence Venuti, 'Translating Derrida on Translation: Relevance and Disciplinary Resistance', *The Yale Journal of Criticism* 16, no. 2 (2003): 240.
90. Ibid. 240.
91. Ibid. 240.
92. Derrida, 'What is a "Relevant" Translation?', 181.
93. Ibid. 183.
94. Ibid. 196.
95. Ibid. 196.
96. Derrida, *Specters of Marx*, 11.
97. Joseph Conrad, 'The Secret Sharer', in *'Twixt Land and Sea: Tales*, ed. J. A. Berthoud, Laura L. Davies and S. W. Reid (Cambridge: Cambridge University Pres s, 2008), 90.
98. Derrrida, 'What is a "Relevant" Translation?', 199.
99. Ibid. 177.
100. Derrida, 'Qu'est-ce qu'une traduction "relevante"?', 24.
101. Venuti, 'Translating Derrida on Translation', 253.
102. Derrida, 'What is a "Relevant" Translation?', 198.
103. Derrida, 'Che cos'è la poesia?', 223.
104. Ibid. 226/227.
105. Derrida, '*Istrice 2: Ick bünn all hier*', 303.
106. Derrida, 'Che cos'è la poesia?', 235.

CHAPTER 5

GIVING THE GREATEST CHANCE TO CHANCE

Derrida (Almost) Reads King Lear

Derrida's 'My Chances/*Mes Chances*: A Rendezvous with Some Epicurean Stereophonies' is in many ways a companion piece to 'Aphorism Countertime'. Here, we re-encounter themes of translation, of those strange movements in 'tr', intertextual travel, and lost or erring letters, as well as the uncanny thinking processes of *lettres*, which, as I have shown in the preceding chapter, are intrinsic to Derrida's understanding of 'Shakespeare's genius'. If I turn to 'My Chances' now, however, it is mainly because this text deals with the thorny but central issue of chance in Derrida's approach to reading, writing and thinking.

The ways Derrida reads Shakespeare may not leave everyone with the aftertaste of the inevitable. Chance, indeed, orchestrates them, whether this be the unprogrammatic character of his engagement with the plays, the seemingly fortuitous routes he takes from one decontextualised passage to the next, the often surprising appearance of Shakespeare at the most unexpected argumentative junctions, and, perhaps most importantly, his dedication to tracing the seemingly aleatory but argumentatively absolutely pivotal lexical and phonetic movements of the Shakespearean porpentine.

The chances a reading takes, as well as the chances it does not take, and the routes of reading that it therefore skirts, are my subjects here, just as they are Derrida's. What chances, then, does Derrida take with Shakespeare in this text on chance and on reading? Given that 'My Chances' is in silent conversation with his engagement with *Romeo and Juliet* and with Shakespeare more in general, it is perhaps not surprising that, nestled towards its very end, we find a direct reference to Shakespeare, but this time to *King Lear*. As we shall see later in more detail, Derrida is here talking about his decision to cite Freud citing Leonardo da Vinci citing *Hamlet* as a way of thinking about the role the chances of literature and reading play for psychoanalysis, but also for Derrida himself:

> Giving the greatest chance to chance, it reappropriates chance itself into necessity of fatality. Literature plays nature for fortune – and art. ('Nature's above art in that respect' – *King Lear*.) Consequently, the third reason for this citation: it appeases the sense of remorse or misfortune ('How malicious is my fortune', says the bastard Edmund in *King Lear*), the regret I feel in not having attempted with you, as I initially projected, an analysis of *King Lear* that would take us beyond Freud's observation in *The Theme of the Three Caskets* (1913). I would have followed the play of Nature and Fortune there, the words 'nature' and 'fortune,' and also the abundantly numerous 'letters' (for example, the 'thrown letter'), the 'wisdom of nature,' 'prediction' ('there's son against father: the king falls from bias of nature'), 'planetary influence' for 'a sectary astronomical,' of 'epicurism,' 'posts,' letters and lips to unseal, 'gentle wax' and the 'reason in madness' of Lear ('I am even / The natural fool of fortune'). And taking more time, but that will be for another time, I would have attempted to read with you together, between the lines of Shakespeare, Freud and Heidegger's reflection on *Moira* (in *The Theme of the Three Caskets* and in *Moira*).[1]

There is something rather baffling about Derrida's somewhat reparative, apologetic final gesture here. This mention of *Lear* is disorienting not merely because, in bringing 'My Chances' to an end, Derrida refers us palintropically back to its beginning. The reference to the reading of *King Lear* he might have given, and indeed was intending to give, is also astounding due to its telegrammatic, and thus almost completely hypothetical, character. It would not be difficult to find other passages in Derrida where entire arguments are compressed, concertina-like, within a few sentences. Derrida's texts are full of them, particularly in their concluding passages. To be sure, lifting the curtain at the end of a, by all accounts, highly sophisticated reading performance, allowing a glimpse of other, untaken avenues, only increases the impression of exhaustive textual mastery. Their effect is, however, also one of textual tilt; in such asides whole thought-worlds remain suspended. By mentioning the chances not or almost not taken with *King Lear*, Derrida highlights the fact that the routes 'My Chances' *does* take through Freud, Leonardo da Vinci, Shakespeare and others to think about the relationship between chance, literature and psychoanalysis are themselves given by nothing but chance. The text's masterful performance turns out to be nothing but a *malchance*, a bit of bad luck. The master here it seems to be not Derrida, but chance itself.

How does Derrida fall upon the words of a literary work he will come to find, immediately or perhaps only upon repeated perusal, significant enough to base a philosophical reading on? How do any of us? Whatever the method or madness, these are, as Derrida already admits in 'Aphorism Countertime', quickly isolated, taken 'out of context', or *counter-timed* to use that text's idiom. Thus, in the final pages of 'My Chances', a text which not only does not offer a comprehensive Shakespearean reading, but which in fact proposes to think about something else entirely, *King Lear* is 'deconstructed' according to 'an implacable program', which, as Derrida writes elsewhere in this text, 'requires cutting solids into certain sequences (stereotomy), intersecting and adjusting subsets, mingling voices and proper names . . .'.[2] And yet, despite the fact that the direct citations from Shakespeare are here kept even shorter and more isolated than in 'Aphorism Countertime' or 'What is a "Relevant" Translation?', it would not be difficult to place them once again within the solidity of what we may think of as their original context.

'Nature's above art in that respect' (IV, vi, 86) marks Lear's disjointed response, if it is one, to Edgar near the cliffs of Dover. 'How malicious is my fortune, that I must / repent to be just?' are the words with which Edmund shows Cornwall a letter documenting his father's supposed treason (III, v, 9–10). There is no direct mention of a 'thrown letter' in the play, although Edmund reports that the letter 'was not brought me, my lord, there's the cunning of it. I found it thrown in at the casement of my closet' (I, ii, 59–61). In the same scene, Gloucester evocates 'the wisdom of Nature' (I, ii, 104) when making a link between 'these late eclipses in the sun and moon' (I, ii, 103) and Edgar's treachery: 'This villain of mine comes under the prediction – there's son against father. The King falls from bias of nature – there's father against son' (I, ii, 109–10). 'Planetary influence' appears in Edmund's soon-to-follow mockery of his contemporaries', including his father's, superstitions (I, ii, 125), whereas Edgar asks him sceptically how long he has been a 'sectary astronomical' (I, ii, 150) after he reports the same astrological predictions that he so derides. Goneril mentions Lear's knights 'epicurism' (I, iv, 235) when banning him from her palace. In Act III, scene vii Cornwall promises to Goneril that 'our posts shall be swift and intelligent betwixt us' (III, vii, 11). Soon Derrida returns to Act IV, scene vi and therefore to the cliffs of Dover, to Lear's madness ('Reason in madness'

(IV, vi, 171)), Lear's fleeing once more from the love of his youngest daughter ('No rescue? What, a prisoner? I am even / The natural fool of fortune' (IV, vi, 186–7)), and finally the 'gentle wax' (IV, vi, 254) of Goneril's letter to Edmund which Edgar takes off a dying Oswald.

Derrida does not provide a detailed abstract of what he would have done with the play of nature and fortune in *King Lear*, although we might guess from his interest in letters in the play that it would perhaps have been not dissimilar to what he says about the necessity of the accidental in his discussion of *Romeo and Juliet*'s straying letters in 'Aphorism Countertime'. It would not be difficult, then, to gather these textual strands up in order to try to guess how Derrida might have, as he puts it, followed the play of nature and fortune in *King Lear*. It would not be impossible to divine what he might have said, particularly given that many of the citations he gives come from Act I, scene ii, which is intensely concerned with the issues of chance on the one hand and predetermination, mostly as symbolised through the rhythms of nature, on the other. Although, with its twenty-five uses of the word 'fortune' or related words, *King Lear* is not dissimilar to other Shakespeare plays, it is its nuanced portrayal of the enmeshment of fortune and nature that explains Derrida's interest in the context of his discussion of the chances psychoanalysis takes with literature.[3] It is true, of course, that *King Lear* reflects Shakespeare's contemporaries' complex attitude towards fortune. Although Augustine had already sought to supplant fortune with divine providence, the classical imagery of, and most importantly the associated notions about, fortune never really went away.[4] As such, the many plays on fortune in Shakespeare derive, as Alan R. Young has argued, not from a Christian but from a classical heritage.[5] Fortune is thus consistently understood to be more fickle, less directed than divine providence may be, with nature standing in seemingly contradictory dynamics to both. Throughout the play, nature is both aligned with and undermined by fortune: in the play storms and planetary influences do fortune's bidding, but at the same time they put pressure on any idea of the legibility of nature's intentions. In fact, *King Lear*'s many allusions to the 'instability, unpredictability, deceptiveness, and destructive potential' of fortune directly 'destabilize[s] assumptions about the natural order and the beneficence of divine power'.[6] As Paul A. Cantor has argued, being a pagan, Lear believes 'that the natural and the divine orders are one and the same, and both are aligned with human justice and law'.[7] At the beginning of the play in particular, Lear is a man who believes that nature, in alliance with divinity, undergirds his actions as a king; the storm, however, confirms that the natural world is, as Cantor suggests, fundamentally unjust and, more importantly, incalculable.[8] Lear's famous, seemingly oxymoronic, 'I am even / The natural fool of fortune' (IV, vi, 186), is but one of the ways in which Shakespeare shows that in the play's cosmos being flesh and blood, and thus being part of nature, means to be subject to the whims of fortune.

There is nothing more human than wanting to master fortune. Derrida's 'almost reading' of *King Lear* shows, I think, that when we read there is something of Lear's facing the storm in us. What we set out to do when we read is, at a very fundamental level, to make sense of something, and by doing so, to re-establish, or establish for the first time, a sense of control, or mastery. It is because of this that Derrida points us towards Freud, a thinker intensely preoccupied with mastering the chances of reading, for example, Shakespeare. It is important to note that Derrida does not merely regret not reading *King Lear*, he laments his not having taken the opportunity to read *King Lear* in light of what Freud says not merely about this play, but also, in another intertextual concatenation, about *The Merchant of Venice*. Let's follow Derrida's pointer.

Freud's *The Theme of the Three Caskets* (1913) sets the scene: in order to win Portia's hand her suitors must choose between a gold, silver and lead casket. Coming up last, Bassanio chooses lead:

> Therefore, then, thou gaudy gold,
> Hard food for Midas, I will none of thee;
> Nor none of thee, thou pale and common drudge
> 'Tween man and man. But thou, thou meagre lead,
> Which rather threaten'st than dost promise aught,
> Thy paleness moves me more than eloquence,
> And here choose I; joy be the consequence.
> (*The Merchant of Venice*, III, ii, 101–7)

Freud does not need fortune's hand to identify the 'ancient theme', which Shakespeare is modulating here.[9] While in the Estonian epic *Kalewipoeg* or in the *Gesta Remanorum* 'the subject is a girl choosing between three suitors', in *The Merchant of Venice*, it is a man's turn to choose the right casket.[10] Although 'the subject is apparently the same ... something appears in it that is in the nature of an inversion of a theme'.[11] Inversion is, of course, an important interpretative tool for Freud, particularly in *The Interpretation of Dreams*. In fact, referring back to this work, Freud suggests that 'if what we were concerned with were a dream, it would occur to us at once that caskets are also women, symbols of what is essential in woman, and therefore of a woman herself – like coffers, boxes, cases, baskets, and so on'.[12] Allowing for inversion then also does something else to this story: it allows us to 'stri[p] the astral garment' from this story and to see that it is at heart a human one.[13] For Freud, this story is really about '*a man's choice between three women*', a choice which itself stands in for a matter more to do with the nature of man's attitude to his mortality, than with the nature of chance.[14]

The idea that Bassanio chooses one of three women allows Freud to link *The Merchant of Venice* to Lear's choice between his three daughters. To use Bassanio's words, Goneril and Regan are too 'gaudy' in their assurances of love. In contrast, 'Cordelia makes herself unrecognizable, inconspicuous like lead, she remains dumb, she "loves and is silent".'[15] Again, drawing on psychoanalytic techniques provides a ready answer to why the choice must fall – like it does in the stories of Aphrodite, Cinderella and Psyche – on the third and youngest woman. As Freud explains, 'in dreams dumbness is a common representation of death'.[16] Another 'unmistakable symbol of death in dreams' is 'a marked pallor, of which the "paleness" of the lead in one reading of Shakespeare's text is a reminder'.[17] For Freud then, the third woman must be chosen because she stands for 'the Goddess of Death' itself, the third of the three Morae, also called 'Atropos, the inexorable'.[18] As Freud explains, the Morae, who are closely related to the Horae, reminded man that he too was 'a part of nature and therefore subject to the immutable law of death'.[19] But why would someone choose the third sister, Atropos, she who points man to the inexorable necessity of his own death? Again, Freud believes that psychoanalysis can shed light on this, because 'contradictions of a certain kind – replacements by the precise opposite – offer no serious difficulty to the work of analytic interpretation' and the goddess of death has been turned into the goddess of love, less in the sense of a 'wishful reversal' than in rebellion.[20] Choice is reintroduced to supplant all necessity, destiny and chance with man's agency and power.

Freud's reading of *King Lear* with *The Merchant of Venice* not merely has the mastering of chance as its subject but is itself a superb example of Freud's abilities as a reader to shepherd the chances of reading into a masterful performance. The importance of this readerly move becomes clear when considering that Freud is, of course, not merely a disinterested reader, but the father of a nascent discipline he was eager to prove to be scientifically sound. In *The Theme of the Three Caskets*, Freud repeatedly draws on the tools of psychoanalysis in ways that legitimate both Freud's interpretation of Shakespeare, as well as their own very efficacy. In Freud's reading of *King Lear* chance is, therefore, sublimated to the point of erasure.

Derrida's 'almost reading' of *King Lear* does not end with Freud. If Derrida had had more time, even more than would have allowed him to read *Lear*'s play of fortune and nature *beyond* Freud, he would have also said something about Freud's and Heidegger's reflections on Moira and he would have done so 'between' Shakespeare's lines.[21] Heidegger appears once before this enigmatic mention in 'My Chances', more precisely in connection with the particular deconstructive dynamism of the falling of chance (what Derrida calls the *clinamen*, to which I shall turn later) in Heidegger's discussion of *Dasein*. Here, Derrida suggest that the 'dispersion and dissemination (*Zerstreuung*)' opened by the '*Geworfenheit* or throwness' of *Dasein* is not disruptive but essential.[22] The implication is that Heidegger does not recognise the essential role chance plays for *Dasein*. Incidentally, his remarks about Moira, to which Derrida refers in relation to *King Lear*, are marked by the same reluctance to, to say it with Derrida, 'giv[e] the greatest chance to chance'.[23]

In 'Moira (Parmenides, Fragment viii, 34–41)', Heidegger stays closely with the pre-Socratic philosopher's discussion, in his only known work, *On Nature*, of the relationship between thinking and saying. Particularly important for my purposes is the beginning of the fragment, given here in the English rendition of the German translation Heidegger himself was working with:

> Thinking and the thought 'it is' are the same. For without the being in relation to which it is uttered you cannot find thinking. For there neither is nor shall be anything outside of being, since Moira bound it to be whole and immovable.[24]

Heidegger goes through great trouble to elucidate that uttering is not what we think it might be. *Noein*, for example, here translated as 'thinking, which is something uttered in being', must be understood in context with the use of *noein* as closely linked to *legein* in Fragment 6:

> Νοεῖν ... is grounded in and comes to presence from λέγειν. In λέγειν the letting-lie-before of what is present in its presencing occurs. Only as thus lying-before can what is present as such admit the νοεῖν, the taking-heed-of ... On that account νοεῖν, is essentially – not peripherally or accidentally – something said. Certainly not everything said need be an utterance. It can also, and sometimes must, be a silence.[25]

As Heidegger is at pains to make clear, *noein* is not linked to what J. L. Austin might have called a 'locutionary act', in other words to uttering or speaking, but rather to a 'letting-lie-before (λογός)' even 'as a bringing-forward-into-view (φάσις)'.[26] Indeed, for Heidegger, the emphasis on saying would be nefarious to thinking about thought because it tempts us 'into a veiling darkness and yields ascendancy to a characterisation of language which relentlessly represents in terms of φονά, vocalization – a system of signs and significations, and ultimately of data and information'.[27] It is important to note at this point that Derrida's repeated suggestions that he reads Shakespeare in darkness and thus with his ears seems to play on Heidegger's fear of the dark and his reluctance to take the work of *phone* and its imbrication with chance seriously. Although Moira is at play in *noien*, its role is to secure 'the presencing of what is present' and the shining through of what Heidegger calls *aletheia*.[28] Like Freud, Heidegger is not content with leaving chance be; it must be the conduit to something more significant, more solid, something indeed approaching a secular iteration of that same divine predestination with which Augustine sought to supplant fortune.

It is not impossible to hazard a guess as to how Derrida might have read Shakespeare beyond Freud and beyond Heidegger. Derrida's talk about his (unfulfilled) intention to read *beyond* Freud must, I believe, be read as the announcement of a commitment to put pressure on Freud's and Heidegger's sublimated view of chance. Wishing to give the greatest chance to chance, he would have, I think, shown the importance of resisting the temptation to sublimate chance like Heidegger and Freud do. Because both thinkers of course strip chance of its very essence when turning it into something more, something that, for example, allows *aletheia* or man to have the final word.[29] Derrida's almost reading of *King Lear* with or beyond Freud and Heidegger is, let us not forget, about reading itself. Any critique of the sublimation of chance, which is both Freud and Heidegger's subject, is more importantly a critique of the ways of reading which lead them to their respective conclusions. For both thinkers, chance's trajectories, however temporarily straying, never miss their intended marks. And for both men a certain kind of reading, a way of reading like their own, plays an important role in piloting chance into the safe haven of a masterful interpretation. This is not the kind of mastery Derrida is interested in when reading Shakespeare.

'How malicious is my fortune.'[30] In Derrida's mouth, these words play, as they do in Edmund's, to the idea of the givenness of chance. This expression of regret at not having been able to give the reading of *King Lear* which he had originally planned is also a nod to the mastery of chance itself. In contrast to Freud and Heidegger, he characterises his reading, perhaps not merely humorously, as a throw of the dice, something that is perhaps out of his hands. While it would, as I have endeavoured to show, not be impossible for us to fulfil or attempt to fulfil the promise of the reading-to-come his brief references to *Lear* amount to, what is important about Derrida's almost reading of *Lear* is not what he might have said, but that their promise remains essentially *unfulfilled*. What counts, I would like to argue, when thinking about the way Derrida reads Shakespeare, is not merely the chances he takes, but also the chances he does *not* take. In leaving his almost reading of *King Lear* suspended, Derrida foregrounds the role of chance in reading, what we might call the 'event' of reading. Why is it, for example, that we take one avenue through a text or a set of questions rather than another? What about the routes we did not or almost did not take? Are they any less valuable and less illuminating? And what effect does the foregrounding of an unexplored reading have on how seriously we might take the reading that did in fact happen? To begin to answer these questions, I will, in what follows, take my own chances and take a route through Freud and Shakespeare, which Derrida does not – not even almost – take.

Taking Chances with Freud

If chance plays a role in Freud's reading of *The Merchant of Venice* and *King Lear*, and I would suggest with Derrida that it always does when we read, it is not as much repressed as sublimated into interpretative necessity. But while he here draws on psychoanalysis to read Shakespeare, more often than not the roles are reversed. The ways in which Freud takes and does not take chances with literature within psychoanalytic interpretation is a crucial reference point for Derrida's own ways of taking chances with Shakespeare.

Freud's description and interpretation of his '*Non Vixit* Dream' is an intricate and, stretching over three different passages in the last part of *The Interpretation of Dreams*, agile creature. Although he treats it as one, Freud's narrative actually comprises two dreams. In the first dream, the curtain opens on Freud alone in Ernst Wilhelm von Brücke's laboratory at night. When somebody gently knocks at the door, Freud opens it and the late Professor Ernst von Fleischl-Marxow and a number of strangers come in and sit down at his table. The second dream is set in Vienna in July. Freud meets his friend Fl. (abbreviated by the same Fl., as Fleischl, but, as will emerge a couple of sections later, this is also Wilhelm Fliess) and their mutual friend P. (Joseph P., the brilliant and younger colleague of Freud who took his place at Brücke's laboratory and who died young). Fl. is talking about his sister, saying that she was dead in a quarter of an hour and something like '*das ist die Schwelle*', or '*that was the threshold*'.[31] P. does not understand and Fl. turns to Freud, asking him how much he has told P. about his affairs. Suddenly Freud is '*overcome by strange emotions*' and tells him that P. could not possibly understand anything because he was not alive.[32] But rather than *non vivit* (he does not live), Freud mistakenly says *non vixit* (he has never lived). As he recognises his mistake, he looks at P., his eyes turn a '*sickly blue*' and he vanishes under the intensity of Freud's gaze. Freud was '*highly delighted at this*' and then realises that '*Ernst Fleischl, too, had been no more than an apparition, a "revenant"* ['ghost' – literally, 'one who returns']; *and it seemed to [him] quite possible that people of that kind only existed as long as one liked and could be got rid of if someone else wished it.*'[33]

What to make of such a dream? Due to the non-creative or reprocessing nature of the dream work, the origin of most of the dream's elements must be extraneous to the dream itself. The scene, in which Freud obliterates P. through his gaze, for instance, 'was unmistakably copied from one which [he] had actually experienced'.[34] As Freud recalls, in his time as a demonstrator, Brücke had once reduced him to nothing with those 'terrible blue eyes' for arriving late.[35] Similarly, the words '*Non vixit*' must have come from somewhere other than the dream itself. Remembering that these words 'possessed their high degree of clarity in the dream, not as words heard or spoken, but as words *seen*', he identifies them as belonging to the inscription of the Kaiser Josef Memorial in the Hofburg in Vienna.[36] He then remembers that this dream came 'only a few days after the unveiling of the memorial to Fleischl in the cloisters of the University' and that, on that occasion, he had seen Brücke's memorial once again and 'must have reflected (unconsciously) with regret on the fact that the premature death of my brilliant friend P., whose whole life had been devoted to science, had robbed him of a well-merited claim to a memorial in these same precincts'.[37]

Yet the abbreviation Fl. in the dream does not only stand for Fleischl but also his friend Wilhelm Fliess. When Freud comes back to this dream in 'The Affects in Dreams', he realises that the dream must have also been triggered by Fliess's letter, in which his good friend tells him of an upcoming operation. Freud writes that he would have very much liked to be able to travel to Fliess, but that his own illness had kept him from it.[38] The reappearance of Fliess's sister, who died as a child after a very short illness, marks the fear of arriving too late, as the fear of Fliess dying before him.[39] The fear of arriving late is echoed in P.'s blue eyes, which in truth belong to Brücke, Freud's scolding superior.

There is a twist, however. The '*Non Vixit* Dream' does not only speak of his fear of losing a good friend and colleague (first P. then, possibly, Fliess). Although P. has Brücke's blue eyes, it is Freud who has the obliterating gaze, and this gaze is directed at P. And because, as Freud notes in *The Theme of the Three Caskets*, pallor stands for death, we might say that, according to the dream's logic, Freud is himself responsible for P.'s death. Freud writes:

> It then struck me as noticeable that in the scene in the dream there was a convergence of a hostile and an affectionate current of feeling towards my friend P., the former being on the surface and the latter concealed, but both of them being represented in the single phrase *Non vixit*.[40]

Two sources are offered for this underlying aggression and for the logic of the dream thought. The first one relates to his early years and involves Fleischl and P.: P. was impatient with the slow progress of his career and expressed a wish to take the place of his superior, who was gravely ill at the time. Although Freud himself had been not dissimilarly impatient, he finds in P.'s behaviour the justification for his obliteration: 'It serves you right if you had to make way for me.'[41] The other justification for his mixed feeling towards P. relates directly to Fliess. A relation of Fliess's had admonished Freud to be discreet about an operation he had had.[42] Freud was angry about this lack of trust but was also simultaneously ashamed, because he had been guilty of just such a lack of secrecy during his time at Brücke's laboratory, when he told one of his colleagues what the other had said about him.[43] The mixed feelings are hence triggered partly by anger at P.'s or Fliess's behaviour, partly by the guilt of self-recognition in that very behaviour.

Again, however, Freud draws on the chances of literature, or, more precisely, Shakespeare. Freud finds 'a similar antithesis, a similar parallel between two opposite reactions to the same person' in Shakespeare's *Julius Caesar*, more specifically in Brutus' famously ambivalent speech in Act III, scene ii: 'As Caesar loved me, I weep for him; as he was fortunate, I rejoice at it; as he was valiant, I honour him: but as he was ambitious, I slew him' (III, ii, 24–7), which thus becomes the second source of the ambivalent feelings voiced in the '*Non Vixit* Dream'. Freud is now angling for more evidence: 'If only I could find one other piece of evidence in the content of the dream to confirm this surprising collateral connecting link!'[44] He finds not one but two explanations for this strange chance event: first, the dream is set in the month of July, named so after Julius Caesar; second, Freud did not only play the Brutus to P. and Fliess in his dream, but he did actually play Brutus, albeit in Schiller's rather than in

Shakespeare's version, as a fourteen-year-old together with his English nephew John, to whom he has a similarly ambivalent relationship.

As William Beatty Warner suggests in *Chance and the Text of Experience*, it is only the introduction of a double literary reference to Shakespeare and Schiller that allows Freud to link 'the scenes and situations of three different epochs of Freud's life: his training in neurology in Brücke's laboratory . . . his intimate relationship with Wilhelm Fliess at the time he is writing *The Interpretation of Dreams* . . . and last, Freud's decisive early relationship with his older nephew John'.[45] The chance encounter of literature – Brutus' speech, Schiller's 'Brutus and Caesar Song' in *Die Räuber* – and the underlying rivalries in Freud's friendships, his difficult and defining relationship with John, to whom he first played the Brutus, seems to play into Freud's hands: the perfect chain of consistencies and coincidences gives Freud's interpretation the smack of the undeniable. But Freud is not taking his chances, or at least not taking all of them. According to Warner, the call for mastery over the psychoanalytic discourse systematically neutralises chance. Parapraxes as well as dreams might give the impression of being aleatory, but their chance element can be and is usually subtracted by his interpretation that uncovers the unconscious element pulling the strings behind the scenes.[46] Freud therefore not only plays the Brutus to John, Fliess, and P., but also to chance itself. Chance is the grist to his interpretative mills, but, recognising the threat of its tyranny, he is reluctant to allow it to reign unbridled, for fear of reducing his nascent discipline to a mere concatenation of chances.

The aleatory element of reading can never be successfully extricated or sublimated from the interpretative fabric. Even if the chances leading to any given interpretation might be reasoned away, the chances of other possible readings, of routes not taken, cannot. There is always textual tilt. The intertextual chain to Shakespeare's Brutus, the justification for his mixed feelings towards Fliess and P., and his decisive childhood relationship to John, could, for example, point towards another kind of justification or reason, one perhaps even less comfortable for Freud. The Schiller passage to which Freud refers is the 'Brutus and Caesar Song' in his play *Die Räuber* (incidentally, a play centring on rivalry). We know that Schiller must have been familiar with *Julius Caesar* because (another chance event tidily following Freud's interpretation) in a letter of 2 February 1789 to Körner he gives his own difficult relation to Goethe the same *Klang* that so fascinated Freud in Shakespeare's Brutus: 'He has roused within me a most curious mixture of hatred and love, a feeling not unlike that which Brutus and Cassius must have entertained for Caesar. I could murder his spirit, and then love him from my very heart.'[47] Schiller's 'Brutus and Caesar Song' could be seen as expressive of the rivalry, which seems to be the main theme in Schiller's play and which allows Freud to articulate his dream thought. Michael Mann, however, has argued that what is expressed in the song is not rivalry but the dualism that so fascinated Schiller in his later plays.[48] The song that Freud and John recited as teenagers is hence not expressive of rivalry for which in Freud's eyes John is the revenant haunting all of his subsequent relationships with peers, but rather of an inner struggle where one is the Brutus to one's own Caesar. While Freud is quite forthcoming with the confession that he has played the Brutus, he is reluctant to admit that he has played Caesar, too. Considering Freud's double agenda in writing *The Interpretation of Dreams* – he was not only interpreting his dreams, he was also founding a discipline and establishing himself as the master over it – his avoidance of any further enquiry into Schiller's 'Brutus and Caesar Song' can be understood as a reluctance to face his possessiveness over his nascent discipline.

For Freud, the dream thought or sentence – 'as my friend P. has deserved well of science, I erect a memorial to him; as he has been guilty of a malicious wish (expressed at the end of the dream) I annihilate him' – is a sentence 'von ganz besonderem Klang', literally 'of a very particular sound' or 'had a quite special cadence', as Strachey has it.⁴⁹ Just as Freud avoids any further analysis of his reference to Schiller's *Die Räuber*, he avoids any further enquiry into the *Klang* of Brutus' speech. Freud's strange avoidance of the question of *Klang* in his interpretation of the '*Non Vixit* Dream' is entangled with its very matter: the primal scene of rivalry, which repeats itself in most other relationships Freud has with his peers, be it John, P., Fliess or other thinkers he worked with or drew upon. Freud's Caesarean behaviour is indeed most evident in the way he references or rather does not reference his peers in his psychoanalytical work. Ernest Jones argues that in contrast to his neurological work, in which 'Freud's bibliographical references had been scrupulously exact and comprehensive', his analytic writings reference other analysts' writings 'on the same principle as the Emperor distributed decorations, according to the mood and fancy of the moment'.⁵⁰

Behind the question of what Freud is avoiding there lurks the question of *whom* he is avoiding. As Barale and Minazzi argue, who is avoided is no one else than Theodor Lipps.⁵¹ From his letters to Fliess we know that Freud was reading Theodor Lipps's *Grundtatsachen des Seelenlebens* (published 1883) when he was working on the *Interpretation*. As Barale and Minazzi note, Freud felt that Lipps had forestalled many of his own discoveries and Freud explicitly draws on Lipps's work twice in *The Interpretation*: when he discusses the somatic source of dreams – 'in the copy of Lipps's book preserved in Freud's library, the underlining of a passage on the processes underlying dreams is clearly visible' – and when he argues for the primacy of the unconscious over the psychic life.⁵² Freud seemed to be feeling uneasy about the 'uncanny resemblance' between his work and Lipps's.⁵³ This is what he writes to Fliess on 31 August 1898:

> In Lipps I have rediscovered my own principles quite clearly stated – perhaps rather more than suited me. 'The seeker often finds more than he seeks.' Lipps regards consciousness as only a sense organ, the contents of the mind as ideation, and all mental processes as unconscious. In details the correspondence is close too; perhaps the divergence on which I shall be able to base my own contribution will come later. I have only read about a third of him. I got stuck at the treatment of tone-relations, which I have always had trouble, lacking the most elementary knowledge of the subject because of my stunted acoustic sensibility.⁵⁴

We do not know where exactly Freud got stuck in his reading of Lipps's *Grundtatsachen des Seelenlebens*, but perhaps it was in Chapter 11 when Lipps turns to tone relations and rhythm. After observing that harmonic tones seem to pull towards each other while disharmonic tones seem to repel each other, Lipps argues that this has to do with the micro rhythms that constitute the tone.⁵⁵ For Lipps, rhythm is the 'fundamental principle of' the 'organization' of music: 'harmony and musical consonance', for example, have to do with 'the relationship between the internal "microrhythms" of each sound'.⁵⁶ Rhythm was of great interest to many of Lipps's contemporaries (rhythm, for instance, plays a central part in the aesthetic of *Einfühlung*). Lipps, however, went beyond his contemporaries and argued for rhythm as a more general organisational principle of psychic experience.⁵⁷ Via tone relations and rhythms he therefore establishes an analogy between the way we perceive sound (the way our ear is equipped to pick out the right micro rhythms to what he calls the *Stimmung*, the fundamental 'tuning' of psychic life: just as our ear pushes towards harmony and halts before disharmony, so every rhythm of a psychic process is attracted by the same rhythm in other simultaneous or shortly following psychic processes).[58] Barale and Minazzi argue that Freud had to halt before Lipps's discussion of tone relations because the inclusion of rhythm, sound and music, tapping into the preverbal realm, would have significantly shifted the focus of his research, which at the time was the representational unconscious and infantile sexuality.[59] This can certainly not be disregarded, and neither can the resonances Lipps's work might have with Freud's formulation of the *Zauderrhythmus* in 'Beyond the Pleasure Principle', but on this occasion I would like to think of Freud's 'stunted acoustic sensibility' in light of the type of deafness that Shakespeare attributes to Julius Caesar.

In Act I, scene ii of Shakespeare's eponymous play, Julius Caesar asks Antony to 'Come on my right hand, for this ear is deaf' (I, ii, 212). Caesar's deafness may as well have been Shakespeare's invention, since none of the ancient sources, including Plutarch, mention this deafness. As Garber suggests, Caesar's deafness is, however, not necessarily a physical one: 'There was a popular saying that a king's left ear was for flattery and private favors, his right ear for truth and for public concerns.'[60] Caesar's deafness in his left ear, therefore, suggests that he is deaf to the private sphere, deaf therefore to his own mortal existence. Perhaps Freud's 'stunted acoustic sensibility' in reading Lipps is not unlike the 'psychic deafness' Royle diagnoses in Shakespeare's characters in *In Memory of Jacques Derrida*: a selective deafness hearing only what it wants to hear, picking out only what harmonises with one's own view (of things and of oneself) and excluding any disruptive dissonance.[61] However, unlike Caesar, Freud is deaf in his right ear, not his left. He is therefore, keeping with Garber, conversely deaf to public matters and receptive to flattery and personal matters. Freud's halting before Lipps's work on tone relation can therefore be understood as a ruse to force a divergence that would allow Freud to avoid having to affiliate himself with the philosopher from Berlin. Freud's deafness here is therefore to be understood as an unwillingness to lend his ear too much to the work of an other, an other who already forestalled too many of his ideas, infringed too much on his claim for originality, primacy and mastery.

Against Mastery

It is of course difficult, indeed near impossible, to withstand the temptation to sublimate the chances of reading into something more than 'mere' chance. Derrida himself acknowledges the temptation to sublimate chance in his way of reading not merely Shakespeare, but also, as here for instance, Poe:

> You may think that I am juggling. For when chances increase steadily, and too many throws of the dice come to fall well, does this not abolish blind Chance (*le hasard*)? It would be possible to demonstrate that there is nothing random in the concatenation of my findings. An implacable program takes shape through the contextual necessity that requires cutting solids into certain sequences (stereotomy), intersecting and adjusting subsets, mingling voices and proper names, and accelerating a rhythm that merely gives the *feeling* of randomness to those who do not know the prescription – which incidentally, is also my case.[62]

Although Derrida does not talk about reading Shakespeare here, this methodological admission would do very well to sum up the contretemps of his rendezvous with, for example, *Hamlet*, *The Merchant of Venice* and *Romeo and Juliet*: solids (plays, but also single words) are cut into seemingly random sequences and voices and proper names mingle into new and unforeseen constellations (as, for example, the voices and proper names of Marx and *Hamlet*). Like in 'Aphorism Countertime', Derrida does not dodge incredulity or accusation and – the conditional of proving the supposed underlying necessity of his readings never actualised – he lets his juggling with Shakespeare stand.

Like all of his work, and particularly his readings of Shakespeare, 'My Chances' thus poses the question of its own practice, indeed of its own right to exist as a reading. Very much following the often indirect routes traced by chance, this text does not address the question of what roles chance or necessity play in his ways of reading directly. Instead, it asks a question, which is as impossible to answer as it is easy to pose: what are the chances of psychoanalysis? By virtue of asking this question, Derrida is, it turns out, already taking a chance; he was invited not to talk about chance, but about the relationship between literature and psychoanalysis. Yet, Derrida's deviation from the programme is, of course, no accident. By the end of his talk these strands – chance, psychoanalysis, literature, Shakespeare— will have been weaved together, according to a kind of mastery, which does not need to turn chance into predetermination, but which lets it stand, or rather *fall*.

Much of the discussion in 'My Chances' aims at turning our idea of chance, how it relates, even undergirds, the way we approach or find our ways through texts, on its head. Chance, then, is at the heart of the way Derrida reads Shakespeare. And his open avowal of his debts to chance constitutes one of his most important challenges to our understanding of what reading can do, also for philosophy. Giving such weight to the chances of reading unsettles something about literature that we have come to believe in our bones, namely that the principle or aim of the reader and certainly the critic is to unlock a text, to make it give up its secrets. Those who believe the secret to be at the text's surface and those who search for it deep in its folds share the, often implicit, conviction that the job of the reader or indeed the critic is to *master* the text. In

Derrida's view, the fact of chance frustrates any ambitions for such textual mastery.

Like 'Aphorism Countertime' did for contretemps and 'The Time is Out of Joint' and *Specters of Marx* did for the out-of-jointness of time, here chance is shown to be fundamental to what it is usually thought to disrupt. Chance is, in other words, not the perversion or interruption of something linearly determined, but is something absolutely necessary and unavoidable, ingrained in being itself. Thus, Derrida identifies a link between chance and what he most famously calls *différance*, but which here is addressed as the divisibility of the mark. In order to mark, 'a mark must be capable of being identified, recognized as the same, being precisely *re-markable* from one context to another', by being 'more than one', by 'multipl[ying] and divid[ing] itself internally'.[63] For Derrida, the divisibility of the mark opens the space that allows for, or indeed guarantees, the falling of chance. Starting from the etymological correspondence between chance and the Latin *cadere*, or 'to fall', Derrida links the divisibility of the mark to Epicurus' image of atoms falling in empty space. In the course of their fall in the void, atoms are driven by a supplementary deviation, by the *parenklisis* or *clinamen* that, impelling an initial divergence, produces 'the "concentration of material (*systrophè*) thus giving birth to the worlds and things they contain" (J. and M. Bollack, H. Wissman, *La Lettre d'Epicure*, p.182.3)'.[64] This *clinamen* is, Derrida suggests, the inescapable chance element opened by the mark's divisibility. Derrida also repeatedly highlights the etymological correspondence between chance, cadence and falling, for example towards the beginning of the piece:

> As you know, the words 'chance' and 'case' descend, as it were, according to the same Latin filiation, from *cadere*, which – to indicate the sense of the fall – still resounds in 'cadence,' 'fall' (*choir*), 'to fall due' (*échoir*), 'expiry date' (*échéance*), as well as in 'accident' and 'incident'.[65]

Chance, with its 'descending trajectories' and its 'perturbations' and 'deviations', is then, Derrida argues, a necessity dictated by *différance*:

> The same semantic register supposes the idea of whatever falls (*ce qui est échu*) to someone's lot – that lottery said to be attributed, distributed, dispensed, and sent (*geschickt*) by the gods or destiny (*moira, nemein, nomos, Schicksal*), the fatal or fabulating word, the chance circumstances of heredity, the game of chromosomes – as if this gift and these givens obeyed, for better or for worse, the order of a throw coming down from above. We are in fact dealing with a logic and *topos* of the dispatch (*envoi*). Destiny and destination are dispatches whose descending trajectories or projections can meet with perturbation, which, in this case, means interruption or deviation.[66]

In 'My Chances', Derrida asks what we should make of this structural unavoidability of the (be)falling of chance when it comes to psychoanalysis, a discipline heavily reliant on ideas of 'determinism, necessity or chance', as well as dependent in its interpretations on 'writing, the signifier and the letter, the simulacrum, fiction or literature'.[67] As I have shown, in practising his nascent discipline Freud takes his chances; he often does so with or through literature. In 'My Chances', Derrida turns to Freud's *Leonardo da Vinci and a Memory of His Childhood* to think about both the issue of chance in psychoanalytic interpretation and its relation to literature. In concluding *Leonardo da Vinci and a Memory of Childhood*, Freud very explicitly poses the question of a kind of psychoanalytic determinism, by hypothesising that perhaps 'only a man who had had Leonardo's childhood experiences' could have become the artist and thinker that he was.[68] And yet, the particularly difficult constellations of Leonardo's childhood 'misfortunes' were, Freud himself acknowledges, due to seemingly nothing else than chance.[69] But isn't chance,

Freud suggests, an essential ingredient of life? Derrida follows Freud's text very closely here:

> At the same time we are all too ready to forget that in fact everything to do with our life is chance, from our origin out of the meeting of spermatozoon and ovum onwards – chance which nevertheless has a share in the law and the necessity of nature, and which merely lacks any connection with our wishes and illusions. The apportioning of the determining factors of our life between the 'necessities' of our constitution and the 'chances' of our childhood may still be uncertain in detail; but in general it is no longer possible to doubt the importance precisely of the first years of our childhood. We all still show too little respect for Nature which (in the obscure words of Leonardo which recalls Hamlet's lines) 'is full of countless causes ["*ragioni*"]' that never enter experience.[70]

When, Derrida asks, is it 'moderate' or 'reasonable' to rely on chance and the chances of literature in psychoanalytic interpretations? The frequency with which literature is drawn upon to clinch an interpretation would suggest that Freud has no qualms about giving a certain weight to chance. And yet, he is, as Derrida notes, defensive in differentiating the method of his nascent (scientific, he insisted) method of psychoanalysis from superstition or pure chance on the other hand.[71] For Freud, there is, Derrida writes, 'no chance in the unconscious. The apparent randomness must be placed in the service of an unavoidable necessity that in fact is never contradicted.'[72] There is, it seems, no place for chance when mastery over an emergent discourse needs to be established. But throughout 'My Chances' Derrida argues that any of Freud's claims to mastery are complicated by the 'singularity' and hence 'eventness' of the psychoanalytic discourse which opens it to the fortunes and mishaps of the *clinamen*. And nowhere is the *clinamen* more pronounced than in literature.

The path towards mastery, Freud's as well as ours or indeed anyone's, is complicated by the chances of literature, and by what they throw at us, like arrows. If Derrida then concludes his discussion of Freud by referring to the very end of Freud's *Leonardo da Vinci and a Memory of His Childhood*, he does so not merely to make a point about the dependence of psychoanalysis on the chances of literature, but also about the travel or the erring of the *clinamen*, literature's complication of any linear or perfectly faithful transmission, as it affects the way he reads Shakespeare. To say it with Derrida:

> Once again indebtedness and filiation. Freud cites Leonardo da Vinci, whom he had come to recognize as being out of the reach of analytic science by virtue of a certain random enigma. But Freud cites da Vinci approximately citing Shakespeare, or rather Hamlet the son: '*La natura é piena d'infinite ragioni che non furono mai in insperienza,*' in place of 'There are more things in heaven and earth Horatio / Than are dreamt of in your philosophy.'[73]

Here we encounter again the Shakespearean porpentine: moving catachrestically across lectures, disjointedly across time – and perhaps all by chance. And here we also re-encounter the question of literature's ability to '*performatively* circumscrib[e] its own context for its own event' elaborated in 'Aphorism Countertime'. In this brief but significant gesture towards the end of his essay, Derrida thus implies that a literary oeuvre, for example Shakespeare's, is such not because it is any different from the mark, but because in contrast to the mark it reflects, as it were, its own chances: 'art, in particular the "art of discourse" and literature' are able to '*performatively* circumscrib[e] [their] own context for [their] own event, that of the oeuvre', he wrote a couple of lines earlier.[74] In contrast to the mark, we overtly recognise the oeuvre as the 'locus of luck and of chance'.⁷⁵ We are conscious of the chances that befall us while reading; we are conscious of what is called 'the freedom' of having this 'large ... stereotomic margin'.⁷⁶ Literature, as Derrida writes, 'giv[es] the greatest chance to chance' and thus 'reappropriates chance itself into necessity or fatality'.⁷⁷ This is, as we shall see, a different kind of reappropriation or sublimation of chance than Freud's or Heidegger's. One furthermore having to do with the often aural movements of the Shakespearean porpentine, that very same *Klang* that both Heidegger and Freud, in their different ways, wanted to avoid. Let's return once more to *Julius Caesar*.

Julius Caesar is perhaps the Shakespeare play that most explicitly addresses this link between chance and falling. It is a play about chance, about what happens (a word that incidentally and etymologically has also to do with falling) and what comes to pass. It is also a play about falling. The verb 'to fall' appears eleven times in the play, five of which are in the crucial first scene of the third act when the falling that is so central to the play occurs: the falling of Caesar ('*Et tu, Brute?* – Then fall, Caesar' [III, i, 77]). Like in *King Lear* or *Romeo and Juliet*, again there are letters (that fall through windows) and there is the falling to their knees of two adoring wives, and of the flattering and persuasive Cassius. Like in *Lear* in particular, there is again the pervasive fear of what may fall and befall: storms, death, dishonour and dreams. *Julius Caesar* is also a play about how what happens is dealt with, and most importantly for our purposes, it directly links whether or not a character is quick of hearing to his or her ability to make the most of the chance events that befall him. Although Shakespeare is fond of homophonic plays and links, Brutus' speech is free of them. Freud, indeed, does not dwell on the *Klang* of Brutus' speech or its formal and rhetorical properties. *Klang* or 'cadence' is rather used to describe the speech's and the dream's 'antithetical' structure, or the 'juxtaposition ... of two opposite reactions towards a single person, both of them claiming to be completely justified and yet not incompatible?'[78] Yet, from its very opening scene, which hinges on the Cobbler's homophonic puns, *Julius Caesar* is also play that repeatedly underlines the importance of hearing.

> MURELLUS You, sir, what trade are you?
>
> COBBLER Truly, sir, in respect of a fine workman, I am but as you would say, a cobbler.
>
> MURELLUS But what trade are thou? Answer me directly.
>
> COBBLER A trade, sir, that I hope I may use with a safe conscience, which is indeed, sir, a mender of bad soles.
>
> FLAVIUS What trade, thou knave? Though naughty knave, what trade?
>
> COBBLER Nay I beseech you, sir, be not out with me: yet if you be out, sir, I can mend you.
>
> MURELLUS What mean'st thou by that? Mend me, thou saucy fellow?
>
> COBBLER Why, sir, cobble you.
>
> FLAVIUS Thou art a cobbler, art thou?
>
> COBBLER Truly, sir, all that I live by, is with the awl: I meddle with no tradesman's matters, nor women's matters; but withal I am indeed, sir, a surgeon to old shoes; when they are in great danger, I recover them.
>
> (*Julius Caesar*, I, i, 9–25)

The wordplay snowballs. The initial pun hinging on the homonym 'cobbler' (meaning both a mender of shoes and a thief) slips into a homophonic pun of 'soles' and 'souls', later sliding into the quibble of 'to cobble' and 'to couple', ending in yet another homophonic pun between 'all' and 'awl'. Since the tribunes are unable to pick up the homophonic puns, the joke is on them. In the rest of the play a lack of aural discernment, however, has more wide-ranging repercussions. Shakespeare added deafness to Caesar's historically documented 'falling disease' or epilepsy. Caesar's partial deafness (manifesting itself especially in his unwillingness to lend an ear to the soothsayer and his wife's dream) is not only indicative of a reluctance to consider what concerns him personally, but is also indicative of an inability to have an open ear for events that befall the play, seemingly without reason, as if by chance. Although Caesar turns his good ear to the Soothsayer ('Caesar is turned to hear' [I, ii, 17]), he does not deem his warning 'Beware the Ides of March' (I, ii, 18) worthy of his serious attention: 'He is a dreamer. Let us leave him. Pass' (I, ii, 24). In contrast Cassius, the most cunning of the conspirators who at every turn well knows how to take his chances, is praised for having a good ear ('Your ear is good' [I, iii, 42]).

In light of Freud's supposed 'stunted acoustic sensibility', it is fascinating that Freud should use the word *Klang*, especially since he does not dwell on the aural nature of Brutus' speech, which is also quoted in the German translation and not in Shakespeare's English. At the same time, it is striking that Freud does not dwell longer on the sound-relations that are an important part of his dream's fabric. It is also interesting in light of the role of sound in the chances Derrida takes with Shakespeare (or perhaps which Shakespeare takes with Derrida), as well as Heidegger's avoidance of sound in 'Moira (Parmenides, VIII, 34–41)', which Derrida might have elaborated reading *King Lear* between the lines with Freud and Heidegger, but which he does not.

For Freud, the dream work also moves through sound. After one of their frequent fights from which uncharacteristically Freud had risen victorious, John 'hurried to his grandfather – my father – and complained about me, and I defended myself in the words which I know from my father's account: "I hit him 'cos he hit me"'.[79] As Freud remarked earlier, 'It must have been this scene from my childhood which diverted "*Non vivit*" into "*Non vixit*," for in the language of later childhood the word for to hit is "*wichsen*".'[80] In the language of earlier childhood, hitting is *schlagen*, or '*ge(sch) lagt*', as the child Freud cried, and not *wichsen*, which in some parts of the German-speaking world also denotes masturbation. Warner argues that the shift between *non vivit* and *non vixit* is motivated by the other signification of *wichsen* and its substitution for *ge(schl)agt*. Although I do not believe that Warner is wrong in detecting a significant sexual charge in Freud's relationship with John, and although the repressed memory of that episode with John only came back *nachträglich*, after that word *wichsen* had obtained a heightened signification for Freud during his teenage years (perhaps around that time when he played Brutus to John's Caesar), I am more interested in the partial homophony between *wichsen* and *vixit*, which seems to link a childhood scene (furthermore a scene Freud only knew through hearsay because he was too young to remember it himself) and his mixed feelings towards P.[81]

Although Freud mentions the partial homophony between *wichsen* and *vixit*, he protests (perhaps too much) that the clarity of the expression *non vixit* suggests that he had seen and not heard it (a claim seemingly corroborated by the fact that he misquotes the inscription, substituting via sense and not sound). In the interpretation of the '*Non Vixit* Dream', the aural component of the dream work is only half-heartedly gestured towards. Even though he is obviously intrigued by it, he merely dismisses the aural dimension of this by noting, almost apologetically, that 'the dream-work is not ashamed to make use of links such as this one'.[82] While Freud goes about unpicking this manifest content of his dream with his usual aplomb, and while he gives us many reasons for why he could have replaced a 'v' with an 'x', turning *non vivit* to *non vixit*, these do not seem to fully satisfy him – the rest of *Klang* remains unanalysed. Freud, in truth, has quite an acute ear for the workings of the psychic apparatus. Although he does not seem to want to give the partial homophony between *wichsen/vixit* great importance, he does turn to homophony with considerable interest when adding a footnote about a neurotic patient in the passage in which he distinguishes between dream thoughts and dream speech: 'I know a patient one of whose symptoms is that, involuntarily and against her will, she hears – i.e. hallucinates – songs or fragments of songs, without being able to understand what part they play in her mental life.'[83] The song '"*Leise, Leise, fromme Weise!*" [literally, "Softly, softly, devout melody"]' is, for instance, misheard as '"*Leise, Leise, fromme Waise*"', literally '"Softly, softly, pious orphan"'.[84] The unconscious takes advantage of the homophony between *Weise* and *Waise* and mishears in a significant manner: this mishearing, though of a haphazard nature, allows Freud, the reader, the analyst, to link it back to the fact that his patient is an orphan. The path leading the word *wichsen* to Freud's secondary revision of his dream is, despite his protestations to the contrary, aural: there is not only the significant *Klang* of *wichsen* in *vixit*, directly linking his ambivalent feelings for P. to his relationship with John, but the very story about his victory over John reaches Freud only through hearsay. And then there is the 'schw' sound connecting the strange sentence 'Das ist die Schwelle' to Fliess's sister, or *Schwester* in German, as well as the 'fl' sound that Fliess and Fleischl share. In the '*Non Vixit* Dream' the chance connections of *Klang* are crucial to Freud's interpretative process, yet he remains unwilling to acknowledge their importance. Freud's attitude towards the realm of sound seems to confirm Jones's depiction of a whimsical tyrant. When it suits his purpose he uses it, when it undermines it he turns a deaf ear. The *Klang* element is not only avoided because of Lipps but also because it is just in *Klang* that chance, that very element Freud is eager to subtract from his psychoanalytic discourse, seems to be most at work.

In his translation for the English Standard Edition of Freud's work, James Strachey mistakenly translates *Klang* with 'cadence', not with 'sound'. While Strachey's mistranslation to some extent echoes Freud's avoidance of *Klang*, I believe its significance to go deeper. His translation for *Klang* retains the aural aspect that Freud timidly gestures to, while offering a word – 'cadence' – that etymologically does not only comprise the aural aspect but also the idea of falling and, through that, of chance. Strachey's merit lies precisely in the fact that his translation renders the implicitness of sound and chance that Freud, like Heidegger, is trying to circumnavigate.

In contrast, Derrida could not be clearer in 'My Chances' that we often take our chances with literature with our ears. Let's return once more to its beginning:

> The 'things' that I throw, eject, project, or cast (*lance*) in your direction to come across to you fall, often and well enough, upon you, at least upon certain of those among you. The things with which I am bombarding you are linguistic or non-linguistic signs: words, sentences, sonorous and visual images, gestures, intonations, and hand signals.[85]

Although the aural seems to play only a marginal role in Derrida's piece he will repeatedly return to the 'sonorous images' he is alluding to here:

> For a while now, I have been speaking to you about chance [*du hazard*], but I do not speak haphazardly [*au hazard*]. Calculating my chances of reaching you through my speech [*parole*], I have above all spoken to you of speech.[86]

Derrida does not write *mot* but *parole*. The slight semantic difference between these words is crucial. For Derrida the chances of languages lie not only in *mot*, a fixed grouping of sounds corresponding to a meaning – in short, a word – but in the sounds, measure, flow and rhythm of *parole*, speech, that cannot be linked to only one signification.[87] With this differentiation in mind let us turn to Derrida's brief mention of the 'classical philological problem concerning the indeterminate reading of the word *voluptas* or *voluntas*' in Lucretius.[88] As with the change of a single letter between *vivit* and *vixit* in Freud's dream, the change of one letter between *voluntas* and *voluptas* can already provoke a *clinamen*. Derrida writes: 'The mere difference of a letter introduces a *clinamen* precisely when Lucretius is at the point of explaining the extent to which the *clinamen* is the condition of the freedom and will or voluptuous pleasure that has been wrested from destiny.'[89] As the subtitle for 'My Chances' – 'Some Epicurean Stereophonies' – suggests, Derrida, however, understands the slip from *voluntas* to *voluptas* not as a slip of the pen but as a slip of the ear. According to the *Oxford English Dictionary*, stereophony denotes 'sound recording and reproduction using two of more channels so that the reproduced sound seems to surround the listener and to come from more than one source'. For Derrida, the indecision around whether Lucretius' text reads *voluntas* or *voluptas* creates an Epicurean stereophony, because due to the logic of the mark, the possibilities of both letters 'n' and 'p' always ring in the other, because both meanings, though following or falling through two different channels of reading, are simultaneously present in the text.

It is, I believe, this location of the *clinamen* in the ear, as well as Derrida's insistence on *parole* rather than *mot*, that invites us to re-examine Freud's double avoidance of *Klang* and chance and infer that perhaps there is a greater correlation between *Klang* and chance in the dream work and his use of Shakespeare in the interpretation of his dream than he is willing to acknowledge. We know that the link Freud makes to Shakespeare, even if it was aleatory in the first place, is soon subsumed in Freud's strategy to attain mastery over the psychoanalytic discourse. As I have shown, however, the mention of Shakespeare has kicked off a mechanism far beyond the reach of the kind of mastery Freud might have aspired to.

It would be impossible to understand Derrida's contribution to the relationship between philosophy and Shakespeare, and thinking more in general, without taking Derrida's challenge to our traditional understanding of the reader as master seriously. In *Without Mastery*, Sarah Wood remarkably 'tak[es] seriously' Derrida's 'proposal' that 'the trace is the erasure of selfhood, of one's own presence, and is constituted by the threat or anguish of its own irremediable disappearance, of the disappearance of its disappearance'.[90] This is the sort of mastery that concerns Derrida here: the mastery of the text itself, the mastery of unselfing. Taking Derrida's proposal of the erasure of selfhood seriously would also mean letting go of, for example, Bloom's notion of Shakespeare's omniscient genius, his invention of the human and consequent sublimation of the human self and its potentialities. It is significant that, when Derrida chooses a figure – and very often he does not (remember the trajectory of an arrow, the rhythm of frequencies) – to think about the genius of a great literary work, it is nothing at all pompous, certain, or even entirely present: the humble *hérisson*, the punctuating voice of a spectre. The way Derrida reads and writes is not, as Nussbaum suggests in relation to Butler, an attempt to rule by obfuscation. It is quite the opposite: an attempt at radical unselfing, a total capitulation and surrender to the uncanny mastery, the genius even, of reading itself.

Notes

1. Jacques Derrida, 'My Chances/*Mes Chances*: A Rendezvous with Some Epicurean Stereophonies', in *Taking Chances: Derrida, Psychoanalysis, and Literature*, ed. Joseph H. Smith and William Kerrigan (Baltimore and London: Johns Hopkins University Press, 1984), 29.

2. Ibid. 14.
3. Alan R. Young, 'Fortune in Shakespeare's *King Lear*', in *Fortune: 'All is but Fortune'*, ed. Leslie Thomson (Washington, DC: The Folger Shakespeare Library, 2000), 59.
4. Werner Gundersheimer, 'Foreword', in *Fortune: 'All is but Fortune'*, ed. Leslie Thomson (Washington, DC: The Folger Shakespeare Library, 2000), 7.
5. Young, 'Fortune in Shakespeare's *King Lear*', 59.
6. Ibid. 57.
7. Paul A. Cantor, 'The Cause of Thunder: Nature and Justice in *King Lear*', in *King Lear: New Critical Essays*, ed. Jeffrey Kahan (New York and London: Routledge, 2008), 232.
8. Ibid. 232.
9. Sigmund Freud, 'The Theme of the Three Caskets', in *The Standard Edition of the Complete Psychological Works of Sigmund Freud*, vol. XII, trans. and ed. James Strachey (London: The Hogarth Press, 1995), 291.
10. Ibid. 292.
11. Ibid. 292.
12. Ibid. 292.
13. Ibid. 292.
14. Ibid. 292.
15. Ibid. 294.
16. Ibid. 295.
17. Ibid. 295.
18. Ibid. 296.
19. Ibid. 299.
20. Ibid. 298–9.
21. Derrida, 'My Chances', 29.
22. Ibid. 9.
23. Ibid. 29.
24. David Farrell Krell, 'Introduction', in *Early Greek Thinking*, trans. David Farrell Krell and Frank A. Capuzzi (New York: Harper & Row, 1975), 5–6.
25. Martin Heidegger, 'Moira: Parmenides VIII, 34–41', in *Early Greek Thinking*, trans. David Farrell Krell and Frank A. Capuzzi (New York: Harper & Row, 1975), 89–90.

26. Ibid. 91.
27. Ibid. 91.
28. Ibid. 93.
29. Derrida, 'My Chances', 29.
30. Ibid. 29.
31. Sigmund Freud, *Die Traumdeutung* (Leipzig: Franz Deuticke, 1930), 287; Sigmund Freud, 'The Interpretation of Dreams', in *The Standard Edition of the Complete Psychological Works of Sigmund Freud*, vol. V, trans. and ed. James Strachey (London: The Hogarth Press, 1995), 421.
32. Freud, *Interpretation of Dreams*, 421.
33. Ibid. 421.
34. Ibid. 422.
35. Ibid. 422.
36. Ibid. 422.
37. Ibid. 423.
38. Ibid. 480.
39. Ibid. 481.
40. Ibid. 423.
41. Ibid. 484.
42. Ibid. 481.
43. Ibid. 482.
44. Ibid. 424.
45. William Beatty Warner, *Chance and the Text of Experience: Freud, Nietzsche, and Shakespeare's* Hamlet (Ithaca and London: Cornell University Press, 1986), 56.
46. Ibid. 44.
47. Friedrich Schiller and Christiam Gottfried Körner, *Correspondence of Schiller with Körner, Comprising Sketches and Anecdotes of Goethe, the Schlegels, Wieland, and Other Contemporaries* (London: Richard Bentley, 1849), 330.
48. Michael Mann, *Sturm-und-Drang-Drama: Studien und Vorstudien zu Schiller's 'Räubern'* (Bern und Munich: Francke Verlag, 1974), 107.
49. Freud, *Traumdeutung*, 289; Freud, *Interpretation*, 423.
50. Ernest Jones, *Sigmund Freud: Life and Work*, 3 vols (London: Hogarth Press, 1953–7), 411–12.

51. Francesco Barale and Vera Minazzi, 'Off the Beaten Track: Freud, Sound and Music. Statement of a Problem and Some Historico-Critical Notes', *The International Journal of Psycho-analysis*, 89 (2008): 943.
52. Ibid. 943.
53. Ibid. 943.
54. Sigmund Freud, *The Origins of Psycho-Analysis: Letters to Wilhelm Fliess, Drafts and Notes: 1887–1902*, ed. Marie Bonaparte, Anna Freud and Ernst Kris, trans. Eric Mosbacher and James Strachey (London: Imago, 1954), 262–3.
55. Theodor Lipps, *Grundtatsachen des Seelenlebens* (Bonn: Verlag von Max und Cohen & Sohn (Fr.Cohen), 1883), 240.
56. Francesco Barale and Vera Minazzi, 'Off the Beaten Track: Freud, Sound and Music', 944.
57. Ibid. 944.
58. Lipps, *Grundtatsachen des Seelenlebens*, 242, 268.
59. Barale and Minazzi, 'Off the Beaten Track: Freud, Sound and Music', 937.
60. Marjorie Garber, *Shakespeare after All* (New York: Anchor Books, 2004), 414.
61. Nicholas Royle, *In Memory of Jacques Derrida* (Edinburgh: Edinburgh University Press, 2009), 148.
62. Derrida, 'My Chances', 14.
63. Ibid. 16.
64. Ibid. 7.
65. Ibid. 5.
66. Ibid. 7.
67. Ibid. 10.
68. Freud, 'Leonardo da Vinci and a Memory of His Childhood', in *The Standard Edition of the Complete Psychological Works of Sigmund Freud*, trans. and ed. James Strachey, vol. XI (London: The Hogarth Press, 1995), 136.
69. Ibid. 136–7.
70. Ibid. 137.
71. Derrida, 'My Chances', 23.
72. Ibid. 24.
73. Ibid. 28.

74. Ibid. 28.
75. Ibid. 16.
76. Ibid. 28.
77. Ibid. 29.
78. Freud, 'The Interpretation of Dreams', 424.
79. Ibid. 484.
80. Ibid. 425.
81. Warner, *Chance and the Text of Experience*, 61.
82. Freud, 'The Interpretation of Dreams', 425.
83. Ibid. 418–19.
84. Ibid. 419.
85. Derrida, 'My Chances', 3.
86. Ibid. 4.
87. Ibid. 4.
88. Ibid. 7.
89. Ibid. 7.
90. Sarah Wood, *Without Mastery: Reading and Other Forces* (Edinburgh: Edinburgh University Press, 2014), 5–6; Jacques Derrida, 'Freud and the Scene of Writing', in *Writing and Difference*, trans. Alan Bass (London: Routledge, 2001), 289.

CHAPTER 6

THE POLITICS OF RE-READING

Political Aporias

Among Derrida's texts on Shakespeare, *Specters of Marx* has attracted by far the most interest, albeit more for the fact that it is considered to be Derrida's most overtly 'political' book than because it is a book that closely engages with Shakespeare. Derrida tackled overtly political themes in the last two decades of his life. It would, nonetheless, be wrong to speak of a political turn in Derrida's work, as his readings of Shakespeare show. As I will argue, what is often called the 'political' dimension of his work is intrinsic to and present in it from the very beginning under the guises of a performance of and meditation on what reading can do.

In 1993, when it seemed that Marxism had once and for all been consigned to history, Derrida argued not only that Marxism was and would never be quite gone, but also confessed his indebtedness to a certain spirit or spectre of Marx. The striking image Marx and Engel's chose to open their 1848 *Manifesto of the Communist Party* ('A spectre is haunting Europe – the spectre of communism') thus becomes occasion for Derrida to suggest that there is something essentially spectral about Marxism. Like Shakespeare, indeed like any other 'signature', Marx is subject to the twinned movements of *différance* and iteration and welcomes, even demands, the incalculable event of reading and of countersigning, singularily. There could, in this sense, perhaps not be anything more political than reading and thus countersigning Marx, or indeed Shakespeare or Celan or any other *génie*. As Simon Morgan Wortham suggests, it is in this injunction to inherit and to choose one, singular response here and now that Derrida locates 'the possibility of justice in radical excess of existing apparatuses of law, morality, duty or right'.[1] He continues: 'in its profound affirmation of an unprogrammable justice always remaining possible in the "here-now", deconstruction inherits a certain spirit of Marx, a certain messianic remains'.[2]

For many of its left-leaning critics, *Specters of Marx* chartered an impassable political route, no doubt also because this characterisation of a haunting and iterable Marx does in fact not amount to a backing of Marxism, or in fact any '-ism'. Derrida's very notion of the spectre – sharing, as we shall see, certain moves or movements with *différance and* trace *and* supplement *and* the remaining chain of quasi-synonymous terms around which Derrida's work organises itself – resists any linear or teleological account of history, whether it works towards the crowning or ousting of a political system. As such, what makes *Specters* so remarkable is perhaps the fact that, although it is an intensely political book, it does not offer passage (*poros*) to a political stance; Derridean political discourse remains aporetic (*a-poros*, without passage).

For many, such aporetic politics amount to a betrayal, even a bastardisation, of Marx. *Specters*' immediate wake was indeed filled with impassioned critical responses, defending Marx and finding fault with Derrida's reading. Many Marxists critical of what Derrida seemed to be doing in *Specters* took to the stage in a symposium published in 1999 as *Ghostly Demarcations: A Symposium on Jacques*

Derrida's Specters of Marx. Among Derrida's critics were Terry Eagleton and Aijaz Ahmad, both of whom took the literary nature of Derrida's reading of Marx in particular – understood here not merely as his reading of Marx with *Hamlet*, but also as the emphasis of the political and ethical potentialities of the act of reading itself – at best as a sign of political timidity, and at worst as pseudo-intellectual escapism from the strictures of 'real' political engagement. Eagleton's 'Marxism without Marxism' begins with the backhanded compliment that, although Derrida 'has always been a man of the Left', he is so 'in some suitably indeterminate sense'.[3] In contrast to the 'genuine radical' whose 'hearty desire' is 'to stop having to be so obdurately oppositional', Derrida is characterised here as 'an exasperating kind of believer who holds what he does until he meets someone else who holds the same'.[4] For Eagleton, Derrida only reaps Marxism's negative lessons, its critique, its questioning, leaving its 'positivity', its political actualities to Marxists like Eagleton himself. Starting from a single-minded idea of what political engagement is and can be, Eagleton concludes that Derrida's 'curiously empty, formalistic messianism' does not amount to an 'effective socialism', but merely remains an

> ultimate poststructuralist fantasy . . . a dissent beyond all formulable discourse, a promise which would betray itself in the act of fulfilment, a perpetual excited openness to the Messiah who had better not let us down by doing anything as determinate as coming.[5]

Ahmed argues along the same lines in lambasting Derrida's '*messianic* tonal register' as not merely politically ineffective but in fact nefarious.[6] Like in Nussbaum's critique of Butler, discussed in Chapter 2, here 'poststructuralist fantasy' and all its stylistic and argumentative hallmarks and its attention to the performativity of writing and reading are seen to stand in the way of political commitment, whether it be to feminism or Marxism:

> Feminist thinkers of the new symbolic type would appear to believe that the way to do feminist politics is to use words in a subversive way, in academic publications of lofty obscurity and disdainful abstractness. These symbolic gestures, it is believed, are themselves a form of political resistance; and so one need not engage with messy things such as legislatures and movements in order to act daringly.[7]

Parallel to this, we might say that Eagleton's critique aims at Marxist of the new symbolic type who believe that doing fancy things to words is in itself political resistance. We could then add a third meaning of Nussbaum's charge of 'bloodlessness': a squeamish reluctance to get involved in politics in a manner, which might actually bring about change.

A politics which would be 'less bloodless' would, however, also be a politics of the bloodline, of tribalism and of the exclusions this entails. In 'Ghostwriting', Gayatri Chakravorty Spivak strikes a particularly proprietorial note. At the beginning of her piece, Spivak admits that she has 'always had trouble with Derrida on Marx'; according to a friend of hers, it is 'maybe because [she] feel[s] proprietorial about Marx'.[8] Like Eagleton and Ahmed, Spivak feels that 'the ghost of Marx that Derrida is most haunted by returns to the bosom of Abraham, shorn of all specificity, mark of a messianism without content, carrier of merely the structure of a promise which cancels the difference between democracy and Marxism'.[9] Here, like in Eagleton's or Ahmed's response, Derrida's 'politics' is judged by its adherence to *their* Marx. Indeed, these pieces clarify just how strong the link between the two dominant themes of politics and inheritance in late Derrida are. For Samir Haddad, in fact, Derrida's 'democracy to come' cannot be separated from a particular understanding of inheritance, which I believe is markedly different from the kind of jealous propriety displayed in Spivak.[10]

It would be just as inaccurate to speak of a Derridean politics, as it would be to talk about a political turn in Derrida. What is present in his oeuvre from the beginning – the radical responsiveness which constitutes his way of approaching texts, problems or questions – is the same thing that makes the extrapolation of a generalised politics from his work as a whole impossible. The positing of a political programme, perhaps like the one Eagleton, Ahmed or Spivak miss in *Specters*, would, for Derrida, in fact be a profoundly apolitical gesture. As Geoffrey Bennington writes reviewing Michael Ryan's *Marxism and Deconstruction: A Critical Articulation* (which incidentally predated *Specters*) paradoxically the 'very insistence on a given notion of the political' can limit political efficacy.[11] If what they seek is political tribalism Eagleton, Ahmed and Spivak are right to criticise Derrida's reading of Marx. Deconstruction is incompatible with the mechanisms of identification, annexation and exclusion that underpin such tribalism. In *Legislations*, Bennington notes that in their criticisms of deconstruction authors such as Ryan or Eagleton (Bennington speaks of his *Criticism and Ideology*) 'appeal . . . to the concepts of "history" and/or "politics"', which in their texts ultimately work as 'uncriticized and uncritical transcendental terms'.[12] It is a tautological move: history and politics are called upon to criticise deconstruction on the grounds that it 'does not accept the transcendental concepts of history and politics invoked against it'.[13] Criticising deconstruction for not subscribing to a particular understanding of 'politics' or 'history' has no real bite, because 'the effort of deconstruction is precisely to question just such transcendental concepts, and more generally the transcendental position in itself'.[14] Furthermore, calling on transcendental terms such as '(a) politics' or '(a) history' would precisely hinder their event. As Bennington shows throughout *Legislations*

> This attempt to enforce institutionalised rules (and there is no suggestion here that institutions and therefore rules are Bad Things, or could ever be simply avoided), even if it be done in the name of revolution (and more especially 'the' revolution) is fundamentally reactionary, and therefore profoundly anti-political, because it forecloses the possibility that the other be a legislator, and that possibility just is the possibility of the political as such.[15]

If deconstruction can speak politics at all, it can only do so, to quote Bennington again, 'improperly' by 'nam[ing] the impropriety of the political in its dispersion'.[16] For Derrida, politics happens not in the comfort of a settled, pre-existing position; it may also not happen in opposition, but in a-position, in other words in that space which belongs to no one, not even Marx. The apoliticality and apositionality that his critics decry is thus precisely where Derrida locates his most significant 'political' move.

If *Specters* presents the reader with an aporetic political discourse – in other words, a political discourse that does not allow passage to a position, a manifesto or a party – it does so not to thwart but to enable action in the political sphere. There is an important difference between what one might call Derrida's politics and his commitment to a 'democracy to come'. While one's politics may be understood as the inheritance of and subscription to a position (a process inextricable from questions of identity, belonging, legacy and legitimacy), the 'democracy to come' is dependent on an ability to eschew this type of thinking in favour of a commitment to an absolute and impossible responsiveness, and hence also to a radical a-positionality. In Derrida, then, rather than an aporetic politics, a politics of inaction, there is a politics of aporia, or a politics of absolute openness and responsiveness that never settles into a position, which would not survive the specific readerly encounter it arises from. It is this centrality of responsiveness that connects the politics of aporia and the act of reading in Derrida.

To read, to respond to the singular with a countersignature of one's own is not to evade political commitment but to turn towards it. For Derrida '*re*-politicisation' always means a *re*-reading which, inverting Feuerbach's eleventh thesis, posits that philosophers can change the world *because* they can interpret it. Indeed, central to Derrida's reading of Marx is 'an interpretation that transforms the very thing it interprets'.[17] Such performative acts of reading cannot lead towards the formulation of political action; they rather posit the New International as 'an inoperative community of transformative interpretation'.[18] Therefore, at the heart of Derrida's understanding of repoliticisation as re-reading lies the Derridean paradox that, as Bennington writes, 'theorising and interpretation are structurally interminable and can *never* prepare for the interruptive and precipitate moment of decision and action, but that the decisiveness of the decision depends none the less on its structural relation to interminable analysis'.[19] It is for this reason that we cannot grasp *Specters*' political import if we do not understand it primarily as an act of reading, or rather re-reading. What is, in this sense, perhaps the most astonishing feature of many critical responses to *Specters* is that the vast majority of scholars seem to ignore or misunderstand the role Shakespeare plays in this text. Neither Eagleton, Ahmed nor Spivak give a satisfactory account of what Shakespeare is doing in *Specters* and this is one of the reasons why they misinterpret Derrida's project. Like in Keston, Sutherland's *Stupefaction* – which portrays the relationship between Derrida and Marx as largely adversarial – here a misreading of what Derrida is doing with Marx, is linked to a blindness to what Shakespeare is doing in *Specters*, indeed what, as I have shown in Chapter 4, Shakespeare is doing to some of Marx's own texts.[20]

Shakespeare also gets short shrift in sympathetic readings of *Specters*, for example Ernesto Laclau's 'The Time is Out of Joint' and Christopher Prendergast's 'Derrida's Hamlet'. Laclau rightly argues that 'the logic of the specter (the hauntology)' cannot be separated from 'the category of messianism'.[21] In other words, 'the messianism we are speaking about', the one 'without eschatology, without pregiven promised land, without determinate content', is dependent on a thinking of hauntology as what fissures the present, 'resulting from the radical opening to the event, to the other', which in turn is 'the very possibility of justice'.[22] Like Laclau, Prendergast recognises the two interconnected, deep-structural, and persistently recurring preoccupations of deconstruction: ontology (the philosophy of Being) and justice (the sphere of the politico-ethical).[23] But although Prendergast asks the right questions – 'What is Hamlet doing in a book about Marx and ghosts (...)?' – like Laclau, he does not really engage with the subject.[24] Laclau's and Prendergast's readings are representative of most good criticism on *Specters* in that, although they acknowledge the opening of 'the very possibility of justice' in Derrida's reading of Marx they do not explicitly link its dependence on a certain thinking of hauntology to the way Shakespeare haunts Marx in Derrida's text.[25] Put differently, the question of how Shakespeare is imbricated in the hauntological textuality *Specters* describes – a textual hauntology Prendergast aims at with this question: 'How is it that Derrida, citing an essay by Blanchot, in which Blanchot uses the expression "since Marx," can add that Blanchot's "since Marx" could easily have been "since Shakespeare"?' – is never broached.[26]

A Finer Ear

Understanding what the act of reading entails and what it demands for Derrida is key to fathoming the 'political' wisdom of *Specters*. Derrida in fact rebukes his critics by highlighting their failure to appreciate the importance of reading. In 'Marx & Sons', Derrida's response to *Ghostly Demarcations*, Ahmed is, for example, criticised for being too cavalier in his admission that he only read *Specters* on his flight to Ljubljana a day before giving his response.[27] He also points out that some of Spivak's 'errors stem from an outright inability to read, exacerbated here by the wounded resentment of her "proprietoriality about Marx"'.[28] Derrida illustrates this with Spivak's misreading of 'there will be no re-politicization, there will be no politics otherwise' as 'We won't repoliticize!'[29] What is at stake here for Derrida is not only a lack of attention in reading, as well as a complete misunderstanding of his idea of political commitment, but more importantly how they are connected.

In 'Marx & Sons', Derrida understands the failure to engage in an appropriate act of reading *Specters* in terms of an aural insensitivity. For Derrida, 'Ahmed is as insensitive as Eagleton to variations of tone' in this text.[30] Here he means, of course, 'the irony and humor that [he is] fond of cultivating in all [his] texts'.[31] But Derrida's reference to tone also goes beyond this. As he suggests a moment earlier, in order to understand *Specters*' 're-politicization' we would have to be able to truly listen to its 'tone', which would mean obtaining 'a slightly more elaborate concept of tone, of its fusion with concept, meaning and . . . performativity'.[32] One must therefore have 'a finer ear for the differential, unstable, shifting qualities of a tone – for example, the tonal value that signal irony or play, even at the most serious moments, and always in passages where the tone is, precisely, inseparable from the content'.[33] One must therefore have a 'finer ear' for the differential tones that shift and destabilise what Derrida does with Marx beyond sudden register changes, precisely in those moments when tonal vibrations become constitutive of, and thus, inseparable from the content. This is to say that I read this criticism of Ahmed's and Eagleton's hardness of hearing as an indication that, to borrow Bennington's term, the 'interminable analysis' of the act of reading and re-reading must be understood in terms of hearing.[34] That in order to understand what Derrida does with Marx we must listen to the 'differential vibrations of a tone' in *Specters of Marx*, which resonate in the space between Derrida's reading of Marx and his reading of *Hamlet*.[35]

Sound is important in Derrida's acts of reading Shakespeare. 'Aphorism Countertime', for instance, plays on the double meaning of contretemps, which, in French, can also mean 'syncopation' or 'being "out of time"'.[36] No love, of either man or text, then, without syncopation, without the missing beat of a rhythm. A similarly aural vocable resonates in Derrida's affirmation that there would have been neither Romeo and Juliet's love, nor its theatre, without the 'discordance' of contretemps.[37] In French, just as in English, *discordance* means both difference and conflict, as well as musical discord, understood as a 'lack of harmony between notes sounding together', or 'a chord which is regarded as displeasing or requiring resolution by another', more specifically 'any interval except unison, an octave, a perfect fifth or fourth, a major or minor third and sixth, or their octaves' (*OED*).

Derrida's relationship to sound is complex. In 'The Spatial Arts', an interview with Peter Brunette and David Wills, Derrida admits to his love for words, his way of making them 'explode so that the nonverbal appears in the verbal', that is to say his way of using words so 'that at a certain moment they no longer belong to discourse, to what regulates discourse – hence the homonyms, the fragmented words, the proper names that do not essentially belong to language'.[38] Indeed, if Derrida loves words, 'it is also because of their ability to escape their proper form, whether they interest me as visible things, letters representing the spatial visibility of the word, or as something musical or audible'.[39] Derrida continues:

> I rarely have my breath taken away by a painting. On the other hand, that does sometimes happen with music or when I hear the spoken word or read texts – by listening to the voice, that is – and it often happens in the cinema, but only to the extent that it comes from what works through the voice as desire [*ce qui dans le désir travaille la voix*].[40]

'Music' is, Derrida confesses, 'the object of my strongest desire, and yet at the same time it remains completely forbidden', perhaps because of the fact that he does not have 'any truly presentable musical culture'.[41] As Marcel Cobussen remarks, Derrida is concerned with 'the idea that texts, either spoken or written, are marked by a certain (non-sonorous) tone, or better, a multitude of (non-sonorous) tones'. As Cobussen points out, this does not mean that he 'pay[s] no attention to sonority, sound, music'. As I have shown in the preceding chapters, homophones or the reverberations of *syllabes* and *lettres* are a crucial part of Derrida's acts of reading. Cobussen, in fact, notes that 'his play with words, his fascination for the materiality of words, the working of dissemination is certainly also influenced by their sounds, their audibility'.[42]

Derrida's love for words is related to what in 'The Spatial Arts' he calls his 'paralyzed' desire for music; it is a desire not for music as an independent art form, but rather for something music-like that he recognises in the 'nondiscursive sonority' of words.[43] The porpentine – the figure through which I thought about what role Shakespeare's English plays in Derrida's French in Chapter 4 – is itself silent, although it opens up the question of the role of sound in inter- and intratextual translation and reading. Indeed, in *Hamlet*, the porpentine does not actually hear; rather, it trembles for fear of hearing. In Derrida's text, too, the *hérisson*/porpentine, as already noted, balances on the edge of hearing. Like *Hamlet*'s porpentine, the *hérisson* is 'a silent incantation', an 'aphonic wound'.[44] The *hérisson*, Derrida writes in 'Che cos'è la poesia?', is blind but listens for death's arrival. Death is in earshot, but these things are not for 'ears of flesh and blood' to hear. Our porpentine is not listening, not yet, or not actually. The musical analogy does not aim at presentness, however momentary it may be, but rather at an absence: not something that creates sound, but something that lets the other's sound resonate. (Remember, the porpentine is armed with teleiopoetic arrows.)

Derrida's concern with the aural is thus twofold: he is not only interested in what ears can pick up, but also in how the act of listening can figuratively represent his acts of reading. Sound must be understood both materially and, to anticipate one of Cixous's terms, 'philosophonically'.[45] In Derrida's readings of Shakespeare, the ear not only picks up homophonies and syllables that alloy and forge new connections and new meanings; it also hears the spacing of the mark or trace, in other words, *différance*. Musical or aural analogies therefore also trace the relationship between text and reader. We must, therefore, listen not merely to the syllabic travel of the idiom, its *lettre* or *parole* and its inter- and intratextual reverberations, but also to the interminable and indeterminable resonances and echoes the 'differential, unstable, shifting qualities of tone' effect in the resonant space between text and reader, between Shakespeare, Marx and Derrida and between *Specters* and us.

Frequencies – Listening to Hamlet's Ghost

Derrida's insistence on a certain auricular sensitivity when criticising Ahmed is striking because *Specters* is a remarkably clairaudient text. In fact, quite often in Derrida's writing on Shakespeare, we are asked to sharpen our philosophical ears by the onset of penumbra or darkness. Let us listen, for example, into the dark of the balcony scene in 'Aphorism Countertime'. Juliet is here speaking 'in the night, and there is nothing to assure her that she is addressing Romeo himself, present in person'.[46] Everything revolves around the setting of this reading scene – in the dark and in the night. Derrida writes:

> 20. Night. Everything that happens at night, for Romeo and Juliet, is decided rather in the penumbra, between night and day. The indecision between Romeo and the bearer of this name, between 'Romeo,' the name of Romeo and Romeo himself. Theater, we say, is visibility, the stage [*la scène*]. This drama belongs to the night because it stages what is not seen, the name; it stages what one calls because one cannot see or because one is not certain of seeing what one calls. Theater of the name, theater of the night. The name calls beyond presence, phenomenon, light, beyond the day, beyond the theatre. It keeps – whence the mourning and survival – what is no longer present, the invisible: what from now on will no longer see the light of day.[47]

Listen closely to what Derrida is saying. The night, and Romeo's subsequent stepping into the 'penumbra' where Juliet can see him, illustrates the 'indecision between Romeo and the bearer of this name'. Derrida is here, of course, referring to the scene's context, but Juliet's location in the dark on the balcony, addressing these words perhaps to nobody but the darkness, is also representative of what, for Derrida, happens whenever we call somebody, perhaps a loved one, by their name, which he bears (*porte*) despite himself: 'Roméo et Juliette portent ces noms. Ils les portent, les supportent même s'ils ne veulent pas les assumer.'[48] Here the dark and the night illustrate and illuminate 'the lack of distinction between the name and the bearer of the name'.[49] For the moment, Derrida notes, Romeo, who is lingering somewhere in the darkness, in the shadow, is not sure whether he should 'take her at her word', which would mean 'committing himself to disowning his name', and decides, for the time being 'to wait and carry on listening'.[50] As Juliet cannot see him, he who is 'bescreen'd in night' (II, ii, 52), and as her 'ears have yet not drunk a hundred words' (II, ii, 58) uttered by his voice, she too must listen to him. Not being able to see him, in the night, Juliet, as Derrida puts it, '*identifies* him on the one hand by the timbre of his voice, that is to say by the words she hears without being able to see'.[51]

What voice is Juliet listening to in this darkness?[52] 'Speaking to the one she loves within herself and outside herself, in the half-light, Juliet murmurs the most implacable analysis of the name. Of the name and the proper name.'[53] For Derrida, her analysis 'is implacable for it announces or denounces the inhumanity or the ahumanity of the name'.[54] For Juliet, 'a proper name does not name anything which is human, which belongs to a human body, a human spirit, an essence of man'.[55] As Derrida paraphrases: 'Romeo *himself*, the bearer of the name is not the name, it is *Romeo*, the name which he bears.'[56] All Juliet hears in *Romeo* are names, and 'the circle of all these names in o: *words, Romeo, words, love*'.[57] Juliet's recognition of Romeo is not dependent on the recognition of a voice that is present to itself, rather, it is dependent on a voice that speaks because it denounces itself, because it is what it is. He is listening for something disembodied, something altogether louder, but more difficult to hear; he is listening for what in *Paper Machine* he calls 'a trace' that is 'never present, fully present, by definition', but that 'inscribes in itself the reference to the specter of something else'.[58] He is, in other words, listening for spectral or spectred voices.

When Derrida claims that *Romeo and Juliet* is a 'theater of the night', he is also saying that, in staging the name, 'it stages what one calls because one cannot see or because one is not certain of seeing what one calls'.[59] *Specters of Marx*, too, is about the night. Indeed in the 'Exordium', Derrida writes that *Specters* 'advances like an essay in the night – into the unknown of that which must remain to come'.[60] For Royle, 'Derrida's published texts on Shakespeare are night letters of a sort, essays about *the night*.'[61] When Derrida writes that Shakespeare is the theatre of the night, he is, however, not only saying that the plays are about the night, but that they themselves are *of* the night. 'Theater', Derrida writes, 'is visibility, the stage [*la scène*].'[62] But this theatre stages what belongs to the night, what cannot be seen. This theatre is about the name as what 'calls beyond presence, phenomenon, light, beyond the day, beyond the theatre'.[63] When Derrida therefore writes that *Specters* advances like an essay in the night, he is also saying that he advances with his ears.

Nancy is perhaps the thinker of 'deconstruction' who has dwelt most upon the *philosophical ear*, arguing that 'the visual persists until its disappearance; the sonorous appears and fades away into its permanence'.[64] Like Derrida, Nancy understands the process of listening as reaching beyond presence or *Dasein*:

> To be listening is thus to enter into tension and to be on the lookout for a relation to self: *not*, it should be emphasized, a relationship to 'me' (the supposedly given subject), or the 'self' of the other (the speaker, the musician, also supposedly given, with his subjectivity), but to the *relationship in self*, so to speak, as it forms a 'self' or a 'to itself' in general,

and if something like that ever does reach the end of its formation. Consequently, listening is passing over to the register of presence to self, it being understood that the 'self' is precisely nothing available (substantial or subsistent) to which one can be 'present,' but precisely the resonance of a return [*renvoi*].[65]

Although Nancy at no point mentions Derrida or, indeed, frequencies, the terms he uses to speak about the sonorous are strikingly similar. Nancy matches frequency's waves, cycles, periods and rhythm, with 'amplitude', 'density', 'vibration' and 'undulation'.[66] Like Nancy's resonance, frequencies allow us to make sense of the musical analogy and most importantly of the moment of silence, caesura or rhythm encased in it. As Cobussen notes, 'Derrida's ear develops into an organ that needs to train itself in receiving the unpredictable, the uncanny, the "unheard".'[67] Here is Derrida again in 'The Spatial Arts':

> It has something to do with tone, timbre, voice, something to do with the voice – because contrary to the nonsense that circulates in this regard, nothing interests me more than the voice, more precisely the nondiscursive voice, but the voice all the same.[68]

Speech and Phenomena, his critique of what Morgan Wortham calls Husserl's desire to 'understand the expressive and logical purity of meaning in terms of logos', and to understand logos as a self-given meaning, does not banish voice from philosophy, but rediscovers it for its use.[69] Husserl's phenomenological project, Derrida argues in *Speech and Phenomena*, is founded on the assumption that this self-presence can then be transposed, so to speak, to the voice: 'my words are "alive" because they seem not to leave me: not to fall outside me, outside my breath'.[70] Voice and speech give themselves out in this manner, because '*I hear myself* [je m'entende] *at the same time that* I speak.' 'The signifier,' Derrida continues, 'animated by my breath and by the meaning-intention ... is in absolute proximity to me.'[71] For Husserl, meaning can be self-present, because it can be present to the self, in a manner which is unmediated by signs: 'if "mental acts" are not announced to themselves through the intermediary of a "*Kundgabe*," if they do not have to be informed about themselves through the intermediary of indications, it is because they are "lived by us in the same instant" *(im selben Augenblick)*'.[72] Although Husserl uses a visual metaphor of the *Augenblick*, this blink of an eye is also to be understood as a caesura, a moment of silence. For Husserl, meaning can be present, because the 'relationship to self' is absolutely silent: 'expressive language itself would be something supervenient upon the absolute silence of self-relationship'.[73] In Bennington's paraphrase: 'the internal voice with which I express myself to myself in the *silent* selfpresence of my consciousness preserves meaning in its purity, with respect to which all the forms of indication must be considered as secondary and derivative'.[74] Husserl's 'phonocentrism' – the 'unfailing complicity here between idealization and speech [*voix*]' – is paradoxically founded on a silencing of voice, and Derrida's critique depends to some extent on making this voice and its 'silence' heard.[75]

This then is what is signalled by Derrida's night writing and reading in *Specters*. He listens to Shakespeare in the dark because he wants to make that other spectral voice, that voice which is so important for his understanding of the to come, heard. Let us listen then to the way Derrida listens to *Hamlet*. In *Hamlet*, Derrida writes in *Specters of Marx*, 'everything begins by the apparition of a specter'.[76] He immediately qualifies. In *Hamlet* everything begins 'by the *waiting* for this apparition'.[77] 'The anticipation is at once impatient, anxious and fascinated: this, the thing ("this thing") will end up coming. The *revenant* is going to come. It won't be long.

But how long it is taking.'[78] I will qualify even further: in *Hamlet*, everything begins with waiting to *hear*. From the very beginning of *Hamlet* something ghostly happens to our ears. If Shakespeare '*wrote for sound*', as Bruce Johnson has argued in '*Hamlet*: Voice, Music, Sound', then *Hamlet* is a 'noisy play'.[79] This noise is not only produced by 'around a dozen heraldic flourishes involving trumpets, drums and ordnance' and 'instrumental and vocal music' but also 'includes references to the voice and hearing, and vocalisation which is purely sonic rather than lexical', as well as sounds which are 'acousmatic' or 'acousmêtric', in other words, sounds which have 'no visible source'.[80] *Hamlet* begins with an example of such an acousmatic effect: 'it begins with disembodied voices in the darkness'.[81] For Johnson, moments such as these not only pose unsettling epistemological questions – 'what may be known of a thing that is heard but not seen . . .' – but also unsettle our understanding of ontology.[82]

BARNARDO	Who's there?
FRANCISCO	Nay, answer me. Stand and unfold yourself.
BARNARDO	Long live the King.
FRANCISCO	Barnardo?
BARNARDO	He.
FRANCISCO	You come most carefully upon your hour.
BARNARDO	'Tis now struck twelve. Get thee to bed, Francisco.
FRANCISCO	For this relief much thanks. 'Tis bitter cold And I am sick at heart.
BARNARDO	Have you had quiet guard?
FRANCISCO	Not a mouse stirring.

(I, i, 1–8)

When we first hear Barnardo's question in the dark, we, like him, do not know that he is not calling to a ghost, but rather to his friend Francisco, who has come to *relieve* him ('relevant' translations are always within earshot). And yet, from the very start of the play, the Ghost is already on the stage, already in our ears. There are no stage directions specified but, according to Bernice W. Kliman, the text's graphics can function as 'explicit directions, which can guide elocution and determine pace and effect'.[83] Both the Second Quarto and the First Folio use full stops and not commas. Although the first Sentinel and Barnardo's dialogue in the First Quarto is different, it too is punctuated by full stops, achieving a similar effect. Elizabethan printers might have used a period, such as that after 'Long live the King', 'to indicate ... an interrupted or unfinished speech'; eager to ascertain their identities, Francisco and Barnardo interrupt each other.[84] Lines overlap, creating a ghostly effect of non-sequiturs that trail off the stage and confuse our ears. At the beginning of *Othello* our ears are similarly confused. A night-screened Roderigo asks old Brabantio whether he recognises his voice (I, i, 92). Brabantio does not, and answers: 'what are you?' (I, i, 93). In 'The Ear, Who?' Kamuf wonders about this use of 'what', where a 'who' would have sounded more natural to our ears.[85] Similarly, when Barnardo throws his question – 'Who's there?' – into the night air, he is really asking: 'what are you? Are you a ghost?' In the night of this theatre, the 'who' and the 'what' mingle. Like Brabantio, who, as Kamuf notes, seems to be 'calling upon the voice to attach itself again to a name, an identity', Barnardo seems to be listening out and addressing a disembodied, spectral voice ringing in the dark.[86] A voice is never single, or present; it never belongs to a body.

> Voice can betray the body to which it is lent, it can make it ventriloquize as if the body were no longer anything more than the actor or the double of another voice, of the voice of the other, even of an innumerable, incalculable polyphony.[87]

What we are listening out for when we are listening for the Ghost's voice is what in 'Dialanguages' Derrida calls the 'writing in the voice', its 'differential vibration'.[88] It is what in 'How to Avoid Speaking: Denials' is called a kind of prayer, a 'pure address, on the edge of silence, foreign to every code and to every rite, hence to every repetition'.[89] It is what Kamuf calls

> the *donner lieu*, that place-less place in which the impossible encounter takes place as a giving of place beyond or before any give-and-take. A place-less place or a silent word, unballasted of even the slightest weight, a breathless word, perhaps.[90]

Let's call it *différance and* contretemps *and* frequency and so forth.

The Ghost is in the ear; it is to be *apprehended* by tuning into frequency. Nowhere is the enmeshment of philosophonic listening and the listening for the idiom's uncanny *lettres* more provocatively formulated than in Derrida's definition of 'frequencies'. The concept of 'frequencies' is interspersed throughout *Specters* but it is only defined once in relation to Marx's Dissertation: 'Frequency counts. The experience, the apprehension of the Ghost is tuned into *frequency*: number (more than one), insistence, rhythm (waves, cycles, and periods)', or, in the original French, 'la fréquence compte. L'expérience, l'appréhension du fantôme s'accorde à la *fréquence*: le nombre (plus d'un), l'insistance, le rythme (des ondes, des cycles et des périodes).'[91] When Derrida writes that the apprehension of the Ghost is tuned into frequency, he is not only listening out for the haunting sounds of Shakespeare's language but he is using a philosophical understanding (*entendre*) of the act of hearing (also, *entendre*) to think about how the Thing Shakespeare haunts us. Frequencies, in fact, allows us to reconsider, once again, what the contretemps, the out-of-jointness of time and being, the teleiopoetic arrow, as well as the porpentine mean for Derrida's understanding of the act of reading as a 'political' act.

What then are these frequencies that allow us to understand what the Thing Shakespeare does in a text on Marx? According to *Le Grand Robert*, *fréquence* is a '*réitération, répétition*'. Enter GHOST (I, i, 38). *Exit Ghost* (I, i, 50). Enter GHOST (I, i, 124). [*Exit Ghost*] (I, i, 140). Thus the ghost of Hamlet's father enters and *re*-enters the stage, amid waiting men, some of them soldiers, some of them scholars, some of them both. First there is speculation as to its existence; later there is speculation as to what its appearance might mean. What is certain, however, is that the Ghost's first stage-entrance is a *return*. Derrida: 'everything begins in the imminence of a *re*-apparition, but a reapparition of the specter as apparition *for the first time in the play*'.[92] The spectre is a 'revenant', Derrida writes, 'because it *begins by coming back*'.[93] For Derrida, the Ghost in *Hamlet* is returning 'from what could be called the other time, from the other scene, from the eve of the play, the witnesses of history fear and hope for a return, then, "again" and "again, a coming and going (*Marcellus*: 'What, ha's this thing appear'd againe tonight?')"'.[94] The frequentation of the Ghost is a frequency, a repetition: 'repetition *and* first time, but also repetition *and* last time, since the singularity of any *first time*, makes of it also a *last time*. Each time it is the event itself, a first time is a last time. Altogether other.'[95] For Michael Naas, indeed, 'in any consideration of the phantasm one must emphasize less the ontological status of the phantasm than its staying power, its returning power, I would be tempted to say its *regenerative* power'.[96] Even when the Ghost in *Hamlet* is on the stage, it does not belong to presence, Being or *Dasein*. 'There is no *Dasein* of the specter, but there is no *Dasein* without the uncanniness, without the strange familiarity (*Unheimlichkeit*) of some specter.'[97] Rather than imagining a *Dasein* for the spectre, we must think of the spectre in terms of this repetition that fissures every presence and makes every presence spectral; because the spectre is a revenant, there cannot be an ontology of a spectre, but only a spectral ontology (say hauntology). The spectre is in this sense teleiopoetic.

Frequency is also what the *Le Grand Robert* calls a *période*, or as the *OED* has it, 'the rate per second of a vibration constituting a wave, e.g. sound, light, or radio waves'. Frequency is a cycle, it counts the *'nombre de cycles identiques d'un phénomène par unité de temps (en général, par seconde)'*. We cannot see the ghost: it goes beyond hearing and beyond sight. The waves, periods and cycles of frequency mark the rhythm that is beat out between the ghost's *re*-apparitions. The ghost *is* not; it is a rhythm. What is also inscribed in the elliptical mention of rhythm in Derrida's definition is not only the insistence or repetition of frequency, but also the fissuring of presence. As Derrida writes in 'Introduction: Desistance', 'rhythm – the spaced repetition of a percussion, the inscriptive force of a spacing – belongs neither to the visible nor to the audible'.[98] Rhythm in this sense is also what in *Monolingualism* is called the missing beat, the 'incalculable origin', which always begins 'before the beginning'.[99] It corresponds with what in 'Rams', a text about Celan, is called the 'spacing that does not pertain to meaning'.[100] It is the 'rhythm, caesura, hiatus, interruption' that exceeds meaning and that makes Derrida 'listen for something that [he] cannot hear or understand'.[101] What is here called 'rhythm' is, in other words, the possibility of audibility and visibility itself. When we listen, therefore, for the ghost and for spectral rhythms, we are listening into that space or spacing which, although being beyond presence and phenomena, makes them possible. In *Specters*, Derrida writes that the ghost is the *'frequency* of a certain visibility'.[102] 'And visibility, by its essence, is not seen, which is why it remains *epekeina tes ousias*, beyond the phenomenon or beyond being.'[103] Rhythm also marks the temporality of the spectre and of literature. It marks what in *Mémoires: For Paul de Man* Derrida speaks of as a 'rhythm without rhythm', which does not 'designate a particular rhythm, a measurable or comparable speed, but a movement which attempts through an infinite acceleration to win time, to win time over time'.[104] One might say that this rhythm outstrips, it *'gagne de vitesse'*.[105] It opens time and opens it for the other who has already been there, listening: 'The poem falls to me, benediction, coming of (or from) the other. Rhythm but dissymmetry', Derrida writes in 'Che cos'è la poesia?'[106] The spectre is contretemps.

Enter GHOST (I, i, 38). *Exit Ghost* (I, i, 50). *Enter* GHOST (I, i, 124). [*Exit Ghost*] (I, i, 140). The appearance of the Ghost marks its frequency. But the appearance of the Ghost also escapes frequencies. In *Specters*, Derrida writes that frequency also counts and it does so quite literally: it is the *'fréquence d'un mot'*, it is the number of times a word reoccurs in a corpus. We might, for instance, be familiar with the idea of a frequency of a Shakespearean word, or the amount of times it appears in his work. Of all the attempts to order and categorise Shakespeare's words, none is more ludic than the work done in concordances. Marvin Spevack's *Harvard Concordance to Shakespeare* is a veritable Shakespearean treasure trove. As outlined in its 'Introduction', it

> lists alphabetically all words exactly as they appear in Shakespeare' and 'each different word (or linguistic type) – a word is defined as a graphic unit – is followed by a line of statistical information: its absolute frequency (FR), its relative frequency (REL FR), the number of occurrences in verse passages (V), and the number of occurrences in prose (P).[107]

This task is, as Spevack himself is the first to admit, 'not without problems', and not only because mistakes are bound to occur 'when one is dealing with almost a million words in a myriad of configurations'.[108] The problem is also Spevack's definition of context, namely 'the typographical line (often the contents of one punch-card) in which the indexed word or lemma appears', because words in Shakespeare exceed their immediate context and always resonate with another frequency and use of that word.[109] The first meaning given for 'frequency' in the *OED* is 'state or condition of being crowded'. In this sense every frequency listed in Spevack's *Concordance* is also a frequency in the sense that it is crowded, inhabited, frequented if you will, by its other frequencies, or occurrences. Whenever Derrida plays on this word – frequency – he is also playing on the frequentation of ghosts, who are always more than one, who, according to *Le Grand Robert*, are always a *fréquence*, which also means a *foule*, or crowd. Frequency is the babel within in each language *and* the crowd of countersignatures present at the very heart of Shakespeare's iterable signature.

Most importantly, however, for our thinking about Derrida's 'politics', frequencies also mark the absolute otherness of the spectre. One does not see 'this Thing that is not a thing, this thing that is invisible between its apparitions, when it reappears'.[110] The Ghost is shielded from our sight by its full armour, what Horatio the scholar calls its 'warlike form' (I, i, 46). For Derrida, the armour allows 'the so-called father to see and to speak ... some slits are cut into it and adjusted so as to permit him to see without being seen, but to speak in order to be heard'.[111] He, of course, knows that the Ghost's visor was raised, but for him the mere 'possibility' of the visor, the possibility of seeing 'without being seen', suffices.[112] And yet, although we cannot see 'this Thing', it sees us. Derrida calls this 'the *visor effect*: we do not see who looks at us'.[113] This Ghost is therefore looking at us 'outside of any synchrony, even before and beyond any look on our part, according to an absolute anteriority (which may be on the order of generation, of more than one generation) and asymmetry, according to an absolutely unmasterable disproportion'.[114] Since we cannot see the Ghost, we must, like

Juliet in the darkness of the balcony scene, listen for it: 'we must fall back on its voice'.[115] But since, as Kamuf argues, 'the visor effect [is] also a prior pluralization of every one, everyone', this voice is, albeit singular, not single.[116] It is what in 'Ulysses Gramophone' is called 'a skein of voices'.[117]

In reading the frequencies of *Specters of Marx*, I have reiterated movements discussed in relation to contretemps *and* the time is out of joint *and* the signature *and* the arrow *and* the porpentine. Frequency is now also part of that quasi-synonymous chain to which Shakespeare's contretemps *and* signature *and* out-of-jointness *and* his arrows *and* porpentine belongs, and yet it is, like all of them, more than this: it is *nombre (plus d'un)*. Like the spectre, frequency is 'the *more than one/no more one* [le plus d'un]'.[118] The spectre that is 'listened' to in the night of Shakespeare's text is a 'remainder' which '*is* not', and which thus remains 'inaccessible to a straightforward intuitive perception (since it refers to something wholly other, it inscribes in itself something of the infinitely other), and it escapes all forms of prehension, all forms of monumentalization, and all forms of archivation'.[119] It is, it seems, a paraphrase of *différance* and the chain of terms it belongs to: 'Differance, which (is) nothing, is (in) the thing itself. It is (given) in the thing itself. It (is) the thing itself. It, differance, the thing (itself). It, without anything other. Itself, nothing'.[120] *Le plus d'un* is a spectrally polyphonic term, its definition comprises insistence, rhythms, waves, cycles and periods. As Kamuf notes, 'depending on whether or not one pronounces the "s": *plu(s)/plus*, the expression shifts registers from that of counting by ones to that of counting without number one, or of taking account of the other than one'.[121] It is perhaps because its definition is so wide-meshed that this net of a term can be thrown over the Ghost, which can only be apprehended if it is allowed to unfold.

It is, however, significant that Derrida modulates these movements philosophonically when thinking about what the haunting of the Thing (and the genius of) Shakespeare means politically. Although frequencies should not be understood as a 'master term' (as I have argued, mastery is not an applicable concept here), it is, I have tried to suggest, particularly illuminating for the study of Derridean acts of reading: in comprising both valences of the ear and listening in his writing – both actual and philosophical – it allows us to understand the modes of his acts of reading – characterised by the inter- and intratextual travel of the *lettre* – as directly linked to his theorisation of the trace. Simply put, there cannot be resonance and echoes if there is no resonant space. Frequencies account for how words can resonate with other words, uttered, written or read by somebody else and in a different context. It is also what in 'Anachronistic Reading' J. Hillis Miller calls a 'future *chiming*', or 'an anticipatory allegory or, perhaps, a prophecy, or, perhaps, a miniature apocalypse in the etymological sense of an enigmatic unveiling of what has not yet happened'.[122] For Royle, these 'peculiar ways in which specific words in Shakespeare come to be traced, in a sort of "now without present", by other appearances or apparitions of the "same" words' belong to a logic 'of another time, a "dead time" perhaps, or time without time. It is a matter of dramaturgic telepathy, the iteraphonic and iteraesthesia.'[123] This idea of the 'iteraphonic' functions as 'a sort of guiding thread' for much of Royle's work on Shakespeare and is in many ways close to my notion of frequencies.[124] Like frequencies, the iteraphonic does not only denote the telepathic echoing of something that could not have been heard. It also means hearing something differently, the ear changing something. Moreover, it means allowing for ghostly frequencies in Shakespeare's corpus, like, for instance, Derrida's 'Shakespearean word' 'relevant'. And it allows for an echoing of something that was never sounded; for a hearing of what is not yet there but still to come. It is precisely such a hearing of what is yet still to come that is performed in *Hamlet* and in *Specters*. And it is precisely this kind of hearing (*entendre*) as philosophical understanding (*entendre*) which is key to understanding the political repercussion that the genius of a work such as Shakespeare's can have.

Re-politicise!

At the beginning of the 'Exordium', we hear a voice ringing in the dark. It belongs to 'you or me', Derrida writes, and says: '*I would like to learn to live finally [je voudrais apprendre à vivre enfin]*.'[125] At once this '*mot d'ordre*' is linked to Shakespeare. The usual translation of *mot d'ordre* as 'watchword' immediately resonates with the image of the genius Shakespeare watching over the English language by shooting arrows at it. This watchword, indeed, Derrida continues, 'vibrates like an arrow in the course of an irreversible and asymmetrical address, the one that goes most often from father to son, master to disciple, or master to slave ("I'm going to teach you how to live")'.[126] In *Hamlet* and in *Specters*, everything turns on this desire to speak with this spectral voice and its *mot d'ordre*. Again, the visor effect and its frequencies are quivering. For Derrida, there is no to come without such an asymmetrical address.

How do we listen to this voice, which is both the voice of the spectre in *Hamlet* and Marx, as well as the voice of the 'Thing Shakespeare'? While most scholars believe that 'looking is sufficient', one of the most radical claims made by *Specters* is that, in order to respond to Marcellus' call for the scholar of tomorrow, we must not only look at but also learn to listen to the spectre.[127] Let us turn to *Hamlet*, whose theatre of the night in the cellarage scene is also a theatre of what Nancy calls '*acousmatics*, or the teaching model by which the teacher remains hidden from the disciple who listens to him'.[128]

HAMLET As you are friends, scholars and soldiers,
Give me one poor request.
HORATIO What is't, my lord? We will.
HAMLET Never make known what you have seen tonight.
HORATIO, MARCELLUS My lord, we will not.
HAMLET Nay, but swear't.
HORATIO In faith, my lord, not I.
MARCELLUS Nor I, my lord, in faith.
HAMLET Upon my sword.
MARCELLUS We have sworn, my lord, already.
HAMLET Indeed, upon my sword, indeed.
GHOST (*Cries under the stage*) Swear.
HAMLET Ha, ha, boy, sayst thou so? Art thou there, truepenny?
Come on, you hear this fellow in the cellarage?
Consent to swear.
HORATIO Propose the oath, my lord.
HAMLET Never to speak of this that you have seen,
Swear by my sword.
GHOST Swear.
HAMLET *Hic et ubique*? Then we'll shift our ground.
Come hither, gentlemen, and lay your hands
Again upon my sword. Swear by my sword
Never to speak of this that you have heard.
GHOST Swear by his sword.
HAMLET Well said, old mole, canst work i'th' earth so fast?
A worthy pioner! Once more remove, good friends.
HORATIO O day and night, but this is wondrous strange.

(I, v, 140–63)

This scene is characterised by a strange polyphony and counterpoint of Horatio and Marcellus' voices, speaking as one and then after the other. There is a strange repetition or circularity about Hamlet's demands, based perhaps on a distinction between sight and hearing and on a desire to match the word (swear) to the deed (the laying of hands on swords). The strangest element is, however, the contretemporal voice of the Ghost. The scene is marked by both a temporal and a spatial disjunction: the Ghost's 'Swear!' always comes after Hamlet's 'Swear!' and the Ghost is under the stage, in the cellarage, while Hamlet is on at least two different spots on the stage, as he asks Marcellus and Horatio to follow a curious choreography. As Samuel Weber has argued, that the cellarage 'suddenly reveals itself to be the haunt of a ghost allows his voice, echoing words of the others, to interrupt and impede the action they intend'.[129] For Weber the Ghost's 'utterance is both eminently theatrical, bringing into play – in the play – all of its theatrical elements, and eminently anti-performative: it renders impossible the performance of an act and the continuation of the plot'.[130]

Asking Marcellus and Horatio to swear, Hamlet speaks of the spectre, but he also speaks to the spectre, replying, himself, to the spectre's injunctions. Hamlet's words, to the spectre and of the spectre, however, do not return to him as his own but return strangely altered and only after a delay. The Ghost's cellarage is a veritable resonance chamber. The Ghost's first interpunctuating 'Swear' comes three whole lines after Hamlet's 'Nay, but swear't' (I, v, 149; 144). The Ghost's second 'Swear' is again heard three lines after Hamlet's 'Consent to swear' and one line after 'Swear by my sword' (I, v, 155; 152; 154). Before they are allowed to resonate, the cellarage's resounding membrane keeps Hamlet's words a while. Finally the spectre is made or allowed to speak: Hamlet's 'Swear by my sword' is echoed as 'Swear by his sword' (I, v, 158; 159). Like at the beginning of *Hamlet*, where our ears are haunted by resonating and intermingling voices, in the cellarage scene we are not dealing with two distinct and corporal voices. We are not listening, or not only listening, to the voice(s) of the spectre, but also to the spectral voice, the 'arch-music of that resonance where it *listens to itself* [s'écoute], by listening to itself *finds* itself [se trouve], and by finding itself *deviates* [s'écarte] from itself in order to resound further away'.[131] By 'differing/deferring itself', by speaking 'at the same time several times – and in several voices', this spectral voice also says: 'choose and decide from among what you inherit'.[132] It says: choose what you listen to, choose what to echo.

Letting the spirit speak, Hamlet also speaks with and to the Ghost. As in Derrida's account of Echo in 'Veni' in the cellarage scene, we are not only confronted with an echo, but with iteration. In 'Resonances of Echo: A Derridean Allegory', Pleshette DeArmitt points out that 'what Derrida hears in Echo's reply to Narcissus is by no means an empty reduplication or a hollow reverberation of the same, but a unique and inventive response'.[133] In Derrida's words: 'Echo thus lets be heard by whoever wants to hear it, by whoever might love hearing it, something other than what she seems to be saying.'[134] Just as Echo who 'might have feigned to repeat the last syllable of Narcissus in order to say something else or, really, in order to sign at that very instant in her own name', in allowing the Ghost to speak and to echo him, Hamlet obeys the injunction by 'tak[ing] back the initative of answering or responding in a responsible way, thus disobeying a sovereign injunction'.[135] In DeArmitt's reading, Echo can 'passionately' open herself 'to the future, to what is to come',[136] precisely because, as Derrida writes in 'Psyche: Inventions of the Other', she passes 'through the economy of the same, indeed, while miming or repeating it ("*Par le mot* par . . .")'.[137] It is just in this moment of resonance, this 'intersection of repetition and the unforeseeable', that we find 'the call for a thinking of the event *to come*, of the democracy *to come*, of the *reason to come*'.¹³⁸

Enter GHOST (I, i, 38). Exit Ghost (I, i, 50). Enter GHOST (I, i, 124). [Exit Ghost] (I, i, 140). As Attridge reminds us in 'Ghost Writing', it is not only 'possible to talk about the ghost *in* literature; we can say that the ghost *is* literature (as long as we're cautious about that word "is")'.¹³⁹ When Derrida asks us to listen to the Ghost's voice in *Hamlet*, he is also asking us '*to make or to let* a spirit *speak*'.¹⁴⁰ We must 'speak *of the ghost*, indeed *to the* ghost and *with it*', meaning that we must not only speak of, to and with the Ghost in *Hamlet* but also the ghost of the play *Hamlet*.¹⁴¹ We must look at the minutiae of Derrida's reading of *Hamlet* to sound out how he allows himself to be ghosted by Shakespeare; indeed, how he ghosts him in turn. And it is precisely this reciprocal haunting that the theatre of Derrida's philosophical-literary writing opens that marks how different Derrida's use of Shakespeare is compared to other philosophers'. It is, so Timothy Clark argues, 'one thing to come up with a general defence of the institution of literary writing', it is 'another thing, however, to put such thinking in practice in the minutiae of how to read, interpret and talk about specific texts'.¹⁴² And even among the most literarily attuned philosophers, Derrida does stands out 'in the variety and minutiae of his practice of reading'. ¹⁴³

In *Specters*, 'the Thing Shakespeare', its genius, is made to, or let speak, in particular through an intricate play on the appearance:disappearance of *Hamlet*'s Ghost. In the first two parts of *Specters*, the Ghost's appearance:disappearance is evoked three times. What we lose in translation is that when echoing the Ghost's frequencies Derrida always echoes Shakespeare's English. The first time is in the 'Exordium': 'Furtive and untimely, the apparition of the spectre does not belong to that time, it does not give time, not that one: 'Enter the ghost, exit the ghost, re-enter the ghost' (*Hamlet*) ["*Enter the*

Ghost, *exit the Ghost, re-enter the Ghost*" (*Hamlet*)].'[144] The second time is at the beginning of 'Injunctions of Marx', the part of *Specters* in which Derrida interweaves *Hamlet* and Marx most tightly, when, answering his own question 'what goes on between these generations?' Derrida responds: 'An omission, a strange lapsus. *Da*, then *fort*, exit Marx [*Da*, puis *fort*, exit Marx].'[145] The third time is also in 'Injunctions of Marx', where Derrida notes that 'this first theatrical apparition already marked a repetition'.[146] Again, Derrida inserts Shakespeare's English in parentheses: '(*Marcellus*: "What, ha's this thing appear'd againe tonight?" Then: *Enter the Ghost, Exit the Ghost, Enter the Ghost, as before*) [Puis: "*Enter the Ghost, Exit the Ghost, Re-enter the Ghost*")].'[147]

The Ghost is in the detail. In the first play on the Ghost's frequency, Derrida does not italicise *Hamlet*, whereas the translator Peggy Kamuf does. What enters and returns is thus not only Hamlet the father of Hamlet, Hamlet the Ghost, but also *Hamlet* the play. What returns are also the resonances of this play, and the differential vibrations of Derrida's rendition of them. In the third reiteration of the Ghost's enter:exit, Kamuf changes Derrida's 'Re-enter the Ghost' to 'Enter the Ghost, as before'. It is, I believe, crucial to hold on to Derrida's original rendition, because we cannot think of this reading scene without this 're-'. This is, of course the 're' in 'Aphorism countertime's' 'rejette', the 're-' of Shakespeare's arrow, the 're-' of the impossible 're-semanticization of the letter', or porpentine.[148] This 're-' which has been haunting us ever since Nancy's resonance, through to Derrida's 're-politicization' that Spivak misheard.[149] What do we make of this 're-'? Nancy writes: 'Meaning consists in a reference [*renvoi*].'[150] According to *Le Grand Robert*, *renvoi* is

> 1) *le fait de porter une affaire devant un autre juge*, the recourse to another judge; 2) *marque invitant le lecteur à se reporter*, or in other words a footnote or reference; 3) *le*

fait de renvoyer, or a revocation; 4) *le fait de retourner*; 5) *action de renvoyer*; 6) un *ajournement*. *Renvoi*: a return, a sending back, a dismissal, a suspension, a postponement, a cross-reference, even a footnote. In music, a *renvoi* is a da capo sign.

The common denominator of *renvoi*'s meanings might be understood as a certain movement traced by the prefix 're-': a movement indicated by the *OED* as one of repetition or return to a previous state (first meaning), one of mutuality (second meaning), one of coming behind or after (third meaning), and finally a movement of frequentative or intensive force (fourth meaning).

Here the 're-' marks the resonating space of the arrow and the inauguration of a different understanding of time, what Nancy calls a 'sonorous time',

> [a] present in waves on a swell, not in a point on a line; it is a time that opens up, that is hollowed out, that is enlarged or ramified, that envelops or separates, that becomes or is turned into a loop, that stretches out or contracts, and so on.[151]

In this reverberation chamber, the present is made to resonate as a 'successive addition of presents' where every 'reprise' of present is both past and '(still) to come'.[152] 'To listen is to enter that spatiality by which, *at the same time*, I am penetrated, for it opens up in me as well as around me, and from me as well as toward me.'[153] We must understand the 'Re-' of 'Re-Enter the Ghost' as 'a Derridean performative', which, in J. Hillis Miller's words, 'creates an absolute rupture between the present and the past. It inaugurates a future that Derrida calls a future anterior, or an unpredictable *à-venir*.'[154] The re-politicisation at the heart of *Specters* lies in the 're-' and in the resonances of Derrida's performative acts of reading Shakespeare. Without such acts of reading there will be 'no future, no time-to-come [*à-venir*], no other, otherwise; no event worthy of the name, no revolution. And no justice'.¹⁵⁵

Playing on the Ghost's appearance, its frequencies, Derrida is letting it speak. But as in the cellarage scene, the Thing is also spoken *with*. The frequencies of the Thing are frequented in turn. Deconstruction is just visiting *Hamlet*. As Derrida writes in 'The Time is Out of Joint': '(Deconstruction is just visiting – and from visitation one passes quickly to the visor, to the visor and haunting effect in Hamlet – return to Hamlet's father).'¹⁵⁶ The visitation or frequentation of deconstruction is intrinsically linked to the visor effect, the Ghost's unmasterable asymmetry and voice, its frequency. What is at stake when Derrida writes about *Hamlet* (and Marx), 'visit upon visit', is hence 'the recurrence or returning, the frequency of a visitation', because 'visitare', Derrida reminds us, is the 'frequentative of visere (to see, examine, contemplate)'.¹⁵⁷ We always need to go back and see, or rather be seen by the Ghost whom we cannot see, but whose voice we must learn to hear. It is just in this spectral resonance that the impossible injunction of the Ghost, and the Thing Shakespeare, can be fulfilled.

In an academic context *renvoi* can also mean expulsion (*Grand Robert*). We must listen to the Ghost and balance on the suspended edge of this 're-' – at once expulsion and reincorporation. For scholars, it has perhaps never been more important to learn

> not how to make conversation with the ghost but how to talk with him, with her, how to let them speak or how to give them back speech, even if it is in oneself, in the other, in the other in oneself: they are always *there*, specters, even if they do not exist, even if they are no longer, even if they are not yet.¹⁵⁸

I would like to learn to speak *to* and *with* the Ghost. Faced with the Ghost, Marcellus defers to Horatio: 'Thou art a scholar – speak to it, Horatio' (I, i, 41). At first Horatio does his best 'to call it, interpellate it, interrogate it, more precisely, to question the Thing that it still is'.[159] He says: 'What art thou that usurp'st this time of night' (I, i, 45). Who or what is this ghost? The scholar does not receive an answer; the Ghost remains silent. What or who is a scholar? For Kamuf, 'taking account of the general condition of spectrality has to displace the limits of scholarship and even redefine altogether the role of scholars'.[160] In Derrida's reading, Marcellus calls for 'a reader, an expert, a professor, an interpreter', a '*scholar* classique'.[161] As Sutherland points out, here 'Derrida's use of an English word in italics cannot be unimportant'.[162] Perhaps, Derrida suggests, Marcellus was 'anticipating the coming, one day, one night, several centuries later, of another "scholar"', a scholar who would know all about how in this drama of the night the who and what bleed into each other. For Derrida, this scholar 'would finally be capable, beyond the opposition between presence and non-presence, actuality and inactuality, life and non-life, of thinking the possibility of the specter . . . he would know how to address himself to spirits'.[163] How does such a scholar come into being? In Elizabethan England, a scholar was also someone 'who had studied at the university, and who, not having entered any of the learned professions or obtained any fixed employment, sought to gain a living by literary work'.[164] But what is literary work?

Notes

1   Simon Morgan Wortham, *The Derrida Dictionary* (London: Continuum, 2010), 195.
2. Ibid. 195.
3. Terry Eagleton, 'Marxism without Marxism', in *Ghostly Demarcations: A Symposium on Jacques Derrida's* Specters of Marx, ed. Michael Sprinker (London: Verso, 2008), 83.

4. Ibid. 86, 85.
5. Ibid. 86, 87, 86, 87.
6. Aijaz Ahmad, 'Reconciling Derrida: "Specters of Marx" and Deconstructive Politics', in *Ghostly Demarcations: A Symposium on Jacques Derrida's Specters of Marx*, ed. Michael Sprinker (London: Verso, 2008), 90.
7. Martha Nussbaum, 'The Professor of Parody: Review of Four Books by Judith Butler, *Excitable Speech*; *The Psychic Life of Power*; *Bodies that Matter*; *Gender Trouble*', in *Philosophical Interventions: Reviews 1986–2011* (Oxford: Oxford University Press, 2012), 199.
8. Gayatri Chakravorty Spivak, 'Ghostwriting', *Diacritics* 25, no. 2 (Summer 1995): 65.
9. Ibid. 66.
10. Samir Haddad, *Derrida and the Inheritance of Democracy* (Bloomington and Indianapolis: Indiana University Press, 2013), 3.
11. Geoffrey Bennington, *Legislations: The Politics of Deconstruction* (London and New York: Verso, 1994), 97.
12. Ibid. 4.
13. Ibid. 4.
14. Ibid. 4.
15. Ibid. 4.
16. Ibid. 97.
17. Jacques Derrida, *Specters of Marx: The State of the Debt, the Work of Mourning and the New International*, trans. Peggy Kamuf (London: Routledge, 2006), 81.
18. Martin McQuillan, *Deconstruction after 9/11* (London: Routledge, 2009), 102.
19. Geoffrey Bennington, *Interrupting Derrida* (London: Routledge, 2000), 25.
20. Keston Sutherland, *Stupefaction: A Radical Anatomy of Phantoms* (London: Seagull Books, 2011), 10.
21. Ernesto Laclau, 'The Time is Out of Joint', *Diacritics* 25, no. 2 (1995): 87.
22. Ibid. 91.
23. Christopher Prendergast, 'Derrida's Hamlet', *SubStance* 34, no.1 (2005): 44.

24. Ibid. 44.
25. Laclau, 'The Time is Out of Joint', 91.
26. Ibid. 44.
27. Jacques Derrida, 'Marx & Sons', trans. G. M. Goshgarian, in *Ghostly Demarcations: A Symposium on Jacques Derrida's* Specters of Marx, ed. Michael Sprinker (London: Verso, 2008), 264.
28. Ibid. 223.
29. Derrida, *Specters of Marx*, 109; Spivak, 'Ghostwriting', 69.
30. Derrida, 'Marx & Sons', 234.
31. Ibid. 234.
32. Ibid. 234.
33. Ibid. 234.
34. Bennington, *Interrupting Derrida*, 25.
35. Derrida, 'Marx & Sons', 234.
36. Jacques Derrida, 'Aphorism Countertime', trans. Nicholas Royle, in *Acts of Literature*, ed. Derek Attridge (London: Routledge, 1992), 414, 416.
37. Jacques Derrida, 'L'aphorisme à contretemps', in *Psyché: Inventions de l'autre II* (Paris: Galilée, 2003), 134.
38. Jacques Derrida, 'The Spatial Arts: An Interview with Jacques Derrida', trans. Laurie Volpe, in *Deconstruction and the Visual Arts: Art, Media, Architecture*, ed. Peter Brunette and David Wills (Cambridge: Cambridge University Press, 1994), 20.
39. Ibid. 20.
40. Ibid. 23.
41. Ibid. 21.
42. Marcel Cobussen, *Deconstruction in Music*, www.deconstruction-in-music.com
43. Derrida, 'The Spatial Arts', 21.
44. Jacques Derrida, 'Che cos'è la poesia?' in *A Derrida Reader: Between the Blinds*, trans. and ed. Peggy Kamuf (New York: Columbia University Press, 1991), 233.
45. Aliette Armel, 'From the Word to Life: A Dialogue between Jacques Derrida and Hélène Cixous', trans. Ashley Thompson, *New Literary History* 37, no. 1 (2006): 6.
46. Derrida, 'Aphorism Countertime', 423.
47. Ibid. 425.

48. Derrida, 'L'aphorisme à contretemps', 136.
49. Derrida, 'Aphorism Countertime', 425.
50. Ibid. 424.
51. Ibid. 431.
52. Ibid. 423.
53. Ibid. 427.
54. Ibid. 427.
55. Ibid. 427.
56. Ibid. 423.
57. Ibid. 429.
58. Jacques Derrida, *Paper Machine*, trans. Rachel Bowlby (Stanford: Stanford University Press, 2005), 151.
59. Derrida, 'Aphorism Countertime', 425.
60. Derrida, *Specters of Marx*, xvii.
61. Royle, *The Uncanny*, 124.
62. Derrida, 'Aphorism Countertime', 425.
63. Ibid. 425.
64. Jean-Luc Nancy, *Listening*, trans. Charlotte Mandell (New York: Fordham Unversity Press, 2007), 2.
65. Ibid. 12
66. Ibid. 2.
67. Cobussen, *Deconstruction in Music*.
68. Derrida, 'The Spatial Arts', 21.
69. Morgan Wortham, *Derrida Dictionary*, 200.
70. Jacques Derrida, *Speech and Phenomena and other Essays on Husserl's Theory of Signs*, trans. David B. Allison (Evanston: Northwestern University Press, 1973), 76.
71. Ibid. 77.
72. Ibid. 59.
73. Ibid. 69.
74. Geoffrey Bennington, 'Derridabase', in *Jacques Derrida* (London and Chicago: University of Chicago Press, 1993), 66. The emphasis is mine.
75. Derrida, *Speech and Phenomena*, 75.
76. Derrida, *Specters of Marx*, 2.
77. Ibid. 2.

78. Ibid. 2.
79. Bruce Johnson, '*Hamlet*: Voice, Music, Sound', *Popular Music* 24, no. 2 (2005): 257, 259.
80. Ibid. 259.
81. Ibid. 259.
82. Ibid. 260.
83. Bernice W. Kliman, 'Explicit Stage Directions (Especially Graphics) in *Hamlet*', in *Stage Directions in* Hamlet: *New Essays and New Directions*, ed. Hardin L. Aasand (London: Associated University Presses, 2003), 74.
84. See Thomas Marc Parrott, 'Errors and Omissions in the Griggs Facsimile of the Second Quarto of *Hamlet*', MLN 49 (June 1934): 376–9.
85. Peggy Kamuf, 'The Ear, Who?' *Discourse* 30, Nos. 1/2 (2008): 177.
86. Ibid. 177.
87. Jacques Derrida, 'Voice II', trans. Verena Andermatt Conley, in *Points . . . Interviews, 1974–1994*, ed. Elisabeth Weber (Stanford: Stanford University Press, 1995), 161.
88. Jacques Derrida, '"Dialanguages"', trans. Peggy Kamuf, in *Points . . . Interviews, 1974–1994*, ed. Elisabeth Weber (Stanford: Stanford University Press, 1995), 140.
89. Jacques Derrida, 'How to Avoid Speaking: Denials', trans. Ken Frieden and Elizabeth Rottenberg, in *Psyche: Inventions of the Other, Volume II*, ed. Peggy Kamuf and Elizabeth Rottenberg (Stanford: Stanford University Press, 2008), 194.
90. Kamuf, *Book of Addresses*, 131.
91. Derrida, *Specters of Marx*, 133; Derrida, *Spectres de Marx*, 174.
92. Derrida, *Specters of Marx*, 2.
93. Ibid. 11.
94. Ibid. 11
95. Ibid. 10.
96. Michael Naas, *Derrida from Now On* (New York: Fordham University Press, 2008), 192.
97. Derrida, *Specters of Marx*, 125.

98. Jacques Derrida, 'Introduction: Desistance', in Philippe Lacoue-Labarthe, *Typography: Mimesis, Philosophy, Politics*, trans. Christopher Fynsk (Stanford: Stanford University Press, 1998), 32.
99. Derrida, *Monolingualism of the Other*, 48.
100. Jacques Derrida, 'The Truth That Wounds: From an Interview', trans. Thomas Dutoit, in *Sovereignties in Question: The Poetics of Paul Celan*, ed. Thomas Dutoit and Outi Pasanen (New York: Fordham University Press, 2005), 165.
101. Ibid. 165, 166.
102. Derrida, *Specters of Marx*, 125.
103. Ibid. 125.
104. Jacques Derrida, *Mémoires: for Paul de Man*, trans. Cecile Lindsay, Jonathan Culler and Eduardo Cadava (New York: Columbia University Press, 1986), 62.
105. Derrida, 'L'aphorisme à contretemps', 131.
106. Derrida, 'Che cos'è la poesia?', 233.
107. Marvin Spevack, *The Harvard Concordance to Shakespeare* (Cambridge, MA: Belknap Press of Harvard University Press, 1974), v.
108. Ibid. vii.
109. Ibid. vii.
110. Derrida, *Specters of Marx*, 6.
111. Ibid. 7.
112. Ibid. 8.
113. Ibid. 6.
114. Ibid. 6–7.
115. Ibid. 7.
116. Kamuf, *Book of Addresses*, 234.
117. Jacques Derrida, 'Ulysses Gramophone: Hear Say Yes in Joyce', trans. Tina Kendall and Shari Benstock, in *Acts of Literature*, ed. Derek Attridge (London: Routledge, 1992), 278.
118. Derrida, *Specters of Marx*, xx.
119. Derrida, *Paper Machine*, 151.
120. Jacques Derrida, *Given Time: I. Counterfeit Money*, trans. Peggy Kamuf (Chicago: University of Chicago Press, 1992), 40.
121. Kamuf, *Book of Addresses*, 219.

122. J. Hillis Miller, 'Anachronistic Reading', *Derrida Today* 3, no. 1 (2010): 82. My emphasis.
123. Nicholas Royle, *In Memory of Jacques Derrida* (Edinburgh: Edinburgh University Press, 2009), 33.
124. Ibid. 37.
125. Derrida, *Specters of Marx*, xvi; *Spectres de Marx*, 13.
126. Ibid. xvi.
127. Ibid. 11.
128. Nancy, *Listening*, 3.
129. Samuel Weber, *Theatricality as Medium* (New York: Fordham University Press, 2004), 184.
130. Ibid. 184.
131. Nancy, *Listening*, 35.
132. Derrida, *Specters of Marx*, 18.
133. Pleshette DeArmitt, 'Resonances of Echo: A Derridean Allegory', *Mosaic* 42, no. 2 (2009): 95.
134. Jacques Derrida, 'Preface: Veni', trans. Pascale-Anne Brault and Michael Naas, in *Rogues: Two Essays on Reason* (Stanford: Stanford University Press, 2005), xii.
135. Ibid. xi–xii.
136. DeArmitt, 'Resonances of Echo: A Derridean Allegory', 95.
137. Jacques Derrida, 'Psyche: Inventions of the Other', trans. Catherine Porter, in *Psyche: Inventions of the Other, Volume I*, ed. Peggy Kamuf and Elizabeth Rottenberg (Stanford: Stanford University Press, 2007), 45.
138. Derrida, 'Preface: Veni', xii, xv.
139. Jacques Derrida, 'Ghost Writing', in *Deconstruction is/in America: A New Sense of the Political*, ed. Anselm Haverkamp (New York and London: New York University Press, 1995), 224.
140. Derrida, *Specters of Marx*, 11.
141. Ibid. xviii.
142. Timothy Clark, *The Poetics of Singularity: The Counter-Culturalist Turn in Heidegger, Derrida, Blanchot and the later Gadamer* (Edinburgh: Edinburgh University Press, 2005), 130.
143. Ibid. 130.
144. Derrida, *Specters of Marx*, xix; *Spectres de Marx*, 17.

145. Derrida, *Specters of Marx*, 3; *Spectres de Marx*, 23.
146. Derrida, *Specters of Marx*, 11.
147. Derrida, *Specters of Marx*, 11; *Spectres de Marx*, 32.
148. Derrida, 'L'aphorisme à contretemps', 134; Jacques Derrida, '*Istrice 2: Ick bünn all hier*', trans. Peggy Kamuf in *Points ... Interviews, 1974–1994*, ed. Elisabeth Weber (Stanford: Stanford University Press, 1995), 311.
149. Nancy, *Listening*, 40; Spivak, 'Ghostwriting', 69.
150. Nancy, *Listening*, 7.
151. Ibid. 13.
152. Ibid. 18.
153. Ibid. 14.
154. J. Hillis Miller, *For Derrida* (New York: Fordham University Press, 2009), 152.
155. Derrida, 'Marx & Sons', 251.
156. Jacques Derrida, 'The Time is Out of Joint', trans. Peggy Kamuf, in *Deconstruction is/in America: A New Sense of the Political*, ed. Anselm Haverkamp (New York: New York University Press, 1995), 29.
157. Derrida, *Specters of Marx*, 126.
158. Ibid. 221.
159. Ibid. 12–13.
160. Kamuf, *Book of Addresses*, 239.
161. Derrida, *Specters of Marx*, 11; *Spectres de Marx*, 33.
162. Sutherland, *Stupefaction*, 8.
163. Derrida, *Specters of Marx*, 13.
164. *Oxford English Dictionary*, meaning 2b.

CHAPTER 7

CONCLUSION, OR *GÉNIE QUI ES TU*

Geneses, Genealogies, Genres, and Genius opens with the question: '*Un génie, qu'est-ce que c'est?*'[1] What is a genius, and what does it do? To us? Derrida notes that the word 'genius' is uncomfortable, that it 'makes us squirm'.[2]

> One is often right to view it as an obscurantist abdication to genes, as it turns out, a concession to the genetics of the *ingenium* or, worse, a creationist innatism, in a word, in the language of another age, the dubious collusion of some sort of biologising naturalism and a theology based on ecstatic inspiration. An irresponsible and docile inspiration, a drunken submission to automatic writing. The muses are never far off. In according the least legitimacy to the word 'genius' one is considered to sign one's resignation from all fields of knowledge, explications, interpretations, readings, decipherings – in particular in what one hastily calls the aesthetics of arts and letters, supposedly more propitious to creation. Such resigning is considered mystical, mysticoïd. One is said to be confessing to dumb adoration of the ineffability of that which, in the usual currency of the word 'genius', tends to link the gift to birth, the secret to the sacrifice.[3]

Nevertheless, Derrida embraces this word, and importantly he does so not merely when thinking about Shakespeare. He acknowledges that genius is at work in the plays; his understanding of genius is, however, distinct from the idea of genius that we might find lurking behind much of philosophy's bardolatry.

A little later on in the text, Derrida notes that Homer's, Joyce's and Shakespeare's Ulysses together with 'their brilliant [*géniaux*] inventors' are 'potentially incommensurable with any library supposed to house them, classify them, shelve them'.[4] This is because 'they derange all the archival and indexing spaces by the disproportion of the potentially infinite memory they condense according to the processes of undecidable writing for which as yet no complete formalisation exists'.[5] It is in the idiom's process of undecidable writing, for which as yet no complete formalisation exists, that the genius of Shakespeare lies. Here, genius lies not in the man but in the work, and not in what it represents but in what it says, more precisely in the spectral, idiomatic, philosophonic bodies of the words themselves.

Let's return to some of the questions I asked at the beginning: Why would philosophers do well to turn to Shakespeare? What might be more valuable about Shakespeare than about other works of literature? Derrida might answer that what makes Shakespeare's work so fruitful for reading/thinking/writing is the genius that does not only exist in Shakespeare. What does, however, only exist in Shakespeare is the particular Shakespearean reincarnation of the genius of writing, this particular body of writing demanding the event of reading, or countersigning Shakespeare, of doing something to *his* body. Between each act of reading and Shakespeare there is an event, and a wound that says: *it only happens to me*.

In *Specters of Marx*, shortly after wondering about how *Hamlet*'s 'the time is out of joint' disjoints its translations,

Derrida speaks of this play as 'a masterpiece, a work of genius, a *thing* of the *spirit* which precisely seems to *engineer itself* [s'ingénier]'.[6] With the play on *génie* and *s'ingénier*, Derrida suggests that the genius of Shakespeare has to do with the ability of Shakespeare's writing to engineer itself, to put itself to work through his words.[7] Here Shakespeare's work itself becomes the 'that thing, the Thing that, like an elusive specter, *engineers* [s'ingénie] a habitation without proper inhabiting, call it a *haunting*, of both memory and translation'.[8] The oeuvre we call Shakespeare's is animated, the words are animated, they engineer themselves, they themselves are thinking, are having ideas, are constructing. As Royle argues in *How to Read Shakespeare*, 'words in Shakespeare seem to take on an autonomous life or machine-like power. They are like little search engines, meddling imps, strange creatures with wills of their own.'[9] Shakespeare's 'stroke of genius' is based precisely on this meddling capacity, not merely of its mercurial lexical meanings, but also because of the workings of its idiom.[10]

There is then perhaps no Shakespeare. In 'Shakespeare Ghosting Derrida', Cixous suggests that Shakespeare 'can be more easily incorporated than others with whom Derrida weaves an alliance (Blanchot for instance)' because he 'does not exist'. She continues:

> Shakespeare is the name of a corpus, of an infinite, unlimited body without ego, without an absolutely identifiable owner, it is the name of the skull which had a tongue which is the whole tongue, Hamlet Derrida gathers him in the graveyard which houses [*où demeurent*] the archives of his innumerable melancholy affects.[11]

Cixous's choice of words – *où demeurent* – is crucial here. In the words of 'Demeure', Shakespeare 'does not remain at home, *abidingly* [à demeure] in the identity of a nature or even of a historical being identical with itself'.[12] Like the spectre in *Hamlet* it '*engineers* [s'ingénier] a habitation without proper inhabiting'.[13] It is because of this that the genius of Shakespeare's writing leaves space for our to come.

The question of the identity of the *génie* – '*qui es tu*' – which is posed at the very beginning of *Geneses, Genealogies, Genres, and Genius* is also its answer.[14] As Beverle Bie Brahic notes, '*génie qui es tu*' is a near-homophone meaning both 'genius who are you' and 'genius who has fallen silent'.[15] The only visual marker, which could keep them apart, namely the *trait d'union* between '*es-tu*', remains silent. Derrida addresses a silent genius: '"Genius, who are you [*qui es tu*]?" I am asking you this question, genius, hear, do you hear?'[16] He addresses this genius, which remains silent, asking it to listen to him and to make itself heard. This then is the stroke of the silent genius. In his description of the silent genius (genius who is you) Derrida seems to be ventriloquising the unprecedented and performative trajectory of the teleiopoetic arrow. Like the teleiopoetic arrow, the work of genius penetrates by withdrawing. It is what in '"A Self-Unsealing Poetic Text"' 'speaks to the other by keeping quiet, keeping something quiet from him. In keeping quiet, in keeping silence, it is still addressing itself.'[17] The stroke of genius – this teleiopoetic arrow – may strike with the engineering sounds of *lettres*, but it withdraws in silence. 'Geniusness is the uniqueness of an impossible arrivingness [*arrivance*] to which one addresses oneself, which is only to the improbable destination of the address – and it is always "*tu*". A silenced [*tu*] instant, the instant of the eternal return.'[18] To listen with our philosophical ears always means, as 'Voice II' suggests, to 'turn one's ears to the other when it speaks to "whom," to "what," to this "who" which has not yet been assigned an identity' and who is perhaps yet to come but who will have been resonating there from the beginning.[19]

Genius is you, and it is silent; it is silent so that you may hear and speak. It is because the genius of writing welcomes the other from the very moment of its inscription that it remains continuously surprising. What Derrida writes about Cixous is also true of Shakespeare:

> I would describe it, this idiom of a signature, as a kind of gift for letting itself be caressed by a genius of the language that cannot get over its utter surprise at the touch that comes out of the blue to move it and that breaks with the genetic filiation it respects and cultivates and enriches even as it betrays it. This betrayal out of faithfulness interrupts with an event the genius of the language, an unconscious genius of the language, unaware it was capable of letting itself be thus regenerated by that which seems to grow out of or derive from it.[20]

For Derrida, we would not do justice to this genius of language if we try to 'limit literature by fixing a mission for it, a single mission'.[21] Literature is 'on the edge of metaphysics', even perhaps 'on the edge of everything, almost beyond everything, including itself. It's the most interesting thing in the world, maybe more interesting than the world.'[22] It is also on the edge of our idea of the human, indeed of any idea, belief or conviction that we take to the plays. You would, of course, not be wrong to protest that this might be true for Derrida. It is true that the Shakespeare I have given you in this book is Derrida's. It is also true that, as anyone who has spent significant time with Derrida's work, I knew in advance what he might find in Shakespeare and what tack he would take. How then can I claim that the genius of language that Derrida finds in Shakespeare, but also in Celan, Austin, Nietzsche and many others surprises even Derrida himself? Because, despite the apparent virtuosity of the way Derrida reads, the very 'logic' that underpins his way of reading also dictates that he too must be countersigned, deconstructed, wounded. His is then perhaps the mastery of vulnerability, the strength of the *hérisson* that exposes itself to its own arrows. And the same is, naturally, true of Shakespeare as it is of any other work that we love. Shakespeare lives on, because with every stroke the work exposes itself to the possibility of its death, of being taken to places no one could ever have foreseen.

Let's think back to the role of *Klang* in Freud's interpretation of his '*Non Vixit* Dream' discussed in Chapter 5. Although Freud does not pay the role of homophones in the dream work the attention it deserves, it is just in the dream work's reliance on sound that one of his greatest and as yet largely unexamined influences on Derrida's writing lies. Although this often gets lost in translation, Derrida's writing and line of thought at certain moments seem to be propelled by the phonic similarities between words. In 'My Chances', for instance, Derrida repeatedly highlights the sound found in all *trajet, jet, ob-jectum, ob-jet, jeté* or *sujet*. One reason why Derrida highlights these words and the sound they have in common is of course that they all derive from the Latin word *icere*, to hit, strike or smite, that they hence are all part of that movement that Heidegger called *Geworfenheit* or *l'être-jeté*, which Derrida recognises in the movement of the *clinamen*. In *Geneses, Genealogies, Genres, and Genius*, a reading of Hélène Cixous's *Manhattan* and *Dream I Tell You* (a collection of some of the innumerable records of dreams she donated to the Bibliothèque nationale de France) that again grapples with the question of literature, Derrida argues that it is just this very sound that works in and through Cixous's dreamlike writing: 'Everything seems contained in the letter *g* (pronounced *gé* in French, as in *génie, générosité* and *généalogie* or as in the *jet* [from *jeter*, to throw] of a toss of the dice, for instance)'.[23] These words – *génie, générosité* and *généalogie* – no longer share an etymological root with *jet*; they are merely linked by a similarity in sound. It is hence, as Derrida notes later, 'the genius of the secret and the genius of the letter, above all of the syllable *gé*, with which we shall never be done, however it is transcribed (the letter g, the whole word "jet", the word fragment "*gé*" [. . .])' that interests him.[24] For Derrida, in Cixous's writings the syllable *gé* is the 'logos'; 'it is everywhere, ever helpful, inspires everything, gets mixed up in everything, keeps watch over everything, it even goes so far as to keep its eye on the unconscious dreams'.[25] When Derrida speaks of *gé* he is certainly also speaking of Cixous's idiom 'as a kind of gift for letting itself be caressed by a genius of the language . . . that breaks with the genetic filiation it respects and cultivates and enriches even as it betrays it'.[26] Although, as Cixous argues in *Manhattan*, this syllable *gé* or 'letter G' is transcribed 'everywhere in disguise in the French language', her genius lies just in her capacity to let this *gé* do its work. Cixous's genius, in other words, lies in her ability to tap into the 'unconscious genius of the language'.[27]

Derrida is, of course, far from suggesting that the idiomatic power of *gé* holds is also transcendental or metaphysical. He rather invites us to think further about what, in this case, the link between *gé* and *jet* is, and whether there is any correlation between the seemingly aleatory play with this syllable and the *jet* of Cixous's writing. What Derrida is, I believe, aiming at is that Cixous's genius with the French language also depends on the *jet* of this *gé*, that in other words literature, as dreams, as philosophical thought, and as the reading or interpretation of all of the above, also works through sound and the chance encounters it creates. It is similarly just Derrida's ability to let sound draw seemingly irrational and aleatory connections in his work, that in turn constitutes part of the literariness of Derrida's philosophical writing, understood both as the literary character of his style and as his use of literature. I furthermore believe that Derrida's and Cixous's ability to let the *jet* work through *gé*, to let the genius of language work and think beyond them and beyond language, must be thought of in connection with the role sound plays in the dream work as described in Freud's *Traumdeutung*. But what happens if we fold Derrida's suggestion that the *jet* of Cixous's writing works through its *gé*, that in other words the genius of language of writing also works through sound, back on to Freud's strange avoidance of *Klang* in his interpretation of the '*Non Vixit* Dream'? Must we conclude that Freud was masterful in ways he could not yet fathom?

By highlighting the *Klang* of Brutus' speech with one hand and sweeping the homophonic play of his dream work under the carpet with the other, Freud sketched a theory of genius underpinning Derrida's reading of Cixous and of Shakespeare, namely the genius of allowing the genius of language to do its work: also, but not exclusively, through chances and sound or the chances of sound. In the introduction to *Dream I Tell You*, Cixous calls Freud 'the Shakespeare of the Night'.[28] What would this mean, to be the Shakespeare of the night? It might mean that Freud, wittingly or not, was able, just as Shakespeare was, to prick up his ears and to play with sounds, to draw connections, to take one's chances and to set in motion the genius of language. Perhaps Freud was the Shakespeare of the night, because his work, as the work of other great literary inventors (*géniaux*) such as Homer, Joyce, and, as Derrida would add, Cixous herself, 'derange[s] all the archival and indexing spaces by the disproportion of the potentially infinite memory they condense according to the processes of undecidable writing for which as yet no complete formalisation exists'.[29] We can only begin to fathom how these 'processes of undecidable writing' work, but I believe that one way they work is through the *lettre*, a sounded idiom.

We do not know where we will end when we start to read Shakespeare; the Thing Shakespeare unsettles everything we bring to it. This is why Kermode has described the canon as 'strange, sublime, uncanny, anxious'.[30] And this is why the Thing Shakespeare – like any other great work of literature – advances not merely research programmes that produce countable and therefore accountable knowledge, but also promotes that kind of thinking that Horatio, the scholar who speaks to and with ghosts, is interested in. It is the ability to live with such anxiety and strangeness, indeed to find the sublime in the uncanny, and, most importantly, to respond, that Derrida calls the ability to learn how to live finally. This is what opens the to come.

It is this understanding of the unsettling, anxious but also creative and creating genius of literature that we must bear in mind when we return finally to Derrida's wish to become a Shakespeare expert. In 'This Strange Institution Called Literature' Derrida says:

> I would very much like to read and write in the space or heritage of Shakespeare, in relation to whom I have infinite admiration and gratitude; I would like to become (alas, it's pretty late) a 'Shakespeare expert'; I know that everything is in Shakespeare; everything and the rest, so everything or nearly.[31]

In French, Derrida leaves the English untranslated: 'Shakespeare expert'. What is a Shakespeare expert? An expert is someone who has 'a special skill at a task or knowledge in a subject' (*OED*). This term resonates with the trappings of professional academia, the professionalisation of research and of thought. It smacks of the categorisation of research interests, of research excellence frameworks, of key word searches. Experts of Shakespeare, declare yourselves if you want to be counted! Deriving from *expertus*, the past participle of the Latin *experiri*, an expert is one who has already gained the experience, already gathered the knowledge of many failed and successful attempts. As the past tense perhaps suggests, an expert is done trying and attempting, he already is in the know. This is not the kind of Shakespeare expert Derrida desires to be, and indeed, already is.

Derrida, he himself readily admits, is no 'Shakespeare expert'. In 'Derrida's Event', Royle notes that the inverted commas here not only suggest 'a characteristic sense of irony and comedy' (Derrida's playful 'tone' again), but also 'draw attention to the connotations of trying, testing and experimentation that belong with the word "expert", the sense of "trying thoroughly"'. Derrida's work shows that the space opened by Shakespeare must always retain something of the future, yet to be tried and experienced. And the same may be true for readers of Derrida (reading Shakespeare) who are faced with the Derridean event of reading which is an event, Bennington writes, 'so worthy of its name that it would suggest a kind of impossibility . . . or unthinkability' that it 'may, in a sense, never quite *happen*'.[32] 'Derrida's event', Bennington suggests a little later, 'is an ongoing series of after-the-event reprises and iterations of an event' that 'never quite or entirely happened, or finished happening, and is to that extent still to come, yet to happen'.[33] Just as one cannot become a Derrida expert, one cannot become a Shakespeare expert, only a experiendum, one who will take his chances with Shakespeare.

'Everything', Derrida writes, 'is in Shakespeare; everything and the rest, so everything or nearly.'[34] Derrida's wish to become a 'Shakespeare expert' is hence articulated as a wish to 'read and write in the space or heritage of Shakespeare'. The field of the Shakespeare expert would hence not only be the corpus of his oeuvre but also what is written after it, what belongs, in other words, to 'the rest' which is already in Shakespeare, as well as the rest of Shakespeare which is still to come. What is this rest? It is us re-reading Shakespeare, as if for the first time. It is us noting that whatever happens between us happens only once and only to us and taking this openness, embrace and vulnerability to the other, whoever she may be.

It is, in short, us learning how to read and to live again, after reading over Derrida's shoulder when he reads Shakespeare.

Notes

1. Jacques Derrida, *Geneses, Genealogies, Genre, and Genius: The Secrets of the Archive*, trans. Beverley Bie Brahic (New York: Columbia University Press, 2006), 1.
2. Ibid. 3.
3. Ibid. 3–4.
4. Ibid. 14–15.
5. Ibid. 15.
6. Jacques Derrida, *Specters of Marx: The State of the Debt, the Work of Mourning and the New International*, trans. Peggy Kamuf (London: Routledge, 2006), 20.
7. Ibid. 20.
8. Ibid. 20.
9. Nicholas Royle, *How to Read Shakespeare* (London: Granta Books, 2005), 5.
10. Derrida, *Specters of Marx*, 25.
11. Hélène Cixous, 'Shakespeare Ghosting Derrida', trans. Laurent Milesi, *The Oxford Literary Review* 34, no. 1 (2012): 17.
12. Jacques Derrida, 'Demeure: Fiction and Testimony' (with Maurice Blanchot's *The Instant of My Death*), trans. Elizabeth Rottenberg (Stanford: Stanford University Press, 2000), 28.
13. Derrida, *Specters of Marx*, 20.
14. Derrida, *Geneses, Genealogies, Genre, and Genius*, 2.
15. Ibid. 92.
16. Ibid. 2.
17. Jacques Derrida, '"A Self-Unsealing Poetic Text": Poetics and Politics of Witnessing', trans. Rachel Bowlby, in *Revenge of the Aesthetic: The Place of Literature in Theory Today*, ed. Michael P. Clark (Berkeley: University of California Press, 2000), 206.
18. Derrida, *Geneses, Genealogies, Genre, and Genius*, 78–9.
19. Jacques Derrida, 'Voice II', trans. Verena Andermatt Conley, in *Points . . . Interviews, 1974–1994*, ed. Elisabeth Weber (Stanford: Stanford University Press, 1995), 163.

20. Derrida, *Geneses, Genealogies, Genre, and Genius*, 22.
21. Jacques Derrida, '"This Strange Institution Called Literature": An Interview with Jacques Derrida', trans. Geoffrey Bennington and Rachel Bowlby, in *Acts of Literature*, ed. Derek Attridge (London: Routledge, 1992), 38.
22. Ibid. 47.
23. Derrida, *Geneses, Genealogies, Genre, and Genius*, 9.
24. Ibid. 28.
25. Ibid. 9.
26. Ibid. 22.
27. Ibid. 94, 22.
28. Hélène Cixous, *Dream I Tell You*, trans. Beverley Bie Brahic (Edinburgh: Edinburgh University Press, 2006), 3.
29. Derrida, *Geneses, Genealogies, Genre, and Genius*, 15.
30. Frank Kermode, 'Strange, Sublime, Uncanny, Anxious', *London Review of Books*, 22 December 1994, https://www.lrb.co.uk/v16/n24/frank-kermode/strange-sublime-uncanny-anxious
31. Derrida, '"This Strange Institution Called Literature"', 67.
32. Geoffrey Bennington, 'In the Event', in *Derrida's Legacies: Literature and Philosophy*, ed. Simon Glendinning and Robert Eaglestone (London: Routledge, 2008), 33.
33. Ibid. 34.
34. Derrida, '"This Strange Institution Called Literature"', 67.

WORKS CITED

Ahmad, Aijaz. 'Reconciling Derrida: "Specters of Marx" and Deconstructive Politics'. In *Ghostly Demarcations: A Symposium on Jacques Derrida's* Specters of Marx, ed. Michael Sprinker. London: Verso, 2008, 88–109.
Alfano, Chiara. 'The King is Dead. Long Live the King'. In *Desire in Ashes: Deconstruction, Psychoanalysis and Philosophy*, ed. Simon Morgan Wortham and Chiara Alfano. London: Bloomsbury, 2015, 161–98.
Armel, Aliette. 'From the Word to Life: A Dialogue between Jacques Derrida and Hélène Cixous', trans. Ashley Thompson, *New Literary History* 37, no. 1 (2006): 1–13.
Atkins, G. Douglas, and David M. Bergeron, eds. *Shakespeare and Deconstruction*. New York: Peter Lang, 1988.
Attridge, Derek. 'Following Derrida'. *Tympanum: A Journal of Comparative Literary Studies. Special Edition Choreographies for Jacques Derrida on July 15, 2000.* https://www.usc.edu/dept/comp-lit/tympanum/4/khora.html (last accessible 11 April 2012)
—. 'Ghost Writing'. In *Deconstruction is/in America: A New Sense of the Political*, ed. Anselm Haverkamp. New York: New York University Press, 1995, 223–7.
—. 'Introduction: Derrida and the Questioning of Literature'. In *Acts of Literature*, ed. Derek Attridge. London: Routledge, 1992, 1–29.
—. *The Singularity of Literature*. London: Routledge, 2004.

Barale, Franceso, and Vera Minazzi. 'Off the Beaten Track: Freud, Sound and Music. Statement of a Problem and Some Historico-Critical Notes'. *The International Journal of Psychoanalysis* 89 (2008): 937–57.

Battisti, Carlo, and Giovanni Alessio, eds. *Dizionario Etimologico Italiano*. Florence: G. Barbera Editore, 1975.

Baxandall, Lee, and Stefan Morawski, eds. *Marx & Engels on Literature & Art: A Selection of Writings*. St. Louis: Telos Press, 1973.

Bielik-Robson, Agata. *The Saving Lie: Harold Bloom and Deconstruction*. Evanston: Northwestern University Press, 2011.

Bell, Millicent. *Shakespeare's Tragic Skepticism*. New Haven: Yale University Press. 2002.

Bennington, Geoffrey. 'Derridabase'. In *Jacques Derrida*. Chicago: University of Chicago Press, 1993.

—. *Interrupting Derrida*. London: Routledge, 2000.

—. 'In the event'. In *Derrida's Legacies: Literature and Philosophy*, ed. Simon Glendinning and Robert Eaglestone. London and New York: Routledge, 2008, 26–35.

—. *Legislations: The Politics of Deconstruction*. London: Verso, 1994.

Bevington, David. *Shakespeare's Ideas: More Things in Heaven and Earth*. Oxford: Wiley-Blackwell, 2008.

Bloom, Harold. *Shakespeare: The Invention of the Human*. London: Fourth Estate, 1999.

—. *The Western Canon: The Books and School of the Ages*. New York: Harcourt Brace & Company, 1994.

Cantor, Paul A. 'The Cause of Thunder: Nature and Justice in *King Lear*'. In *King Lear: New Critical Essays*, ed. Jeffrey Kahan. London: Routledge, 2008, 231–52.

Cascardi, Anthony J. *The Cambridge Introduction to Literature and Philosophy*. Cambridge: Cambridge University Press, 2014.

Cavell, Stanley. *In Quest of the Ordinary: Lines of Skepticism and Romanticism*. Chicago: University of Chicago Press, 1994.

Cixous, Hélène. 'Shakespeare Ghosting Derrida', trans. Laurent Milesi. *The Oxford Literary Review* 34, no. 1 (2012): 1–24.

—. *Dream I Tell You*, trans. Beverley Bie Brahic. Edinburgh: Edinburgh University Press, 2006.
Clark, Timothy. *The Poetics of Singularity: The Counter-Culturalist Turn in Heidegger, Derrida, Blanchot and the Later Gadamer.* Edinburgh: Edinburgh University Press, 2005.
Cobussen, Marcel. *Deconstruction in Music.* www.deconstruction-in-music.com
Conrad, Joseph. 'The Secret Sharer'. In *'Twixt Land and Sea: Tales*, ed. J. A. Berthoud, Laura L. Davies and S. W. Reid. Cambridge: Cambridge University Press, 2008, 79–119.
Connors, Clare. *Force from Nietzsche to Derrida*. London: Legenda, 2010.
Danto, Arthur C. 'Philosophy and/as/of Literature'. In *A Companion to the Philosophy of Literature*, ed. Garry L. Hagberg and Walter Jost. Oxford: Wiley-Blackwell, 2010, 52–67.
Davis, Colin. *Critical Excess: Overreading in Derrida, Deleuze, Levinas, Žižek and Cavell*. Stanford: Stanford University Press, 2010.
De Grazia, Margreta. 'Teleology, Delay, and the "Old Mole"'. *Shakespeare Quarterly* 50, no. 3 (1999): 251–67.
DeArmitt, Pleshette. 'Resonances of Echo: A Derridean Allegory'. *Mosaic* 42, no. 2 (2009): 89–100.
Derrida, Jacques. 'Aphorism Countertime', trans. Nicholas Royle. In *Acts of Literature*, ed. Derek Attridge. New York and London: Routledge, 1992, 414–33.
—. 'L'aphorisme à contretemps'. In *Psyché: Inventions de l'autre II*. Paris: Galilée, 2003, 131–44.
—. 'Che cos'è la poesia?' In *A Derrida Reader: Between the Blinds*, trans. and ed. Peggy Kamuf. New York: Columbia University Press, 1991, 221–37.
—. 'Circumfession', trans. Geoffrey Bennington. In *Jacques Derrida*. Chicago and London: University of Chicago Press, 1993.
—. 'Cogito and the History of Madness'. In *Writing and Difference*, trans. Alan Bass. London and New York: Routledge, 2001, 36–76.
—. 'Demeure: Fiction and Testimony'. In Maurice Blanchot, *The Instant of My Death*, trans. Elizabeth Rottenberg. Stanford: Stanford University Press, 2000, 13–103.

—. '"Dialanguages"', trans. Peggy Kamuf. In *Points . . . Interviews, 1974–1994*, ed. Elisabeth Weber. Stanford: Stanford University Press, 1995, 132–55.
—. 'Différance', trans. Alan Bass. In *Margins of Philosophy*. Chicago: University of Chicago Press, 1982, 1–27.
—. *Dissemination*, trans. Barbara Johnson. London and New York: Continuum, 2004.
—. *The Ear of the Other: Otobiography, Transference, Translation: Texts and Discussions with Derrida*, trans. Peggy Kamuf and ed. Christie McDonald. Lincoln: University of Nebraska Press, 1988.
—. 'Envois'. In *The Post Card: From Socrates to Freud and Beyond*, trans. Alan Bass, 1–256. Chicago: University of Chicago Press, 1987.
—. 'Et Cetera . . . (and so on, und so weiter, and so forth, et ainsi de suite, und so überall, etc.)', trans. Geoffrey Bennington. In *Deconstructions: A User's Guide*, ed. Nicholas Royle. Basingstoke: Palgrave, 2000, 282–305.
—. 'Fidélité à plus d'un'. In *Idiomes, nationalités, déconstruction – Recontre de Rabat avec Jacques Derrida*, special issue of Cahiers INTERSIGNES 13 (1998), 221–65.
—. 'Freud and the Scene of Writing'. In *Writing and Difference*, trans. Alan Bass. London: Routledge, 2001, 246–91.
—. *Geneses, Genealogies, Genre, and Genius: The Secrets of the Archive*, trans. Beverley Bie Brahic. New York: Columbia University Press, 2006.
—. *Given Time: I. Counterfeit Money*, trans. Peggy Kamuf. Chicago: University of Chicago Press, 1992.
—. *Glas*, trans. John P. Leavey, Jr. and Richard Rand. Lincoln: University of Nebraska Press, 1990.
—. 'How to Avoid Speaking: Denials', trans. Ken Frieden and Elizabeth Rottenberg. In *Psyche: Inventions of the Other, Volume II*, ed. Peggy Kamuf and Elizabeth Rottenberg. Stanford: Stanford University Press, 2008, 143–95.
—. 'If There is Cause to Translate I: Philosophy in its National Language (Toward a "licterature en françois")', trans. Sylvia

Söderlin. In *Eyes of the University: Right to Philosophy* 2. Stanford: Stanford University Press, 2004, 1–19.

—. 'If There is Cause to Translate II: Descartes' Romances, or The Economy of Words', trans. Rebecca Comay. In *Eyes of the University: Right to Philosophy* 2. Stanford: Stanford University Press, 2004, 20–42.

—. '"I Have a Taste for the Secret"', trans. Giacomo Donis. In *A Taste for the Secret*, ed. Giacomo Donis and David Webb. Cambridge: Polity Press, 2001, 1–92.

—. '*Introduction: Desistance*'. In Philippe Lacoue-Labarthe, *Typography: Mimesis, Philosophy, Politics*, trans. Christopher Fynsk. Stanford: Stanford University Press, 1998, 1–42.

—. '*Istrice 2: Ick bünn all hier*'. In *Points de Suspension: Entretiens*, ed. Elisabeth Weber. Paris: Galilée, 1992, 309–36.

—. '*Istrice 2: Ick bünn all hier*', trans. Peggy Kamuf. In *Points . . . Interviews, 1974–1994*, ed. Elisabeth Weber. Stanford: Stanford University Press, 1995, 300–26.

—. 'Language is Never Owned: An Interview', trans. Thomas Dutoit and Phillippe Romanski. In *Sovereignties in Question: The Poetics of Paul Celan*, ed. Thomas Dutoit and Outi Pasanen. New York: Fordham University Press, 2005, 97–107.

—. 'Living On: Border Lines', trans. James Hulbert. In *Deconstruction and Criticism*. New York: Seabury Press, 1979, 75–176.

—. 'A "Madness" Must Watch over Thinking', trans. Peggy Kamuf. In *Points . . . Interviews, 1974–1994*, ed. Elisabeth Weber. Stanford: Stanford University Press, 1995, 339–64.

—. 'Marx & Sons', trans. G. M. Goshgarian. In *Ghostly Demarcations: A Symposium on Jacques Derrida's Specters of Marx*, ed. Michael Sprinker. London: Verso, 2008, 213–69.

—. *Mémoires: For Paul de Man*, trans. Cecile Lindsay, Jonathan Culler and Eduardo Cadava. New York: Columbia University Press, 1986.

—. *Monolingualism of the Other; or, The Prosthesis of Origin*, trans. Patrick Mensah. Stanford: Stanford University Press, 1998.

—. 'My Chances/*Mes Chances*: A Rendezvous with Some Epicurean Stereophonies', trans. Irene Harvey and Avital Ronell. In *Taking Chances: Derrida, Psychoanalysis, and Literature*, ed. Joseph H. Smith and William Kerrigan. Baltimore and London: Johns Hopkins University Press, 1984, 1–32.

—. *Of Grammatology*, trans. Gayatri Chakravorty Spivak. Baltimore: Johns Hopkins University Press, 2016.

—. *Paper Machine*, trans. Rachel Bowlby. Stanford: Stanford University Press, 2005.

—. 'Poetics and Politics of Witnessing', trans. Rachel Bowlby. In *Sovereignties in Question: The Poetics of Paul Celan*, ed. Thomas Dutoit and Outi Pasanen. New York: Fordham University Press, 2005, 65–96.

—. *Politics of Friendship*, trans. George Collins. London and New York: Verso Books, 2005.

—. *Politiques de l'amitié: suivi de l'oreille de Heidegger*. Paris: Éditions Galilée, 1994.

—. 'Preface: Veni', trans. Pascale-Anne Brault and Michael Naas. In *Rogues: Two Essays on Reason*. Stanford: Stanford University Press, 2005, xi–xv.

—. 'Psyche: Inventions of the Other', trans. Catherine Porter. In *Psyche: Inventions of the Other, Volume I*, ed. Peggy Kamuf and Elizabeth Rottenberg. Stanford: Stanford University Press, 2007, 1–47.

—. 'Qu'est-ce qu'une traduction "relevante"?' In *Quinzièmes assises de la traduction littéraire* (Arles 1998). Arles: Actes Sud, 1999, 21–48.

—. 'Rams: Uninterrupted Dialogue – Between Two Infinities, the Poem', trans. Thomas Dutoit and Philippe Romanski. In *Sovereignties in Question: The Poetics of Paul Celan*, ed. Thomas Dutoit and Outi Pasanen. New York: Fordham University Press, 2005, 135–63.

—. '"A Self-Unsealing Poetic Text": Poetics and Politics of Witnessing', trans. Rachel Bowlby. In *Revenge of the Aesthetic: The Place of Literature in Theory Today*, ed. Michael P. Clark. Berkeley, Los Angeles and London: University of California Press, 2000, 180–207.

—. 'Shibboleth: For Paul Celan', trans. Thomas Dutoit and Joshua Wilner. In *Sovereignties in Question: The Poetics of Paul Celan*, ed. Thomas Dutoit and Outi Pasanen. New York: Fordham University Press, 2005, 1–64.

—. 'Signature Event Context', trans. Samuel Weber and Jeffrey Mehlman. In *Limited Inc*, ed. Gerald Graff. Evanston: Northwestern University Press, 1988, 1–23.

—. 'The Spatial Arts: An Interview with Jacques Derrida', trans. Laurie Volpe. In *Deconstruction and the Visual Arts: Art, Media, Architecture*, ed. Peter Brunette and David Wills. Cambridge: Cambridge University Press, 1994, 9–32.

—. *Specters of Marx: The State of the Debt, the Work of Mourning and the New International*, trans. Peggy Kamuf. New York and London: Routledge, 2006.

—. *Spectres de Marx: L'État de la dette, le travail du deuil et la nouvelle Internationale*. Paris: Galilée, 1993.

—. *Speech and Phenomena and other Essays on Husserl's Theory of Signs*, trans. David B. Allison. Evanston: Northwestern University Press, 1973.

—. 'The Time is Out of Joint', trans. Peggy Kamuf. In *Deconstruction is/in America: A New Sense of the Political*, ed. Anselm Haverkamp. New York and London: New York University Press, 1995, 14–38.

—. 'The Truth That Wounds: From an Interview', trans. Thomas Dutoit. In *Sovereignties in Question: The Poetics of Paul Celan*, ed. Thomas Dutoit and Outi Pasanen. New York: Fordham University Press, 2005, 164–9.

—. '"This Strange Institution Called Literature": An Interview with Jacques Derrida', trans. Geoffrey Bennington and Rachel Bowlby. In *Acts of Literature*, ed. Derek Attridge. London: Routledge, 1992, 33–75.

—. 'Ulysses Gramophone: Hear Say Yes in Joyce', trans. Tina Kendall and Shari Benstock. In *Acts of Literature*, ed. Derek Attridge. London: Routledge, 1992, 253–309.

—. 'Voice II', trans. Verena Andermatt Conley. In *Points . . . Interviews, 1974–1994*, ed. Elisabeth Weber. Stanford: Stanford University Press, 1995, 156–70.

—. 'What is a "Relevant" Translation?', trans. Lawrence Ventuti. *Critical Inquiry* 27, no. 2 (2001): 174–200.

—. *The Work of Mourning*, ed. Pascale-Anne Brault and Michael Naas. Chicago and London: University of Chicago Press, 2003.

Dutoit, Thomas. 'Jacques Derrida, Anglicist'. *Oxford Literary Review* 25 (2003): 323–36.

Eagleton, Terry. *The Event of Literature*. Newhaven: Yale University Press, 2012.

—.'Marxism without Marxism'. In *Ghostly Demarcations: A Symposium on Jacques Derrida's* Specters of Marx, ed. Michael Sprinker. London: Verso, 2008, 83–7.

Eldridge, Richard, ed. *The Oxford Handbook of Philosophy and Literature*. Oxford: Oxford University Press, 2009.

Emerson, Ralph Waldo. *Representative Men*. London: J. M. Dent & Co., 1901.

Evans, Malcolm. 'Deconstructing Shakespeare's Comedies'. In *Alternative Shakespeares*, ed. John Drakakis. London and New York: Routledge, 2002, 69–96.

Faigenbaum, Gustavo. *Conversations with John Searle*. Buenos Aires: LibrosEnRed, 2003.

Farrell Krell, David. 'Introduction'. In *Early Greek Thinking*, trans. David Farrell Krell and Frank A. Capuzzi. New York: Harper & Row, 1975, 3–12.

Felperin, Howard. '"Tongue-tied our queen?": The Deconstruction of Presence in *The Winter's Tale*'. In *Shakespeare and the Question of Theory*, ed. Patricia Parker and Geoffrey Hartman. New York: Methuen, 1985, 3–18.

Freud, Sigmund. 'Beyond the Pleasure Principle'. In *The Standard Edition of the Complete Psychological Works of Sigmund Freud*, trans. and ed. James Strachey. Vol. XVIII. London: The Hogarth Press, 1995, 7–61.

—. 'The Interpretation of Dreams'. In *The Standard Edition of the Complete Psychological Works of Sigmund Freud*, trans. and ed. James Strachey. Vol. V. London: The Hogarth Press, 1995, 339–627.

—. 'Jokes and their Relation to the Unconscious'. In *The Standard Edition of the Complete Psychological Works of Sigmund Freud*,

trans. and ed. James Strachey. Vol. VII. London: The Hogarth Press, 1995.
—. 'Leonardo da Vinci and a Memory of His Childhood'. In *The Standard Edition of The Complete Psychological Works of Sigmund Freud*, trans. and ed. James Strachey. Vol. XI. London: The Hogarth Press, 1995, 63–137.
—. *The Origins of Psycho-Analysis: Letters to Wilhelm Fliess, Drafts and Notes: 1887–1902*, trans. Eric Mosbacher and James Strachey, ed. Marie Bonaparte, Anna Freud and Ernst Kris. London: Imago, 1954.
—. 'The Theme of the Three Caskets'. In *The Standard Edition of the Complete Psychological Works of Sigmund Freud*, trans. and ed. James Strachey. Vol. XII. London: The Hogarth Press, 1995, 289–301.
—. *Die Traumdeutung*. Leipzig: Franz Deuticke, 1930.
Garber, Marjorie. *Profiling Shakespeare*. New York: Routledge, 2008.
—. *Quotation Marks*. London: Routledge, 2003.
—. *Shakespeare after All*. New York: Anchor Books, 2004.
—. *Symptoms of Culture*. London: Routledge, 2000.
Gaston, Sean. *Starting with Derrida: Plato, Aristotle and Hegel*. London: Continuum, 2007.
Glendinning, Simon. *Derrida: A Very Short Introduction*. Oxford: Oxford University Press, 2011.
Gregory, Johann. 'Wordplay in Shakespeare's *Hamlet* and the Accusation of Derrida's "Logical Phallusies"', *English Studies* 94, no. 3 (2013): 313–30.
Gundersheimer, Werner. 'Foreword'. In *Fortune: 'All is but Fortune'*, compiled and ed. Leslie Thomson. Washington, DC: The Folger Shakespeare Library, 2000, 7.
Haddad, Samir. *Derrida and the Inheritance of Democracy*. Bloomington: Indiana University Press, 2013.
Harries, Martin. *Scare Quotes from Shakespeare: Marx, Keynes, and the Language of Reenchantment*. Stanford: Stanford University Press, 2000.
Hegel, Georg W. F. *Lectures on the History of Philosophy*, trans. E. S. Haldane and Frances H. Simson. 3 vols. Lincoln: University of Nebraska Press, 1995.

Heidegger, Martin. 'Moira (Parmenides VIII, 34–41)'. In *Early Greek Thinking*, trans. David Farrell Krell and Frank A. Capuzzi. New York: Harper & Row, 1975, 79–101.

Heller, Agnes. *The Time is Out of Joint: Shakespeare as Philosopher of History*. Lanham: Rowman & Littlefield Publishers, 2002.

Hillis Miller, J. 'Anachronistic Reading'. *Derrida Today* 3, no. 1 (2010): 75–91.

—. *For Derrida*. New York: Fordham University Press, 2009.

—. *Speech Acts in Literature*. Stanford: Stanford University Press, 2001.

Hobson, Marian. 'Marian Hobson on Reading Philosophy as Translation'. British Academy podcast. https://soundcloud.com/britishacademy/marian-hobson-on-reading-philosophy-as-translation.

Hodge, Joanna. *Derrida on Time*. London: Routledge, 2007.

James, Henry. 'The Birthplace'. In *The Better Sort*. New York: Charles Scribner's Sons, 1903, 245–311.

Johnson, Bruce. '*Hamlet*: Voice, Music, Sound'. *Popular Music* 24, no. 2 (2005): 257-67.

Jones, Ernest. *Sigmund Freud: Life and Work*. 3 vols. London: Hogarth, 1953–7.

Kamuf, Peggy. *Book of Addresses*. Stanford: Stanford University Press, 2005.

—. 'Deconstruction and Love'. In *Deconstructions: A User's Guide*, ed. Nicholas Royle, 151–70. Basingstoke: Palgrave, 2000.

—. 'The Ear, Who?' *Discourse* 30, nos. 1/2 (2008): 177–90.

Keohane, Oisín. 'Tongue-tied Democracy: The Bind of National Language in Tocqueville and Derrida'. *Derrida Today* 4, no. 2 (2011): 233–56.

Kermode, Frank. 'Strange, Sublime, Uncanny, Anxious'. *London Review of Books*, 22 December 1994. https://www.lrb.co.uk/v16/n24/frank-kermode/strange-sublime-uncanny-anxious

Kliman, Bernice W. 'Explicit Stage Directions (Especially Graphics) in *Hamlet*'. In *Stage Directions in* Hamlet: *New Essays and New Directions*, ed. Hardin L. Aasand. London: Associated University Presses, 2003, 74–91.

Kottman, Paul A., ed. *Philosophers on Shakespeare*. Stanford: Stanford University Press, 2009.
Laclau, Ernesto. 'The Time is Out of Joint'. *Diacritics* 25, no. 2 (Summer 1995): 86–96.
Lamarque, Peter. *The Philosophy of Literature*. Oxford: Wiley-Blackwell, 2009.
Laplanche, Jean. 'Notes on Afterwardness'. In *Essays on Otherness*. London: Routledge, 1999, 260–5.
Laplanche, Jean, and Jean-Bertrand Pontalis. *The Language of Psychoanalysis*. London: Karnac Books, 1988.
Lipps, Theodor. *Grundtatsachen des Seelenlebens*. Bonn: Verlag von Max und Cohen & Sohn (Fr. Cohen), 1883.
Lukacher, Ned. 'Shakespeare in the Ear of Hegel'. In *Primal Scenes: Literature, Philosophy, Psychoanalysis*. Ithaca: Cornell University Press, 1986, 178–235.
Mann, Michael. *Sturm und Drang-Drama: Studien und Vorstudien zu Schiller's 'Räubern'*. Bern: Francke Verlag, 1974.
McGinn, Colin. *Shakespeare's Philosophy: Discovering the Meaning Behind the Plays*. New York: HarperCollins, 2006.
McQuillan, Martin. *Deconstruction after 9/11*. London: Routledge, 2009.
Marx, Karl. 'The Eighteenth Brumaire of Louis Bonaparte'. In *Selected Writings*, ed. David McLellan. Oxford: Oxford University Press, 2000, 329–55.
Moi, Toril. 'The Adventure of Reading: Literature and Philosophy, Cavell and Beauvoir'. In *Stanley Cavell and Literary Studies: Consequences of Skepticism*, ed. Richard Eldridge and Bernie Rhie. London: Continuum, 2011, 17–29.
Morgan Wortham, Simon. *The Derrida Dictionary*. London: Continuum, 2010.
Mulhall, Stephen. *The Wounded Animal: J. M. Coetzee and the Difficulty of Reality in Literature and Philosophy*. Princeton: Princeton University Press, 2009.
Naas, Michael. *Derrida from Now On*. New York: Fordham University Press, 2008.
Nancy, Jean-Luc. 'L'Amour en éclats'. In *Une pensée finie*. Paris: Galilée, 1990.

—. *Listening*, trans. Charlotte Mandell. New York: Fordham Unversity Press, 2007.
Nussbaum, Martha. *Cultivating Humanity: A Classical Defense of Reform in Liberal Education*. Cambridge, MA: Harvard University Press, 1998.
—. *Love's Knowledge: Essays on Philosophy and Literature*. Oxford: Oxford University Press, 1990.
—. 'The Professor of Parody: Review of Four Books by Judith Butler, *Excitable Speech; The Psychic Life of Power; Bodies that Matter; Gender Trouble*'. In *Philosophical Interventions: Reviews 1986–2011*. Oxford: Oxford University Press, 2012, 198–222.
—. 'Stages of Thought: Review of A. D. Nuttall, *Shakespeare the Thinker*; Colin McGinn, *Shakespeare's Philosophy*; and Tzachi Zamir, *Double Vision: Moral Philosophy and Shakespearean Drama*'. In *Philosophical Interventions: Reviews 1986–2011*. Oxford: Oxford University Press, 2012, 367–77.
Nuttall, A. D. *Shakespeare the Thinker*. New Haven: Yale University Press, 2007.
Osborne, Peter. 'Problematizing Disciplinarity, Transdisciplinary Problematics'. *Theory, Culture and Society* 32, no. 5–6 (2015): 3–35.
Parrott, Thomas Marc. 'Errors and Omissions in the Griggs Facsimile of the Second Quarto of *Hamlet*'. *MLN* 49 (June 1934): 376–9.
Peeters, Benoît. *Derrida: A Biography*, trans. Andrew Brown. Cambridge: Polity Press, 2013.
Pettman, Dominic. *Human Error: Species-Being and Media Machines*. Minneapolis: University of Minnesota Press, 2011.
Prendergast, Christopher. 'Derrida's Hamlet'. *SubStance* 34, no. 1 (2005): 44–7.
Reinhard Lupton, Julia. *Thinking with Shakespeare: Essays on Politics and Life*. Chicago and London: University of Chicago Press, 2011.
Royle, Nicholas. 'Derrida's Event'. In *Derrida's Legacies: Literature and philosophy*, ed. Simon Glendinning and Robert Eaglestone. London and New York: Routledge, 2008, 36–44.

—. *How to Read Shakespeare*. London: Granta Books, 2005.
—. *In Memory of Jacques Derrida*. Edinburgh: Edinburgh University Press, 2009.
—. 'Nuclear Piece: Memoires of *Hamlet* and the Time to Come'. *Diacritics* 20, no. 1 (1990): 39–55.
—. *Telepathy and Literature, Essays on the Reading Mind*. Oxford: Basil Blackwell, 1991.
—. *The Uncanny*. Manchester: Manchester University Press, 2003.
Scheiner, Corinne. 'Teleiopoiesis, Telepoesis, and the Practice of Comparative Literature'. *Comparative Literature* 57, no. 3 (2005): 239–45.
Schiller, Friedrich, and Christian Gottfried Körner. *Correspondence of Schiller with Körner. Comprising Sketches and Anecdotes of Goethe, the Schlegels, Wieland, and Other Contemporaries*. With Biographical Sketches and Notes, by Leonard Simpson, Esq. Vol. I. London: Richard Bentley, 1849.
Schlegel, Friedrich. *Lucinde and the Fragments*, trans. Peter Firchow. Minneapolis: University of Minnesota Press, 1971.
Shakespeare, William. *Hamlet*, ed. Ann Thompson and Neil Taylor. London: Arden Shakespeare, 2006.
—. *Hamlet: The Texts of 1603 and 1623*, ed. Ann Thompson and Neil Taylor. London: Arden Shakespeare, 2006.
—. *Hamlet*, trans. Yves Bonnefoy. Paris: Gallimard, Folio, 1992.
—. *Julius Caesar*, ed. David Daniell. London: Arden Shakespeare, 2002.
—. *King Henry VI Part 2*, ed. Ronald Knowles. London: Arden Shakespeare, 1999.
—. *King Lear*, ed. R. A. Foakes. London: Arden Shakespeare, 1997.
—. *The Merchant of Venice*, ed. John Drakakis. London: Arden Shakespeare, 2011.
—. *Othello*, ed. E. A. J. Honigmann. London: Arden Shakespeare, 2006.
—. *Romeo and Juliet*, ed. René Weis. London: Arden Shakespeare, 2012.
—. *Troilus and Cressida*, ed. David Bevington. London: Arden Shakespeare, 2006.

Skeat, Walter W., ed. *An Etymological Dictionary of the English Language*, new edn revised and enlarged. Oxford: The Clarendon Press, 1924.
Smith, Barry. 'Letter to *The Times*'. *The Times*, 9 May 1992.
Spevack, Marvin. *The Harvard Concordance to Shakespeare*. Cambridge, MA: Belknap Press of Harvard University Press, 1974.
Spivak, Gayatri Chakravorty. 'Ghostwriting'. *Diacritics* 25, no. 2 (1995): 65–84.
Stevenson, Ruth. '*Hamlet*'s Mice, Motes, Moles, and Minching Malecho'. *New Literary History* 33 (2002): 435–59.
Stewart, Garrett. 'The Word Viewed: Skepticism Degree Zero'. *Stanley Cavell and Literary Studies: Consequences of Skepticism*, ed. Richard Eldridge and Bernie Rhie, 78–91. London and New York: Continuum, 2011.
Sutherland, Keston. *Stupefaction: A Radical Anatomy of Phantoms*. London: Seagull Books, 2011.
Venuti, Lawrence. 'Translating Derrida on Translation: Relevance and Disciplinary Resistance'. *The Yale Journal of Criticism* 16, no. 2 (2003): 237–62.
Vries, Hent De. 'The Shibboleth Effect: On Reading Paul Celan', trans. Bettina Bergo and Michael B. Smith. In *Judeities: Questions for Jacques Derrida*, ed. Bettina Bergo, Joseph Cohen and Raphael Zagury-Orly. New York: Fordham University Press, 2007, 175–213.
Warner, William Beatty. *Chance and the Text of Experience: Freud, Nietzsche, and Shakespeare's* Hamlet. Ithaca: Cornell University Press, 1986.
Weber, Samuel. *Theatricality as Medium*. New York: Fordham University Press, 2004.
Wilson, Richard. *Shakespeare in French Theory: King of Shadows*. London: Routledge, 2007.
Witmore, Michael. *Shakespearean Metaphysics*. London: Continuum, 2008.
Wolfreys, Julian, John Brannigan and Ruth Robbins, eds. *The French Connections of Jacques Derrida*. Albany: State University of New York Press, 1999.

Wolfreys, Julian. 'Justifying the Unjustifiable: A Supplementary Introduction, of Sorts'. In *The Derrida Reader: Writing Performances*, ed. Julian Wolfreys. Edinburgh: Edinburgh University Press, 1998, 1–49.

Wood, Sarah. 'Let's Start Again'. *Diacritics* 29, no.1 (1999): 4–19.

—. 'A New International, Or What You Will'. *Oxford Literary Review* 30, no. 1 (2008): 147–60.

—. *Without Mastery: Reading and Other Forces*. Edinburgh: Edinburgh University Press, 2014.

Young, Alan R. 'Fortune in Shakespeare's *King Lear*'. In *Fortune: 'All is but Fortune'*, compiled and ed. Leslie Thomson. Washington, DC: The Folger Shakespeare Library, 2000, 56–67.

Zamir, Tzachi. *Double Vision: Moral Philosophy and Shakespearean Drama*. Princeton and Oxford: Princeton University Press, 2007.

INDEX

Note: Entries starting with an article have been transposed when entries are in English (e.g. *German Ideology, The*). Entries in other languages have not been transposed (e.g. *Die Räuber*).

acousmatics, 199
Acts of Literature (Derrida), 41
acts of reading, 41, 47–8, 53, 59, 68, 80, 108
    arrow of teleiopoesis, 69–74, 78, 84–5
    frequencies, 198
    homophones, 183
    political aporias, 175, 179
    Specters of Marx (Derrida), 179, 181–2, 205–6
    see also countersigning / countersignatures
Adam, Charles, 92
'Adventures of Reading' (Moi), 6–7
Ahmad, Aijaz, 175–6, 181
alienation, 88–9
'Anachronistic Reading' (Hillis Miller), 198
Anglicist, Derrida as, 86–93
'Aphorism Countertime' (Derrida), 17, 18
    chance, 85
    contretemps, 31–5, 53–4, 65–8, 137, 182

countersignatures, 86
deconstruction, 48–53
iterability, 53–6, 67
listening, 185–7
love, 49–50, 52, 53, 76
aphorisms, 31
aporia, politics of, 173–80
après-coup, 7; *see also Nachträglichkeit*
Arendt, Hannah, 14
arrow of teleiopoesis, 69–74, 78, 218
art, 82–3, 110, 136, 138, 160, 183
'Aschenglorie' (Celan), 81–2
Assises de la traduction littéraire, 121
Athenaeums Fragmente (Schlegel), 110
atoms, 157
Attridge, Derek, 31, 32, 41, 54, 86, 203
'au mot homo', 124; *see also* homophony
Aufhebung, 125, 126
Austin, J. L., 56–7, 144

Index

Barale, Francesco, 152–3, 154
bardolatry, 8–16, 33
Bell, Millicent, 13, 16
Bennington, Geoffrey, 177–8, 179, 189, 224
Bevington, David, 12–13
Beyond Good and Evil (Nietzsche), 69–70
Bielik-Robson, Agata, 11
Blanchot, Maurice, 34
bloodlessness, 44, 56, 79–80, 176
Bloom, Harold, 9–12, 16, 37, 56
Bollack, J. and M., 157
Brahic, Beverley Bie, 218
Brannigan, John, 87
Brunette, Peter, 182
'Brutus and Caesar Song' (*Die Räuber*, Schiller), 150, 151
Butler, Judith, 41–3, 45

cadence, 157, 161–2, 166
cadere, 157
Cambridge affair, 35, 37, 42, 48
canonicity, 9–10, 37, 41, 222
Cantor, Paul A., 140
Cascardi, Anthony, 39
Cavell, Stanley, 102
Celan, Paul, 34, 79, 81–2, 88
chance, 135–8, 155–8
 'Aphorism Countertime' (Derrida), 85
 King Lear, 139, 142, 143, 145–6
 language, 166–7
 literature, 136, 159, 160–1, 166
 Martin Heidegger, 143, 144, 145
 psychoanalysis, 139, 156, 158–60
 Sigmund Freud, 142–3, 145, 146–55
Chance and the Text of Experience (Warner), 150

'Che cos'è la poesia?' (Derrida), 81, 103, 110, 113–14, 116, 118, 184, 195
choice, 141–2
'Circumfession' (Derrida), 85
Cixous, Hélène, 34, 80, 119, 123–4, 217, 220–2
Clark, Timothy, 203
clinamen, 143, 157, 159, 160, 167, 220
Cobussen, Marcel, 183, 188
Collins-Robert French Dictionary, 32, 66, 84
Comedy of Errors, 112
Condillac, Étienne Bonnot de, 57, 58
Connors, Clare, 68
Conrad, Joseph, 126
continental philosophy, 89–90
contretemps, 31–5, 48–9, 53–4, 65–8, 155, 182
corps à corps, 48, 79, 84
countersigning / countersignatures, 78, 219
 'Aphorism Countertime' (Derrida), 86
 '*Fidelité à plus d'un*' (Derrida), 119
 frequencies, 196
 Specters of Marx (Derrida), 108, 174, 179
 'This Strange Institution Called Literature' (Derrida), 47, 85
 see also acts of reading
countertime *see* 'Aphorism Countertime' (Derrida); *contretemps*
coup, 66, 69, 73, 82
Courcelles, Étienne de, 92

da Vinci, Leonardo, 136
Danto, Arthur, 37–8

Dasein, 111, 113, 143, 193
Davies, Colin, 41
De Grazia, Margreta, 101, 103, 109
de Vries, Hent, 83
deadening, 45, 61n
deafness, 154–5, 163
DeArmitt, Pleshette, 202
death, 142
deconstruction, 12, 44–5, 46–8, 177–8, 180
  'Aphorism Countertime' (Derrida), 48–53
  Hamlet, 206
  King Lear, 137–8
  love, 76, 78
  United States, 89
'Deconstruction and Love' (Kamuf), 76, 79
'democracy to come', 176–7, 178
Der Spiegel, 35
Derrida, J.
  as Anglicist, 86–93
  critics, 35–6, 37, 42, 65, 174–7, 180
  readings of Shakespeare, 2–4, 16–23, 75–86
'Derrida's Event' (Royle), 224
'Derrida's Hamlet' (Prendergast), 180
Descartes, René, 91–3
deterministic approach, 7, 8
'Dialanguages' (Derrida), 192
Die Räuber (Schiller), 150, 151
différance, 51–2, 53–4, 59, 87, 157, 158, 184, 197
discordance, 182
Discourse on Method (Descartes), 91–3
Dissemination (Derrida), 22
Double Vision (Zamir), 4, 8, 61n

Dream I Tell You (Cixous), 220, 222
dreams, 141, 142, 146–50, 152, 163–6, 220, 222
Dutoit, Thomas, 88

Eagleton, Terry, 175, 176
ear, 127, 128, 144, 153, 184, 187–8, 198, 218
  Hamlet, 129, 190–1, 192, 202
  Julius Caesar, 154, 163
  'Marx & Sons' (Derrida), 181
  'My Chances' (Derrida), 166, 167
  porpentine, 110, 116, 117
  Romeo and Juliet, 186
  Sigmund Freud, 155, 164–5, 222
  see also hearing; listening
Ear of the Other, The (Derrida), 76, 78, 84
echo, 202–3
Economic and Philosophical Manuscripts (Marx), 104
Eighteenth Brumaire (Marx), 104–6
Eldridge, Richard, 38–9
Emerson, Ralph Waldo, 15
English as discipline, 19
English language, 86–7, 92, 120, 124, 207
'Envois' (Derrida), 50, 73, 74, 76, 85
Epicurus, 157
Essay on the Origin of Human Knowledge (Condillac), 57, 58
'Et Cetera ...' (Derrida), 52
ethical questions, 45
Etymological Dictionary of the English Language (Skeat), 116–17

experts, 33–4, 86, 207, 223–5
Eyes of the University (Derrida), 91–2

falling, 157–8, 161, 166
feminism, 43, 176
  symbolic turn, 43–4
Ferraris, Maurizio, 110
'*Fidélité à plus'un*' (Derrida), 119
'Following Derrida' (Attridge), 86
fortune, 139–40
French Connections of Jacques Derrida, The (Wolfreys, Brannigan and Robbins), 87
French language
  'Che cos'è la poesia?' (Derrida), 113–14
  Discourse on Method (Descartes), 91, 92
  'Following Derrida' (Attridge), 86
  Hélène Cixous, 221
  Monolingualism of the Other (Derrida), 77, 87
  'Translating Derrida on Translation' (Venuti), 124
  'What is a 'Relevant' Translation?' (Derrida), 120
French philosophy, 89–90
French Revolution, 104–5
'French Shakespeare', 9–10
frequencies, 188, 192–4, 195, 196, 197–9, 203–4, 206
Freud, Sigmund, 222
  chance, 142–3, 145, 146–55
  Hamlet's mole, 102–3
  Interpretation of Dreams, The, 141, 146–50, 151–2, 163–6, 222
  Klang, 161–2, 163–6, 167, 220
  Leonardo da Vinci and a Memory of His Childhood, 158–60

  in 'My Chances' (Derrida), 136, 158–60
  Nachträglichkeit, 7
  'Shakespeare of the Night', 222
  Theme of the Three Caskets, The, 140–3, 148
  'Freud and the Scene of Writing' (Derrida), 101

Garber, Marjorie, 15, 106, 154
Gaston, Sean, 17, 18
gé, 220–2
Geneses, Genealogies, Genres, and Genius (Derrida), 215–16, 218, 219, 220–2
genius, 3, 110, 215–16, 217–19, 220–2
German Ideology, The (Marx), 104
German language, 79, 81, 87, 107, 110, 125
Ghost (*Hamlet*), 106, 108, 109, 110, 118, 128–9, 189–99, 199–207
'Ghost Writing' (Attridge), 203
Ghostly Demarcations: A Symposium on Jacques Derrida's Specters of Marx, 174–5
'Ghostwriting' (Spivak), 176
Glas (Derrida), 82
Glendinning, Simon, 12, 52
Goethe, Johann Wolfgang von, 151
Grimm brothers, 111
Grundtatsachen des Seelenlebens (Lipps), 152–4

Haddad, Samir, 176–7
Hamlet, 52, 68, 118, 126, 136
  Ghost, 106, 108, 109, 110, 118, 128–9, 189–99, 200–7
  mole, 101–3, 105–7, 108–10
  mot d'ordre, 199

Hamlet (cont.)
  porpentine, 184
  'the time is out of joint', 50,
    76, 81
  visor effect, 196–7, 199, 206
'Hamlet: Voice, Music, Sound'
  (Johnson), 190
Harries, Martin, 107
Harvard Concordance to
  Shakespeare, The (Spevack),
  195–6
hearing, 162–5, 184, 192, 198–9;
  see also listening
Hecate, 81–2
hedgehog, 114, 129–30; see
  also hérisson; Igel; istrice;
  porpentine
'Hedgehog and the Hare, The'
  (Grimm), 111
Hegel, Georg W. F., 107,
  125, 128
Heidegger, Martin, 19, 111, 143–4,
  145, 163
Heller, Agnes, 14
hérisson, 103, 109, 110, 111–15,
  117–18, 129, 184; see also
  hedgehog; Igel; istrice;
  porpentine
hermeneutic approach, 7–8
hic et ubique, 111, 113, 118
Hillis Miller, J., 73, 198, 205
history, 177–8
History of Philosophy (Hegel),
  107
Hobson, Marian, 90–1, 93
Hodge, Joanna, 51
homophony, 124, 164–5,
  183, 220–2; see also
  iteraphonic functions; lexical
  dismemberment
'How to Avoid Speaking: Denials'
  (Derrida), 192

How to Read Shakespeare (Royle),
  217
humanism, 11, 16, 38–40, 56,
  79–80, 186
Husserl, Edmund, 188–9

'I Have a Taste for the Secret'
  (Derrida), 51, 83
Identity and Difference
  (Heidegger), 111
idiomacity, 80, 92
idioms, 79, 93, 119, 123, 124,
  221
  continental / French philosophy,
    90
  countersigning, 85
  untranslatability, 81, 120–1
  see also porpentine; 'the time is
    out of joint'
Igel, 110–11; see also hedgehog;
  hérisson; hic et ubique; istrice;
  porpentine
'imp words', 102
In Memory of Jacques Derrida
  (Royle), 154
'Injunctions of Marx' (Derrida),
  115
integrated philosophical criticism, 8
interdisciplinarity, 1, 5–8, 19,
  37–40
Interpretation of Dreams, The
  (Freud), 141, 146–50, 151–2,
  163–6, 222
'Introduction: Desistance'
  (Derrida), 194
inversion, 141
istrice, 114, 129; see also hedgehog;
  hérisson; Igel; porpentine
'Istrice 2. Ick bünn all hier'
  (Derrida), 110, 113
Italian language, 113–14
iterability, 53–6, 57–9, 67, 73

iteraphonic functions, 198
iteration, 202

jet, 66, 69, 73, 220–2; *see also*
    rejeter
Johnson, Barbara, 22, 23
Johnson, Bruce, 190
Jones, Ernest, 152
Joyce, James, 34
Julius Caesar, 149–50, 151,
    154, 161–3

Kamuf, Peggy
    'Che cos'è la poesia?' (Derrida),
        116
    donner-lieu, 192
    Hamlet, 204
    istrice, 129
    Le plus d'un, 197
    love, 76
    Othello, 191
    peepholes (*meurtrières*), 119–20
    scholars, 207
    teleiopoesis, 74
    textuality, 79
    visor effect, 197
keeping watch, 75, 76, 87, 89, 103,
    104, 119–20
Kermode, Frank, 20, 41, 222
King Henry VI, 112
King Lear, 136–40, 142–3,
    145–6
Klang, 151, 152, 161–2, 163,
    165–6, 167, 220
Kliman, Bernice W., 191
Kottman, Paul, 9

Lacan, Jacques, 102
Laclau, Ernesto, 180
language, 79, 119, 126, 221–2
    chance, 166–7
    Derrida as Anglicist, 86–93

moles of, 102
poets, 82–3
power of, 12, 21
see also English language; French
    language; German language;
    Italian language; Latin
Language of Psychoanalysis
    (Laplanche and Pontalis), 7
Laplanche, Jean, 7–8
Latin, 91, 92, 125
Le Grand Robert, 193, 194, 196,
    204–5, 206
Le plus d'un, 119, 121, 122–3,
    192, 197
legein, 144
Legislations (Bennington),
    177–8
*Leonardo da Vinci and a Memory
    of His Childhood* (Freud),
    158–60
lettre, 103, 127, 183, 222
    Derrida as Anglicist, 88
    frequencies, 192, 198
    hérisson, 112–13
    'My Chances' (Derrida), 135
    porpentine, 116, 118, 128
    Shylock's oath, 123
    téléiopoièse, 70
lexical dismemberment, 102
Lipps, Theodor, 152–4
listening, 116, 127, 184, 205
    Hamlet, 128–9, 189–99,
        199–207
    Jean-Luc Nancy, 187–8
    Romeo and Juliet, 185–7
    see also hearing
literary excellence, 9, 10
literary theory, 45
literature, 55, 160, 219
    chance, 136, 159, 160–1
    in Derrida's philosophical
        project, 36

literature (*cont.*)
  interdisciplinarity between philosophy and, 1, 5–8, 19, 37–40
  singularity, 59, 83
  transdisciplinarity between philosophy and, 19–20, 40
  translatability, 90
'Living On: Border Lines' (Derrida), 18
locutionary act, 144
love, 49–50, 52, 53, 74–8, 84
Love's Knowledge (Nussbaum), 39–40, 44, 45
Lucretius, 167
Lukacher, Ned, 101
Luke, 9.2 (Gospel), 105

McGinn, Colin, 4, 12
McQuillan, Martin, 70, 73
'"Madness" Must Watch Over Thinking, A' (Derrida), 119
maintenant, 84
Manhattan (Cixous), 220, 221
mark, divisibility of, 157
Marx, Eleanor, 104
Marx, Karl, 104–8
'Marx & Sons' (Derrida), 181
Marxism, 173
'Marxism without Marxism' (Eagleton), 175
mastery, 137, 140, 145, 150, 155–68, 198, 219; *see also* Shakespeare experts
meaning, 189
Mémoires: For Paul de Man (Derrida), 195
Mensah, Patrick, 77
Merchant of Venice, The, 121–3, 140–2
mercy, 121
metaphysics, 13

meurtrières (peepholes), 76, 119–20, 122, 126, 127–8
Minazzi, Vera, 152–3, 154
Moi, Toril, 6–7, 8, 11, 41
'Moira' (Heidegger), 143–4
mole
  Hamlet, 101–3, 105–7, 108–10
  moles of language, 102
Monolingualism of the Other (Derrida), 77, 87, 88–9, 108, 194
Morgan Wortham, Simon, 174
mot, 112, 166
mot d'ordre, 199
mourning, 49–50
Mulhall, Stephen, 39
music, 183
'My Chances' (Derrida), 17, 135–8, 143, 155–61, 166–7, 220

Nachträglichkeit, 7, 8
Nancy, Jean-Luc, 77–8, 187–8, 199, 204, 205
nature, 138, 139–40
New International, 179
Nietzsche, Friedrich, 44, 69–70, 72
noein, 144
noise, 190
'*Non Vixit* Dream', 146–9, 152, 164, 165, 220, 222
nonsynonymous substitutions, 23, 54; *see also* quasi-synonymous substitutions
'Notes on Afterwards' (Laplanche), 7–8
'Nuclear Piece' (Royle), 101
Nussbaum, Martha, 4–6, 8, 39–40, 41–5, 56, 79, 80, 176
Nuttall, A. D., 4, 6

obscurantism, terrorism of, 42
oeuvre, 55, 160–1

Of Grammatology (Derrida), 48
Osborne, Peter, 19, 40
Othello, 191
otherness, 52
out-of-jointedness
  of being, 51
  of time, 50–1
  see also 'the time is out of joint'
overreading, 41
Oxford Dictionary of English Etymology, 114, 116
Oxford English Dictionary (OED), 46, 116, 167, 182, 194, 196, 205, 223

palintrope, 17–18
Paper Machine (Derrida), 186–7
parole, 112, 166
peepholes (*meurtrières*), 76, 119–20, 122, 126, 127–8
performativity, 75
philosophical criticism, integrated, 8
philosophy
  attitude towards Shakespeare, 1–2
  French and continental, 89–90
  as handicraft, 19–20
  interdisciplinarity between literature and, 1, 5–8, 19, 37–40
  recent engagement with Shakespeare, 4–8: bardolatry, 8–16
  three criteria for worthwhile engagement with Shakespeare, 4–5
  transdisciplinarity between literature and, 19–20, 40
  translatability, 90–3
phonocentrism, 189
Po&sie, 113
Poe, Edgar Allan, 155
poems, 76, 91, 93, 110, 118
Poesia, 111, 113

poetry, 111–12, 118
'Che cos'è la poesia?' (Derrida), 103, 110, 113–14, 116, 118, 184, 195
poetry of the past, 105
poets, 82–3
Points de suspension (Weber), 113
political aporias, 173–80
Politics of Friendship (Derrida), 69–72
Pontalis, Jean-Bertrand, 7
popular culture, 106
porcupine, 109, 110, 114, 116–17
porpentine, 109–10, 116–18, 120, 126
  listening, 128–9
  signature, 103
  sound, 183–4
  Troilus and Cressida, 112
  untranslatability, 115
  see also hedgehog; *hérisson*; *Igel*; *istrice*
port, 115, 116
porter, 115
'Preface: Veni' (Derrida), 202
Prendergast, Christopher, 180
Primal Scenes (Lukacher), 101
'Professor of Parody, The' (Nussbaum), 41–4
'Psyche: Inventions of the Other' (Derrida), 202
psychoanalysis, 139, 142, 156, 158–60

quasi-synonymous substitutions, 52, 67, 174, 197; *see also* nonsynonymous substitutions
quotation, 106

'Rams' (Derrida), 194
're-', 193, 194, 204–5, 206; *see also* re-politicisation; re-reading

readers, 38
reading, acts of, 41, 47–8, 53, 59, 68, 80, 108
  arrow of teleiopoesis, 69–74, 78, 84–5
  frequencies, 198
  homophones, 183
  political aporias, 175, 179
  Specters of Marx (Derrida), 179, 181–2, 205–6
  see also countersigning / countersignatures
reading, event of, 224
reading, *King Lear*, 140, 145–6
'Recollections of Mohr' (E. Marx), 104
Reinhard Lupton, Julia, 13–15
rejeter, 66, 71, 204
relevant, 124–5, 127
relevare, 125
relever, 121–2, 125, 126
relief / relieve, 125
renvoi, 204–5, 206
repetition, 193–4
re-politicisation, 179, 181, 205–6
re-reading, 53, 104, 179, 182, 224
research programmes, 19–20
'Resonance of Echo' (DeArmitt), 202
revolutions, 104–5
rhythm, 153–4, 194–5
Richmond, Sarah, 35
Robbins, Ruth, 87
Romeo and Juliet
  contretemps, 31–5, 53–4, 65–8
  deconstruction, 48–53
  'Following Derrida' (Attridge), 86
  iterability, 53–6, 67
  listening, 185–7
  love, 49–50, 52, 53, 76

Royle, Nicholas
  Hamlet's mole, 101–2, 109
  hérisson, 113
  iteraphonic functions, 198
  meurtrières, 76
  night letters, 187
  psychic deafness, 154
  rejeter, 66
  Shakespeare experts, 224
  words, 217

Scheiner, Corinne, 70
Schiller, Friedrich, 150, 151
Schlegel, Friedrich, 107, 110–11
scholars, 206–7
'School of Resentment', 9–10, 12
science, 38
scientific rigour, 37
Searle, John, 42, 56–7
season, to, 121–2, 125, 126
'Secret Sharer, The' (Conrad), 126
selfhood, 168
self-presence, 188–9
'Self-Unsealing Poetic Text, A' (Derrida), 218
Shakespeare, William
  as Anglicist, 88
  Derrida's readings of, 2–4, 16–23, 75–86
  'French Shakespeare', 9–10
  performativity, 75
  philosophy's attitude towards, 1–2
  recent philosophers' engagement with, 4–8: bardolatry, 8–16
  three criteria for worthwhile philosophical engagement with, 4–5
Shakespeare experts, 33–4, 223–5
'Shakespeare Ghosting Derrida' (Cixous), 34, 80, 123–4, 217
Shakespearean Metaphysics (Witmore), 13
Shakespeare's Guide to Life, 14–15

Shakespeare's Ideas (Bevington), 12–13
Shakespeare's Philosophy (McGinn), 4, 12
'Shibboleth: For Paul Celan' (Derrida), 72, 119
signature, 82, 83–4, 103; see also countersigning / countersignatures
'Signature Event Context' (Derrida), 55–9, 72, 84
singular events, 56, 59
singularity, 21, 59, 82, 92, 115, 119
  psychoanalytic discourse, 159
  responsiveness to, 47, 74, 83–4
Singularity of Literature (Attridge), 83
Skeat, Walter W., 116–17
social revolution, 105
sonorous time, 205
sound, 163–7, 182–4, 220; see also Klang
'Spatial Arts, The' (Derrida), 182–3, 188
Specters of Marx (Derrida), 17–18
  acts of reading, 179, 181–2, 205–6
  arrow of teleiopoesis, 68–9
  countersigning / countersignatures, 108, 174, 179
  English language, 87
  frequencies, 192–3, 194, 195, 196, 197–8, 203–4, 206
  genius, 216–17
  Hamlet's mole, 108–9
  listening, 189–90, 199, 203, 205–6
  night, 187
  poetry of the past, 105
  political aporias, 173–80
  porpentine, 117, 120
  'the time is out of joint', 68–9, 75, 115
  translation, 112
speech, 112, 166
speech act theory, 57
Speech Acts in Literature (Hillis Miller), 73
Speech and Phenomena (Derrida), 188–9
speed, 66–7, 68, 71, 72
Spevack, Marvin, 195–6
spirit, 107
Spivak, Gayatri Chakravorty, 176
'Stages of Thought' (Nussbaum), 4–6
Starting with Derrida (Gaston), 17
stereophony, 167
Stevenson, Ruth, 103
Stewart, Garrett, 102
Strachey, James, 166
stroke (*coup*), 66, 69, 73, 82
Stupefaction (Sutherland), 179–80
Sutherland, Keston, 179–80, 207
symbolic feminism, 43–4
syncopation of non-simultaneity, 51

tableau, 86
Tannery, Paul, 92
Taylor, Neil, 116
teleiopoesis, arrow of, 69–74, 78, 218
Telepathy and Literature (Royle), 102
terrorism of obscurantism, 42
texts, 80–1
textual, the, 36
textuality, 40, 45, 79–80
'the time is out of joint', 50, 51, 68–9, 75, 81, 115; see also 'Time is Out of Joint, The' (Derrida); 'Time is Out of Joint, The' (Laclau)

theatre, 185, 187
Theme of the Three Caskets, The (Freud), 141–3, 148
thinking, 143–4
Thinking with Shakespeare (Reinhard Lupton), 13–14
'This Strange Institution Called Literature' (Derrida), 32–3, 34, 47, 85, 223
Thompson, Ann, 116
time, 50–1, 52, 68–9, 71, 72, 74, 75, 205; *see also* contretemps
'Time is Out of Joint, The' (Derrida), 17, 50, 51, 76, 206
'Time is Out of Joint, The' (Laclau), 180
Times, The, 35
Timon of Athens, 104, 106
tone, 181–2, 183
transdisciplinarity, 19–20, 40
'Translating Derrida on Translation' (Venuti), 124
translation, 86–7
 'Che cos'è la poesia?' (Derrida), 113–14, 116
 Hamlet, 204
 Hamlet's mole, 107–8
 idioms, 81, 120–1
 Klang, 166
 literature, 90
 Merchant of Venice, The, 121–3
 meurtrières (peepholes), 119–30
 philosophy, 90–3
 porpentine, 109, 112, 115, 116
Troilus and Cressida, 112

'Ulysses Gramophone' (Derrida), 197
Uncanny, The (Royle), 101, 109–10
United States, 89

Venuti, Lawrence, 120, 122, 124, 127
visibility, 194
visor effect, 196–7, 199, 206
vivit/vixit, 164
voice, 188–9, 191–2
'Voice II' (Derrida), 218
voluntas / voluptas, 167

Warner, William Beatty, 150, 164
watchword, 68, 199
Weber, Elisabeth, 113
Weber, Samuel, 201
'What is a "Relevant" Translation?' (Derrida), 17, 120, 121, 122, 125, 126, 127–8
What is Called Thinking (Heidegger), 19
wichsen/vixit, 164–5
Wills, David, 182
Wissman, H., 157
Without Mastery (Wood), 168
Witmore, Michael, 13
Wolfreys, Julian, 87
Wood, Sarah, 16–17, 168
words, 182–3
Work of Mourning, The (Derrida), 50
Wortham, Edmund, 188–9
wounds, 69, 72, 78, 79, 82, 85, 184, 216
writing, 40–1, 41–3, 57–9, 70

Young, Alan R., 139–40

Zamir, Tzachi, 4, 8–9, 10, 45, 61n

EU representative:
Easy Access System Europe
Mustamäe tee 50, 10621 Tallinn, Estonia
Gpsr.requests@easproject.com

www.ingramcontent.com/pod-product-compliance
Lightning Source LLC
Chambersburg PA
CBHW071830230426
43672CB00013B/2809